How to Buy Your Own Hotel

How to Buy Your Own Hotel

A guide to purchasing a hotel, restaurant or pub
SECOND EDITION

Miles Quest, FHCIMA

Stanley Thornes (Publishers) Ltd
in association with Brodie Marshall Hotels

Originally published by Northwood Publications Ltd 1979
Second edition published by Hutchinson Education 1984

Reprinted in 1990 by
Stanley Thornes (Publishers) Ltd
Old Station Drive
Leckhampton
Cheltenham GL53 0DN

British Library Cataloguing in Publication Data

Quest, Miles
    How to buy your own hotel.
    I. Title
    647'.94'068   TX911.2

    ISBN 0 7487 0355 1

Photoset in Times Roman

Printed and bound in Great Britain by
Courier International Ltd, Tiptree, Essex

To:
Sue, Katie and Stephen and my father
And all those who try

Contents

Foreword

As agents specializing in the sale of hotels, pubs and restaurants, we are in a unique position to see the tremendous efforts people make to start up in the catering industry. No personal or financial sacrifice is ruled out. They will cheerfully sell their houses, cash in insurance and scrape together every last pound to make this most demanding investment of their lives.

Under the pressure of everyday business we do our best to help and advise, but I felt the need for some more formal guidance and practical help for people in this situation. It was on this basis that I approached Miles Quest, who was then editor of *Catering Times* and among the most informed commentators on the catering industry. *How to Buy Your Own Hotel*, first published in 1979 by Northwood Books and ourselves, Brodie Marshall & Company, was the result. I am pleased that Hutchinson have agreed to publish the second edition which has been extensively revised and updated.

The book provides in a very readable form an unprecedented range and depth of information invaluable to a potential buyer. When it was first published it met an enormous need, both as a general introduction to the newcomer, to set him off on the right road, and as a consistently useful handy reference to the established caterer. The second edition provides even more information and guidance.

Anybody who is going to embark on buying their own hotel, restaurant or pub would do well to make this book their first investment.

James H. Nairn
Chairman and Managing Director
Brodie Marshall & Company   *December 1983*

Preface

The process of buying a hotel or catering establishment is long and complicated and can be fraught with pitfalls. Each hotel purchase has to be viewed as an individual undertaking because every hotel, restaurant or pub is different with its own special personality and characteristics. It is true that there are many common problems (which are outlined in this book) but no two hotels or restaurants or pubs are alike and there are no universal answers. This is the most important fact that a would-be purchaser must bear in mind in his search.

The objective of this book is to take some of the complication and mystique out of a hotel or catering purchase and to guide readers around the pitfalls. Not every hotel purchase will involve every consideration mentioned in this book; generally speaking, the smaller the establishment the simpler will be the purchase and the operating problems. But by approaching the search systematically and logically, it is possible to avoid much heartache and save considerable sums of money. The book aims, therefore, to advise the reader step by step from the time of his initial decision to come into the industry through to the day he takes over – and beyond. It does not aim to be a hotel and catering manual but the later chapters outline the most immediate problems that a new owner will have to face and point the way to some solutions.

Incidentally, throughout this book I have referred to hoteliers in the masculine, for reasons of convenience. I should emphasize that few industries offer so many opportunities to women entrepreneurs and there are many examples of hotels and restaurants which they successfully own or operate.

No book of this nature can cover every eventuality. I would welcome suggestions and comments from readers for improvements and additions; all of them will be considered when the book is revised again.

Miles Quest
February 1984

Acknowledgements

After twenty-three years working in the industry, I find it impossible to thank all those who have consciously or unconsciously given me the information that has been used in this book. Some specific acknowledgements are required, however, to those who have particularly helped me with this project – not least to James Nairn, chairman and managing director of Brodie Marshall and Co., whose idea this book was, who encouraged me to write it and who made many helpful suggestions during the preparation of the manuscript. Grateful acknowledgement is due also to Henry Edwards (chairman, Comfort Hotels International) and to David Pinder (David J. Pinder and Partners) for taking the time to read the original manuscript so carefully and for making so many valuable comments.

I must also especially record my appreciation to Michael Brady and to John and Amanda Willmott for providing me with a considerable amount of source materials without which the book would be much the poorer.

Thanks are also due to Christopher Horsman, Tony Rothwell and Geoffrey Pye for their comments on specific chapters; Eric Jolly and Wendy Izod for checking the legal information and Graham Aston (environmental health officer, Epsom and Ewell) for his help on the section on food hygiene regulations.

Other people who have willingly given me their time and attention include Maurice Mason (A. T. James and Co., licensed valuers); Mr R. Vaughan Thomas (manager, Midland Bank, Westbourne, Bournemouth); and Mr D. A. Lloyd (manager, National Westminster Bank, Knowle, Bristol).

Acknowledgement must also be made to the Hotel and Catering Industry Training Board, the British Tourist Authority and the English Tourist Board for permission to reproduce various statistics, tables and other information and to Mrs Jean Webb (marketing director, Moor Hall Hotel and Country Club, Sutton Coldfield) and Mrs Ann Voss Bark (proprietor of the Arundell Arms Hotel, Lifton, Devon) for updating their entries to the Cavendish Cup award scheme.

Needless to say, while the contributions generously made by all these poeple have made the book a far more worthwhile project than would have otherwise been possible, any errors and omissions are entirely of my own making.

Introduction

Few industries have such an attraction for those who want to own their own business as hotelkeeping and catering. It has about it a certain glamour and holds out the promise of considerable personal and financial satisfaction.

The glamour certainly exists. There is something intensely theatrical in running a hotel or restaurant, where new and often surprising events occur every day, bringing the owner into contact with people from many different walks of life, some of them famous people. And there are numerous examples of inexperienced businessmen who have come into the industry, bought their own hotel and secured for themselves a happy and prosperous future.

Without intending to play down the attraction of the industry and its capacity to give a prosperous livelihood to those working in it, this book aims to help you make a realistic decision about buying your own hotel or restaurant. This means that the book emphasizes those many other factors that affect the owner-operator but which lie behind the apparent attraction of the industry.

The glamour exists – but that can soon wear off. Running a hotel or restaurant means hard work and long hours. If you have never dealt with people face-to-face regularly before, be prepared; the public can be critical, irritating, mean and thanklessly demanding. Your guests will not consider your feelings and comfort so don't expect them to respect your privacy and leisure time. They will not want to leave the bar at midnight even though you may be dropping off to sleep, having been on duty since 6.30 a.m. cooking and serving the first breakfast; they will lock themselves out at night and you will have to get up to open the front door at 3.00 a.m. – and still remain cheerful. You may well consider yourself to be mine host; most guests will regard you as their servant.

If they drink too much they may break a valuable antique; if they smoke in bed, they may burn a hole in the sheets and blankets – or at worst, they could set fire to the hotel. At the end of their stay some of them will try to steal your towels, your cutlery, your china – even your toilet rolls!

Too gloomy? Talk to any hotelier running a twenty or thirty room hotel and he will be able to tell you stories far worse than these. To be able to cope with the pressures and aggravations that running a hotel generates you need a powerful sense of humour and a deep conviction that this is the job you want to do. You won't be able to please everyone all the time – but you must want to try.

If you can come to terms with the unpredictable and often unreasonable demands of the public, then hotelkeeping and catering can offer a life that is enjoyable and enormously satisfying. Few hoteliers can describe their feelings precisely but I believe most of the satisfaction comes from the constant face-to-face contact with their guests. A hotelier, if he is a sensible and sensitive fellow, can instantly tell whether his guest has enjoyed his meal or his stay.

The rapport between a satisfied guest and the happy host (perhaps that should be the other way round) is something that has to be experienced to be believed. Without becoming too high flown, it is something that is almost sublime. It is a feeling that generates a communication between guest and host that is impossible in most other areas of commerical – even human – endeavour. Hotelkeeping is an immensely personal activity in which the hotelier expresses his own individuality through his hotel and in the way he runs it. And because he is in constant touch with his guests – unlike the manufacturer of nuts and bolts who may never see his customers – he is able to build up a relationship with them that satisfies some very basic human instincts.

If this sounds too esoteric, then talk to any hotelier running his own hotel and get him to explain why he works such long hours. In the final analysis, what he will say is this: that in spite of the work and the aggravation, there is nothing quite like hotelkeeping to form such a close bond between people unless it be the medical profession and, possibly the theatre. Hotelkeeping is about welcoming and caring and serving and making people happy, so perhaps the exceptions are significant. And it is, of course, about making money.

After reading this book, some readers may be put off the industry and the thought of buying their own hotel or restaurant. Others may become even more enthusiastic. In either case, the result will be worthwhile. Hotelkeeping is a profession requiring considerable technical expertise but it is also a service which implies duties and obligations that have to be appreciated for any hotelier to be commercially successful. This book attempts to outline those duties and obligations, emphasizing the pitfalls and problems of buying and initially running your own hotel. If, after reading it, you still want to become a hotelier – welcome.

1 The basic facts

First, a few facts on an industry that is badly served by statistics and figures.

The hotel and catering industry is one of the largest employers of labour in the country. Depending on whether you count workers at the height of the summer season or in the depths of winter, the industry employs between two million and one million people. Of these, nearly three-quarters are female and over half are part-time. Only the retail distribution industry and, possibly, construction are bigger.

The industry employs so many because it comprises not only hotels and restaurants but pubs and clubs, catering in factories, hospitals and schools, marine and air catering and take-away and outside catering. Hotelkeeping and catering is predominantly a small unit industry – and the units are very much smaller than people realize. It is estimated (again, no one quite knows exactly) that there are some 50,000 hotels and guesthouses in Great Britain and that only about 13,000 of these are licensed. As most reasonable-sized hotels have a licence, the implication of these figures is obvious: there are a great many tiny hotels up and down the country, including boarding houses, guest houses and private hotels in the seaside resorts.

Figures from the British Tourist Authority show that the guest and boarding house sector of the industry is becoming less popular with holiday makers (see Table 4) while the larger hotels are just about holding their own. But larger may be a misnomer. The average-sized British hotel has twenty rooms. If the large 500-room hotels of London were to be excluded from such statistics (which would not be unreasonable as they clearly are the exception) then the average size of hotel would probably fall to about fifteen rooms.

One particular economic fact arises out of these figures which is of interest to the independent operator. It is often the case that one or two major public companies dominate a large, small-unit industry in terms of turnover and number of units. This is not so in hotelkeeping and catering, where even the largest group – Trusthouse Forte (with 230 hotels in Great Britain) – has an almost insignificant share of the total market. There are other major public companies in the industry, such as Bass Charrington, the brewers, who own Crest Hotels and Pontins; Allied Breweries, who own Embassy Hotels; Ladbroke Hotels and Comfort Hotels International. But while THF is the biggest company, the thirty largest hotel companies account for less than 20 per cent of the industry's turnover and less than 15 per cent of the room capacity. In no other major industry do the major companies account for such a small market share.

Advantages and disadvantages

The significance of these figures hardly needs emphasizing. Hotelkeeping and catering is an ideal industry for the eager and able entrepreneur because there are small hotels and restaurants available in almost every part of the country. The major groups may influence the industry in terms of pricing but they do not dominate it. The huge number of owner-operators, independent of any public company, make hotelkeeping and catering a fertile ground for the independent businessman. He can and does provide the kind of product and service that the public wants without interference from any other source. Few other industries, except retail distribution, offer the same commercial opportunities, which explains why so many people find the idea of buying a hotel or retail shop such an attractive proposition.

The same situation is evident to an even greater extent in the restaurant industry where Berni Inns, Wimpy, Little Chef, McDonalds and Kentucky Fried Chicken are perhaps the only truly national catering companies. The situation is quite different in the public house sector. This is still dominated by the major breweries who control the majority of the 66,000 pubs. It is true that the entrepreneur can purchase the tenancy of a public house but his freedom of action is circumscribed by the fact that the brewery retains the freehold of the premises and keeps a tie on supplies.

Another major reason why hotelkeeping and catering is so popular with people starting out on their own is that the capital involved in purchasing a business is realistic. Depending on location and size, a hotel in a resort may cost only slightly more than a large house in an expensive London suburb. With the added benefit of living in the premises and off the business, the financial attraction of owning a hotel is obvious. But there are some disadvantages in ownership and it is best to examine them at this stage, though all of them are discussed more fully in later chapters.

One disadvantage derives from the nature of the industry itself. A hotel is defined in the Hotel Proprietors Act, 1956, as 'an establishment held out by the proprietor as offering food, drink and if so required sleeping accommodation without special contract to any traveller presenting himself who appears able and willing to pay a reasonable sum for the services provided and who is in a fit state to be received.'

The broad meaning of this (there are a number of books that will interpret it precisely – see page 118) is that a hotelier who operates within the meaning of the Act, and who has a room available, cannot turn away any person who arrives providing he can pay and is in a fit state to be received, e.g. he is sober. Within certain limits, he also has to accept responsibility for the guest's property but he has a lien on this if the guest does not pay his bill – in other words, he can retain the guest's luggage and dispose of it to help meet an unpaid account.

The implication of this is that any hotel within the meaning of the Act is a very public place indeed. A hotelier cannot pick and choose his guests though an experienced operator may tactfully (though not legally) refuse a person by saying that he has no accommodation available. Few potential guests, anyway, know the letter of the law. The point to be made, however, is that a hotel is not at all like running a large home.

There is another kind of hotel. These do not consider themselves to be within the meaning of the Act and are usually called 'private hotels'. Most boarding houses and guest houses come into this category and almost all are unlicensed – though a liquor licence is not a requirement for running a hotel within the meaning of the Hotel Proprietors Act.

Any establishment that calls itself 'Such and Such Private Hotel' does not hold itself out to receive 'any traveller presenting himself'. Confusingly, however, some hotels not so plainly labelled are also private hotels and even the display of the Hotel Proprietors Act does not necessarily mean that the Act applies. A private hotel can pick and choose its guests, making it (as its name implies) a much more private establishment to run. It cannot retain luggage to pay unpaid bills but, at the same time, it does not have responsibility for the luggage in the first place if it is mislaid or stolen unless negligence can be proved. If you happen to buy a private hotel, it must be added, you can change it the day you take over by deleting the word 'private'. (The statutory notice is available from the British Hotels, Restaurants and Caterers' Association, 13 Cork Street, London W1X 2BH.)

It is important to understand this rather complicated difference because the choice of whether you run a hotel or private hotel is entirely yours. The obligations on those running a hotel within the meaning of the Hotel Proprietors Act are onerous and there is no doubt that these responsibilities have an effect on the character of the hotel and consequently on the life style of the proprietors.

A second disadvantage of ownership is that you really are on your own. This is often regarded as being a considerable advantage but increasing government legislation, VAT regulations, income tax problems and the difficulty of raising short- and long-term capital all conspire to make the life of the independent businessman more and more complicated every year. Most people coming into the industry have a background in other industries or in the services, perhaps as an executive in a large company that has specialist departments. They are accustomed to having the accounts department to deal with a tax problem or with Mrs Bloggs' wages; the personnel department to hire a new cleaner; the legal department to explain the intricacies of capital gains tax or the Employment Protection Act. If you are used to these support services, don't forget that in your own establishment you will need to be your own accounts expert, personnel manager and wages clerk rolled into one –

although it is true that some of some of these services, particularly those dealing with payroll and accounts, for example, may be available locally. You will also be the person who has to persuade your bank manager to grant you an overdraft. There are many who find these problems challenging and stimulating but be sure that you will be able to cope with them.

The tourist industry

A brief look at the future of the industry and at the main trends shows that an interest in owning a hotel or catering business is amply justified. Tourism, on which many hotels rely, has been an exceptional growth industry and has withstood the effects of the 1980–2 recession much better than most industries.

The number of tourists coming to Great Britain increased regularly until 1978 when it reached 12.6 million (4.8 million in 1968). In the face of the recession, this figure dropped to 11.7 million by 1982 – a remarkable achievement considering the economic circumstances. Tourism is, without being too biased in the industry's favour, one of Britain's greatest post-war industrial success stories, and is one of the country's most buoyant and successful industries. While much of manufacturing industry has experienced unemployment, short-time working and a reduced demand for its products. Britain's tourist industry has developed to such an extent that it earned £4,000 million in 1981 – an amount that makes it one of Britain's biggest foreign currency earners.

Future growth is unlikely to match that of the past but, barring some catastrophic economic event, it is likely to remain successful and prosperous. It must be emphasized that the hotel and restaurant sector both world-wide and in this country is vulnerable to shifts in the economic climate. During the 1974–7 oil crisis, hotels were badly hit by the cutback in domestic business activity. They were again affected by the recession which started in 1979, but not as badly as many manufacturing businesses. The number of overseas visitors did not increase at the previous rate and the strength of sterling vis-à-vis the dollar particularly hit the North American market. At home, companies cut back on their use of hotel accommodation and tended to entertain less, while 1980 and 1981 were poor years for most resort hotels. The British domestic holiday market (see tables at the end of the chapter), though incomparably bigger than the overseas tourist market, declined between 1973 and 1981. In fact, the peak years for domestic holidays of four days or more were 1973–4 when 40.5 million holidays were taken by the British in Britain. By 1981 the figure had dropped to 36.5 million. The upsurge in 1978 to 39 million is a little misleading however; even though three million more British people holidayed in Britain there was a net decline in the number of British people who stayed in hotels. In other words, although more people went on holiday, an even greater proportion stayed with friends or relatives or went into self-catering or camping. One cheerful aspect, however, is the growth in the short holiday (under four day) market. It is clear that while Britain is becoming less popular for British people as a main holiday destination, it is very attractive for weekend breaks or short holidays. Nevertheless, the amount spent on all holidays is not rising even in line with inflation. The attraction of the overseas holiday with guaranteed sun is another powerful attraction the British hotelier has to face. The number of holidays taken by British people abroad rose from 7.25 million in 1976 to over 13.25 million in 1981.

The industry's vulnerability to economic 'stop-go' is due to its dependence on discretionary spending money, the amount that is left over in the average family's budget after such essentials as food, clothing, housing and heating have been paid. To many people, holidays are not an essential part of the family budget and expensive eating out even less so. Nevertheless, the increase in the number of overseas holidays indicates that holiday-taking is becoming a custom which a growing number of people are unwilling to forgo. Wages for many people have increased rather faster than inflation, which has helped the holiday-taking habit. But while increasing affluence has left people with more money in their pockets, other areas of consumer spending, such as colour television, video machines and other luxury goods, as well as overseas holidays, have benefited.

Thus, some resort hotels catering for families have experienced a decline in business. Families are now finding that resort hotels are becoming almost too expensive for them to use or that an overseas package holiday is cheaper. To a certain extent, the ever-rising number of tourists has taken up the slack. More and more foreign visitors are being encouraged by the regional and national tourist authorities to travel out of London into the British countryside and many resorts have made special efforts to attract them. But the sheer size of the domestic holiday market makes any stagnation or decline in it a serious matter for hoteliers.

Despite this situation, however, there are some resort areas that have maintained their share of the market and even improved it. Obviously, those resorts that have maintained their facilities and amenities and have promoted them vigorously have been the most successful in attracting visitors. The south and south-west coast resorts remain the most popular, partly because they have done the most to develop their amenities. Some towns like Brighton, for example, have purposely changed the pattern of their trade away from the traditional holiday by the sea (even so, many of the small hotels in these resorts are still busiest in the summer months). These towns see their future in the conference market and have developed conference facilities, giving a more even, year-round trade. Other conference centres have been developed, such as in Harrogate, while covered leisure centres, such as those in Blackpool, Jersey and the Isle of Man, allow many different activities to be pursued, regardless of the weather.

The traditional holiday by the sea has changed in other ways, too. Hotels have been dramatically affected by the near-universal ownership of the motor car in much the same way that they were affected 100 years ago by the introduction of the modern railway system. Up to the middle 1950s, holiday makers customarily spent a fortnight in a seaside hotel, booked Saturday to Saturday. Now they demand greater flexibility and many want to move on after a few days. The weekend to weekend booking is a thing of the past for many resort hotels. Catering for the holiday maker has thus become much more unpredictable – a trend emphasized by the growing number of people who are booking up later, often to within a week of their arrival.

The wise hotelier will be aware of these trends and will adapt to them. Tourism and home holiday making is one area where there are plenty of statistics and a careful study will reveal the strongest holiday regions. The most significant trends are shown in the tables at the end of this chapter.

Any estimate of the future of tourism to Britain must depend on the state of the world's economy. Tourism is undoubtedly one of the most dynamic growth industries. Aided by cheap air travel, it is likely to continue to expand as more and more people have increasing leisure time and higher standards of living. Historically, the number of visitors arriving in the UK has grown on average by 10 per cent per year but is most unlikely that such a rate of growth will be experienced into the late 1980s.

The American market is sensitive to the sterling/dollar relationship. While Britain became unexpectedly expensive to the US visitor in the 1979-81 period, the stronger dollar subsequently changed the situation to Britain's advantage. Happily, tourists continue to come from other sources, such as Europe (still our biggest market), Scandinavia, the Middle East, Japan and Australasia, and to visitors from these countries, Britain remains competitive and is regarded as a good value destination. It can be said that London for example, is only genuinely full for about 100 days per year and considerable opportunities still remain to enlarge off-season traffic and to build up quieter weeks throughout the year – particularly for smaller provincial hotels.

Few new hotels are being planned or built in Britain. The cost of land and construction makes hotel building uneconomic in London, and planning permission is not easy to obtain. The situation in the provinces is not quite so difficult, but the huge boom in hotel construction, brought about by the Hotel Development Incentive Scheme in 1969, is unlikely to be repeated.

The independent hotelier needs Britain to remain attractive to overseas tourists if only because the home holiday hotel market, though big, is not expanding significantly at present. With more tourists travelling into the provinces, their importance to the small hotelier cannot be overemphasized. But their presence in the future cannot be taken for granted and prospective purchasers should be aware of the situation. The hotel industry needs the overseas tourist as well as the domestic holiday maker, which means that much greater sales promotion efforts must be made to maintain and expand existing markets.

Other Markets

Where does the hotelier look for more business? There are four main areas – home holiday makers, overseas visitors, businessmen and conference delegates. Each hotel has a different mix from these sources.

The commercial businessman is the main source of revenue for many provincial city centre hotels from Monday to Thursday night, leaving the hotel the empty weekend to cope with. One solution to this problem is to offer weekend bargain packages and London hotels have shown how successful these can be. Another solution is to attract conferences at the weekend and, if possible, to fill up with conferences during the week as well. Yet another is to develop food and drink business at the weekend. Many small hotels may find this difficult to achieve, however, because they do not have the space or the opportunity. If this is the case, they will have to rely on their traditional source of business – the commercial representative, the holiday maker or the chance customer.

The future of the conference market again depends on the state of Britain's economy. If business activity is prospering, then industry needs to use hotels to accommodate staff and clients on conferences, courses and meetings. If business activity declines, as it did in 1979-82, hotels are the first to suffer. Sales executives, instead of staying overnight, return home; businessmen stop holding conferences and entertain more modestly at lunch or dinner. Every forecast needs to be hedged with provisos, but there are signs that this sector of the market is now expanding and the future looks hopeful. Providing the small, independent hotelier can produce the right facilities there is no reason why he cannot take his proper share of this profitable market.

Future trends in the restaurant sector are much harder to discern. It is, as the next chapter explains more fully, a difficult sector to define. Restaurants are more localized and draw their customers from a much closer area than does a hotel. The success of a restaurant depends on its atmosphere and ambience, location and on the quality of the food. Restaurants have as many different markets as hotels – the de-luxe, expensive restaurant, the fast, short menu grill, the hamburger bar, the take-away – they all attract their own clientele and make generalization difficult.

It is easy to be misled about the restaurant industry because it is more volatile and fashionable than the hotel industry. A new trend can fundamentally affect many existing restaurants though it is possible to overemphasize the trendy nature of the restaurant business. The basic hamburger and steak menu has been in existence for a long time and will continue to survive for many years to come. The higher-spend restaurants which are dependent on expense accounts and on wealthy local diners will prosper providing they give recognizable value for money. Broadly speaking, the de-luxe restaurant serving haute cuisine food is the most dangerous sector to enter and the most difficult to succeed in. It has an enormous attraction in life-style and status, but serving high quality food, day in day out, means that expensive, skilled kitchen staff and high quality materials are needed – and customers willing to pay for both. There are well-known people who have made a success in this sector but they are outnumbered by the many who have failed.

The most attractive section of the restaurant industry is what the professional caterer calls the 'refuelling' market which has been enormously influenced and developed by the arrival of McDonalds and other American fast food chains. Their emphasis on quality, cleanliness, speed of service and value for money has revolutionized the British approach to popular catering. People who want to live to eat patronize the haute cuisine restaurants; those who need to eat to live visit those many thousands of restaurants that offer simpler, cheaper menus. They are in the refuelling market because they provide food to satisfy the customer's hunger. As everybody needs to eat to survive, it follows that this section of the market is huge and can be highly profitable. Running a café or a tea shop, a small restaurant or a take-away hamburger shop, is often a less than glamorous occupation in catering but there can be no doubt about the profitability of many of these units, providing they are properly run. Just as you would take your car to an efficient garage that is clean, quick and not exorbitantly expensive, so most customers need good quality food and clean, quick and inexpensive service for their own personal refuelling. The capital requirements of a major American-style take-away restaurant are so heavy, however, that it is unlikely that many newcomers to the industry would contemplate such a venture. Franchising (see page 136) is one way into the industry that can be considered and is becoming more significant.

Statistics

The British holiday market has expanded considerably since 1965, but as Table and Figure 1 show, it is clear that it is subject to economic depressions. The sharp fall in the number of holidays taken in 1976 and 1977 followed the 1974 oil crisis, but the total number of holidays taken (49.75 million in 1981) shows that the market is resilient. People are evidently reluctant to forgo their annual holiday. The rising number of overseas holidays is a danger sign to British resorts. It should be remembered that Britain remains overwhelmingly popular for short break holidays (less than four nights) and this is an expanding market for hoteliers. Not all these holidays, of course, were taken in hotels (see Table 4).

Long-term trends show that British people are changing their holiday patterns (see Table 2). Since 1968 there has been a decline in the number of people taking only one holiday a year while the number of people taking two holidays a year has more than doubled. Even more spectacular is the six-fold growth in the number of people taking three or more holidays a year. The

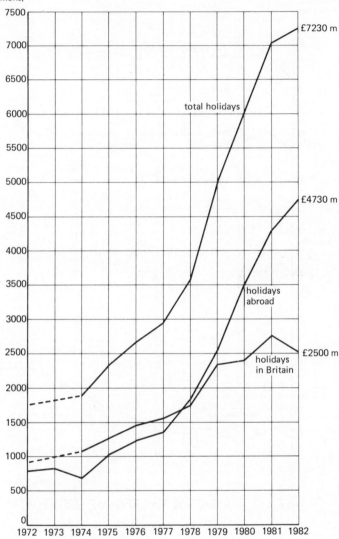

Figure 1   *Trends in holiday expenditure.*
Courtesy: British Tourist Authority

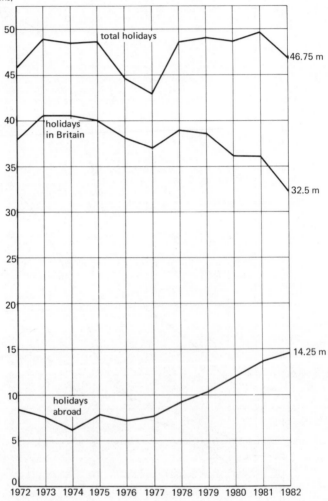

Figure 2   *Trends in the number of holidays taken*
Courtesy: British Tourist Authority

Table 1   *Estimated number of holidays taken by the British population 1965 to 1981*

Year	Britain	Abroad	Total
	millions	millions	millions
1965	30.0	5.00	35.00
1966	31.0	5.50	36.50
1967	30.0	5.00	35.00
1968	30.0	5.00	35.00
1969	30.5	5.75	36.25
1970	34.5	5.75	40.25
1971	34.0	7.25	41.25
1972	37.5	8.50	46.00
1973	40.5	8.25	48.75
1974	40.5	6.75	47.25
1975	40.0	8.00	48.00
1976	37.5	7.25	44.75
1977	36.0	7.75	43.75
1978	39.0	9.00	48.00
1979	38.5	10.25	48.75
1980	36.5	12.00	48.50
1981	36.5	13.25	49.75
1982	32.5	14.25	46.75

Source: BTA British National Travel Survey.

Notes:
   (i)   These figures relate to holidays of four nights or more.
   (ii)   They include both holidays taken by adults and holidays taken by children.
   (iii)   The figures are derived from the percentage of the population taking a holiday in each of the years concerned. These percentage figures are, of course, subject to normal sampling error. When applied to large populations, small variations are greatly magnified. These estimates should therefore be regarded as order-of-magnitude figures for individual years; they do not necessarily reflect a precise relationship with the preceding or succeeding year.

figures have implications for the hotel industry. The traditional fortnight by the sea in a resort hotel, booked Saturday to Saturday, is declining in popularity but other opportunities are opening up – the weekend break in the shoulder months of May, June, September and October and the short winter holiday. It is in these areas that hoteliers have to seek new business opportunities.

The growth of the car as a means of transport on holidays has been striking – over two-thirds of all British people now take their car on holiday (see Table 3). Sudden increases in the cost of petrol, however, have adversely affected many outlying resorts and holiday areas, particularly in Northern Scotland, which are also vulnerable to fuel shortages.

Table 4 shows the general trends of the British domestic holiday market. British licensed holiday hotels are holding their own while the small

Table 2   *Level of holiday taking by number of holidays taken 1968 to 1981*

(Based on the British adult population)

	1968	1973	1974	1975	1976	1977	1978	1979	1980	1981
	%	%	%	%	%	%	%	%	%	%
All taking:										
One holiday	51	43	44	41	44	42	42	43	43	40
Two	6	14	13	15	14	12	14	14	14	15
Three or more	1	6	4	4	4	5	6	5	5	6
All taking:										
One or more	58	63	62	60	61	59	61	63	62	61
No holiday taken	42	37	38	40	39	41	39	37	38	39

Source: BTA British National Travel Survey

Table 3   *Method of transport used on holidays in Great Britain 1971 to 1981*

	Total hols.	Main holidays					Additional holidays				
	1981	1971	1975	1977	1979	1981	1971	1975	1977	1979	1981
	%	%	%	%	%	%	%	%	%	%	%
Car	69	67	71	71	71	68	73	72	72	72	72
Bus/ Coach	13	15	13	12	13	13	12	10	11	11	9
Train	13	13	12	13	13	12	13	11	13	12	14
Other	6	5	4	5	3	6	3	3	4	5	4

Source: BTA British National Travel Survey.

unlicensed hotel and boarding house is suffering a significant decline in both the main and additional holiday markets. That does not mean that these small establishments are unprofitable; in many resorts they can be very busy in the peak summer months and they give good experience of the hotel industry to people who eventually want to purchase a larger property. The popularity of rented accommodation and caravanning may be due to price advantage and to the fact that they provide a greater flexibility for families.

As Figures 3 and 4 show, although the total number of overseas visitors has increased in the last decade, their proportion remains almost the same – 1981 was a poor year for world tourism generally. Holidays in Britain, however, even taking into account the relatively buoyant short-break market, have suffered a dramatic decline of over 13 million from the 1973 peak. Much of this shortfall is accounted for by the growth in overseas holidays – from 8.25 million in 1973, to 14.25 million in 1982.

The West Country and southern England are still by far the most popular holiday regions for British people (see Table 5) but a a similar table for overseas tourists would put London at the top of the list. Nearly 90 per cent of

Table 4 *Accommodation used on holidays in Great Britain 1970 to 1981*

	Total hols. 1981 %	Main holidays 1970 %	1978 %	1979 %	1980 %	1981 %	Additional holidays 1970 %	1978 %	1979 %	1980 %	1981 %
Licensed hotel/ motel	17	15	16	18	18	17	15	18	17	18	17
Unlicensed hotel, board. house, etc.	7	16	10	9	8	7	11	6	9	9	7
Friends'/relatives' home	26	24	22	20	23	23	41	37	37	34	31
Caravan	18	18	20	18	20	20	14	19	15	20	16
Rented accom.	18	11	16	15	17	15	6	10	11	7	13
Holiday camp	6	6	8	8	8	8	2	4	3	4	4
Camping	7	6	5	6	5	6	5	4	4	4	8
Paying guest in private house	3	7	2	3	2	4	5	2	2	2	3
Total (including 'other')	103	107	103	102	106	105	104	104	103	105	103

Source: BTA British National Travel Survey.

Table 5 *Regions stayed in for one night or more on holidays in Great Britain in 1981*

Tourist Board regions	All holidays %	All 1–3 night holidays %	All 4 + night holidays %
Cumbria	2	2	2
Northumbria	2	4	2
North West	4	10	3
Yorkshire and Humberside	5	6	5
Heart of England	2	7	2
East Midlands	3	5	3
East Anglia	6	8	6
Thames and Chilterns	2	5	2
London	3	8	2
West Country	13	9	14
South	7	6	7
South East	6	8	6
	55	77	52
Wales	9	10	8
Scotland	7	9	6
Abroad	30	4	33

Source: BTA British National Travel Survey

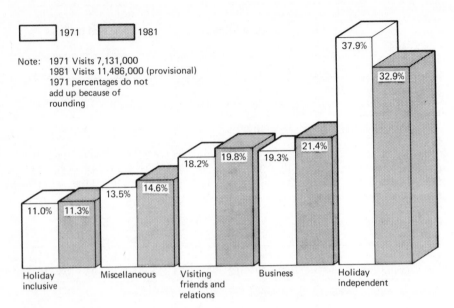

Figure 3   *Overseas visitors to the United Kingdom by purpose of visit 1971 and 1981*
Source: International Passenger Survey

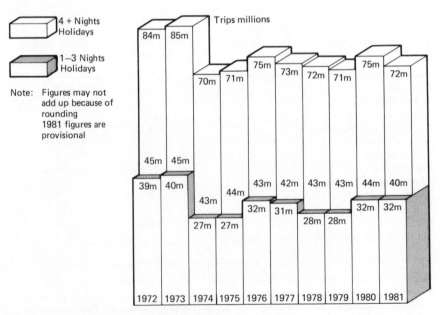

Figure 4   *Holiday tourism in Britain 1972–81*
Source: British Home Tourism Survey

Table 6 *Monthly distribution of holidays in Great Britain 1981*

Holiday began in:	Total hols. %	Main holiday * %	Additional holiday %
May	**10**	10	11
June	**10**	10	9
July	**15**	19	9
August	**19**	26	10
September	**9**	11	9
Other months	**36**	24	52

Source: BTA British National Travel Survey.

* England only

Table 7 *Numbers of hotels in Great Britain in 1981 (by region)*

Region	Total
Cumbria	907
Northumbria	666
North West England	1511
Yorkshire and Humberside	1563
Heart of England	1415
East Midlands	866
Thames and Chilterns	549
East Anglia	1447
London	336
West Country	3277
Southern	2521
South East England	1795
Total England	16853
Scotland	3146
Wales	1321
Northern Ireland	149
Total Great Britain	21469

Source: English Tourist Board

all tourists have at least one overnight stay in London.

The four peak summer months account for over 65 per cent of all main holidays taken in Great Britain, but the situation is sharply reversed with additional holidays (see Table 6). Off-peak holidays, particularly weekend breaks, present considerable marketing opportunities for the hotel industry.

The numbers quoted in Table 7 only cover those hotels for which the national tourist boards have capacity information; they do not aim to represent the total hotel stock, though they do give some idea of the most popular hotel regions. Most of these hotels would be licensed; it is likely that there would be a similar number of unlicensed private hotels and guest houses.

Figure 5   *Percentage bedspace occupancy in the UK, 1981*

Table 8 *Number of registered hotel bedspaces in Great Britain in 1981 (by region)*

Region	Total
Cumbria	19,658
Northumbria	18,562
North West England	59,262
Yorkshire and Humberside	43,286
Heart of England	37,775
East Midlands	21,992
Thames and Chilterns	17,192
East Anglia	37,985
London	97,037
West Country	104,679
Southern	77,408
South East England	57,395
Total England	592,231
Scotland	89,001
Wales	42,964
Total Great Britain	724,196

Source: National tourist boards

About half (11,019) have ten bedrooms or less; there are 3671 with between eleven and fifteen bedrooms; 2878 have between sixteen and twenty-five bedrooms; 2008 have between twenty-six and fifty bedrooms. Only 914 hotels have between fifty-one and one hundred rooms and an even smaller number (516) have over 100 rooms. The industry is clearly dominated by the large number of small hotels.

Table 8 shows that almost half the total number of bedrooms in Great Britain are in coastal resorts, and it is here that many first-time buyers will find their hotel.

2 Hotel, restaurant or pub – which will suit me best?

The decision about which sector to enter is crucial, for each has different characteristics and opportunities. The decision will depend largely on your own inclinations and resources but even if you have already decided to buy a hotel, for example, there are still many other factors that have to be considered before you can seriously begin looking.

What type of hotel are you seeking – one in a resort or in a town, in London or in the countryside? What kind of business attracts you – a steady year-round trade that most city hotels experience or the peaks and troughs of a resort hotel? Do you want to cater for holiday makers or businessmen?

There are advantages and disadvantages to all these options. A seasonal hotel means hard work for four to six months of the year and a long winter of little or no trade; a town hotel may be busy in the week and quiet at the weekends. How do you attract people to Wigan on a Saturday night? London's major hotels are busy all year round but most of their trade comprises foreign businessmen and tourists. Smaller London hotels in areas such as Victoria and Bayswater do not enjoy such a successful pattern of trade and are often quiet in the winter months. Staff are more difficult to find and retain in London and may be a major problem if you are a long way from the city centre. A hotel in the country may sound attractive but who is going to use it?

The type of business you are looking for is the first decision to make because it can save you time, trouble and expense in your search. You can change your mind if you find that what you want is either unrealistic or unavailable but buying a business is rather like buying a house – you need to know what you want, where you want it and how much you can afford.

There are so many different kinds of hotels and restaurants available that an early decision in this area is essential. Hotel estate agents are helpful and pleased to advise but even they can get exasperated when potential purchasers view hotel after hotel and still cannot make up their mind about the type of business they want and where they want it. Much more important, you will save travelling time and considerable sums of money if you know what you are looking for. Even if you do know, you will still need patience – six months is an average time to find a hotel. You may still have to make expensive journeys to far-distant hotels, restaurants or pubs in your search, but if you know what you want, the journeys can be cut down and some of the searches can be undertaken on the telephone. A five minute conversation with the agent or vendor on the telephone could save a long journey. Every time you travel somewhere in your car it is costing you money. It eats into your capital and reduces the amount of cash you can put into the business.

The hotel sector is the most difficult for potential purchasers to enter because a hotel is really three businesses in one – an accommodation business, a restaurant and a pub. This book concentrates on the purchase of a hotel but the principles are the same for buying a restaurant or free house.

Broadly speaking, there are four different types of hotel:

London hotels

In the capital, most hotels depend greatly on tourist traffic but there is much business trade as well, particularly in the larger hotels. London is competitive; when trade is good it can be very, very good but when it is bad it can be disastrous. The many big hotels dominate the capital, most of them operated by the major companies who are constantly seeking new markets and extra revenue. The many independent London hotels prosper on tourism and few make much of a feature of the food and drinks operation – most supply bed and breakfast only. Consequently, operating a London hotel, no matter how small, tends to be a rooming operation – what the professional hotelier calls a bed factory.

London property values are, however, so much higher in comparison to the provinces that most first-time buyers will find it well-nigh impossible to consider purchasing a hotel in the capital. Turnover and profits are also higher as a result of the greater year-round occupancy. London, as the country's capital, attracts over 80 per cent of all tourists and probably has a more secure future than other areas but property prices reflect this factor. It should be said that operating a London hotel may not suit those people who want a rather more personal approach to hotelkeeping.

Provincial town hotels

These hotels can offer the most attractive business opportunities. Unlike London and one or two other major cities, there has been no dramatic increase in the number of hotels in many provincial cities although rooms and other extensions have been added to existing hotels and competition is still keen. Many provincial hotels have built up a steady trade with commercial business traffic or could build it up in the future.

Buying a provincial town hotel needs considerable investigation but providing it has the right facilities, is well located and the town is prosperous, there is almost always scope for an enthusiastic and able newcomer to increase business in such a unit.

Some provincial hotels are similar to their London counterparts, providing bed and breakfast and possibly dinner. Others enjoy a much greater food and drinks trade. The type of hotel that attracts you depends on your own interests and inclinations but the ideal hotel is one in which all three departments – rooms, food and bar – are functioning well and contribute to revenue. Most hotels derive their revenue in the ratio 33 per cent rooms, 33 per cent food and 33 per cent drink. They are thus less vulnerable to economic shifts of fortune than those that are almost totally dependent on room revenue. By far the most profitable source of revenue, however, are the rooms: the importance of food and drink sales is that thay can produce valuable income at the weekends when the rooms may be empty and they supplement room revenue at other times.

Few provincial hotels have built up their reputation on food alone but some produce a much greater percentage of turnover from their restaurant than others. This may be because the proprietor has seen a gap in the market and has exploited it, or he may be particularly interested in food. In many ways, these hotels are more difficult for an inexperienced person to take over. Controlling a kitchen, with a small brigade of chefs, is a difficult enough job for a trained professional. An inexperienced owner could find the problems daunting. It is true that there are examples of outsiders coming in to make a success of this kind of business but it is advisable to think carefully before buying a hotel with an extensive food and beverage operation if you have little or no catering experience. It may be better to build up the restaurant operation after you have had some experience of the hotel.

Country hotels

These are hotels whose siren songs are the most alluring. Treat them with all the caution they deserve. From the outside they look irresistible. There is many a potential purchaser who, walking up the stairs to meet the vendor, sees himself as the local landlord-cum-squire, dispensing hospitality to all. After buying the dream hotel, the reality soon dawns.

Successful country hotels all have two things in common – they have built up their reputation over a long period of time (up to ten years) and have carved a niche in the market by their unique approach to food or accommodation. They experience good occupancy and almost always enjoy high food and beverage turnover. But while there are many that have succeeded there are many that have failed. Either they are badly located or their standards have not been sufficiently high to attract customers from far enough afield; or they are too expensive or too exclusive. They may have failed for any one of a dozen reasons.

Success is difficult to predict because there are so many indefinable qualities that make up a good country hotel. Undoubtedly the atmosphere and the quality of food are the most important but the personality of the owner cannot be underestimated. Buying a country hotel, therefore, can be a hazardous business. Even if the accounts prove that the hotel is sound don't forget that people eat and stay there because of the atmosphere produced by the proprietor. Will they bother to drive miles to visit you? If you do take over a successful country hotel, don't change the formula until you know exactly what you are doing.

Resort hotels

These are by far the most numerous in the hotel market; Bournemouth alone has 1200 hotels and boarding houses. Within this huge market there are many profitable hotels but success depends not only on such things as the facilities of the town but on variables, such as the weather. A resort hotel is, in other words, vulnerable to factors beyond the control of the hotelier.

Trends in holiday making show that many resorts are beginning to lose popularity while many more British people are opting for overseas holidays and self-catering. This trend has been established for too long for it to be reversed now and potential purchasers should be aware of the situation.

Nevertheless, a small resort hotel is an excellent introduction to hotelkeeping for an inexperienced couple. Most of them offer dinner, bed and breakfast only and the majority are small enough for a husband and wife to operate with the help of one or two part-time staff. The demands of the guests are relatively simple even though there are indications that the British holiday maker is becoming more sophisticated, thanks partly to holidays in large, well-equipped foreign hotels. Private bathrooms are now expected on an increasing scale and more imaginative menus are being demanded.

Resort hotels have another advantage for the newcomer. They are generally less expensive to buy than those in other parts of the country. The reason for this is simple. Professional hoteliers do not, by and large, want to enter the resort hotel market and few of the major groups have seaside hotels. Those that have such hotels operate in particularly strong towns like Brighton, Bournemouth and Torquay. The lack of interest by professional operators has had a slightly depressing effect on hotel values, though for every professional hotelier who is not interested there are a hundred amateurs who are. There is no conflict in this situation. A large group, with heavy overheads, cannot afford to shut a resort hotel for six months of the year yet cannot keep it open and operate it with uneconomic occupancy levels. Building up winter business at the hotel would entail a commensurately far greater effort than a similar effort for a hotel in a major provincial city with its much greater spread of business. For this reason, groups do not generally favour investment in seaside resorts; if they have resort hotels, they are now trying to develop conference business.

The independent operator, however, with few overheads and living on the premises, can make his resort hotel highly profitable providing he appreciates that the market is gradually changing and becoming more demanding. Some resorts go out of fashion while others come into favour and it is important to remember that the hotels are dependent on the success of the resort in attracting holiday makers.

Restaurants

The restaurant industry is subject to much greater change than the hotel industry and is more unpredictable. There is a greater element of showmanship in running a restaurant than a hotel and, consequently, there is the need to offer new and interesting dishes. Restaurants are more subject to changing public taste. Once a hotel is constructed and the rooms are equipped, there is little that the hotelier can do to alter his basic product. With a restaurant, the public tires of the same product day after day and demands new ideas, new dishes, a new presentation.

This is not the situation in every case. There are high class restaurants in London and elsewhere which are successful precisely because they have not changed – Simpsons-in-the-Strand in London is one example. Where the restaurant has some particular architectural characteristic, such as a timbered ceiling, then it would be silly not to emphasize the old atmosphere all the time. But even in this type of restaurant, speciality dishes must be offered every day and the menu should be changed from time to time.

Looking back over the last thirty years it is possible to see how trends and fashions affect the popular sector of the restaurant industry. Lyons tea shops and Corner Houses reigned supreme in London and elsewhere for many years until the introduction of the coffee bar in the late 1950s. Selling an expensive cup of coffee, it illustrated an important catering concept – to achieve success, cut the menu to a small number of speciality items but produce them well. Then came (not necessarily in this order) Italian, Chinese, and Indian restaurants, Golden Egg and Wimpy, steak houses, hamburger restaurants and pizza houses, pancake houses, soft ice cream parlours and fast food restaurants. By failing to provide new types of food and new meal experiences, many formerly popular restaurants faded away. Where now do you see a milk bar? Lyons tea shops and Corner Houses no longer exist in their original form and in their place (and even on the same site) McDonald's hamburger restaurants and others have now sprung up.

In the popular sector of the market – now called the fast food sector – American ideas and products have wielded enormous influence. It was an American, Peter Morton, who launched the Great American Disaster hamburger restaurant in London in 1970 and so pointed the British restaurant industry into a new direction. In doing so, he illustrated two fundamental factors about the popular restaurant industry – you need an enticing product and an exciting atmosphere in a good location. Morton's big American hamburger was as different from the popular Wimpy as chalk is from cheese; he realized that it could be transferred to the British scene as a new and exciting product, quickly prepared and served and easily eaten. It was also relatively inexpensive and was perceived as giving value for money.

Whether or not a meal is actually worth the price charged is immaterial. What matters is whether the customer believes it gives value. Perceived value for money is therefore all-important. A meal costing £60 per head can hardly be worth that sum yet people will patronize a restaurant charging such a price because they believe it provides value for money. It follows that the restaurant has to ensure that the customer's perception of value is never undermined – standards have to be rigidly maintained. Once standards start slipping in a high-price restaurant, customers quickly realize that value is not being provided. A restaurant in this situation faces an enormous problem in reimposing high standards because customers who have lost faith will need to be convinced all over again that value for money is once more being provided.

If America has influenced London, the capital sets the pace for catering developments in the provinces. The chief characteristic of the restaurant industry is that it is fast moving in its recognition of new trends and changing public taste. Most restaurateurs in the popular section of the market will say that a restaurant's décor and menu will last about five years. Thereafter, new ideas usually have to be introduced to revive a slowly declining trade. But to re-equip a restaurant can cost anything up to £200,000; such an investment needs to be matched by a similar sized conviction in your ability to provide a product that the public wants.

The key to success, obvious though it sounds, is that a professional restaurateur will give his customers what they want in the way they want it – not what he thinks they should want. This is sometimes the fatal mistake of the amateur who assumes that the public will always like the kind of food that he likes to cook. Such a restaurateur may succeed by his enthusiasm, his cooking skills and by the atmosphere he creates. But more frequently, the commercially successful caterer is the one who provides the kind of food the public wants and is willing to pay for.

Before going into the restaurant industry you must know what you want to do, what kind of restaurant you want to run and what market you are aiming at. Once you have made up your mind you must be determined to provide the highest possible standard of excellence within that market. Berni Inns, for example, has a compact menu consisting of a relatively small number of items and offers simple plate service. It is successful because it provides the public with what the public wants at the price that it is willing to pay. Within the framework of the limited menu and service, Berni aims to provide the best-value steaks on the market. The same situation exists with other successful, limited menu restaurants. There must be no compromise on quality. All the successful restaurant chains – Berni, McDonald's, Beefeater, Strikes – are successful precisely because they have analysed the customer's needs and know what he or she expects. As far as is humanly possible (mistakes occur, as anyone in catering quickly discovers) they refuse to lower the quality of food and service unless it is for a specific marketing reason. If standards are maintained, prices can be increased steadily because customers realize they are constantly getting value for money.

Those thinking of buying a restaurant can learn a great deal from this professional approach. Major chain caterers affect the industry because they can influence the expectation of the public which, in turn, affects the individual restaurateur. Berni, for example, tends to set national standards for the quality and price of steaks in the country. Wimpy, McDonald's and other American hamburger restaurants largely set the standard of hamburgers. A restaurateur in the same market who provides an inferior product to that of Berni or McDonald's is playing hostage to fortune.

For this reason (and partly because they want to stamp their personality on their own operation) independent restaurateurs tend to offer a more individualistic menu. Providing unusual dishes prevents comparison with major chain operations and attracts customers by virtue of their own individuality. Many of these restaurants are highly successful but only because they have wittingly or unwittingly stumbled on a formula that the public likes. There is an element of chance in this as well as of cool calculation; how you, as a restaurateur, combine these elements will determine your success.

If this presents the restaurant industry as a confusing, fast-moving, chancy business, then that is as it should be. There are more bankruptcies in the restaurant sector than in any other sector of the hotel and catering industry. Those who are thinking of entering it need to be aware of the dangers. Cooking commercially for thirty or more people is not just an extension of cooking for a large family. With family parties the host controls the timing of the meal; in a restaurant the customers can be late or can stay too long over drinks; they can be rude and difficult and they can change their minds; too many customers can arrive at the same time; the waiting staff can have an off day – and so can you. All these are hazards that the average restaurateur faces every day. To run a restaurant well so that people actually want to pay to eat your food can be a daunting and exacting experience.

Public houses

Running a public house entails just as long hours as running a hotel or restaurant. Most publicans start work before 8.00 a.m. in the cellar or in the kitchen, working through until 3.30 or 4.00; after a couple of hours rest they are back on duty and they are rarely in bed before 1.00 a.m.

If those are the same sort of hours that most hoteliers and restaurateurs work, the publican has a special cross to bear. As much as any restaurateur, the publican depends on his personality for success. People are attracted to a restaurant by the patron and to be welcomed and recognized by him – a very human form of social acknowledgement. People go to a pub for much the same reason. But because the publican is almost always behind the bar and is readily accessible he is in even greater customer contact than a restaurateur. He has to be prepared to listen to all the joys and woes, all the jokes and stories that his customers want to heap upon him.

It goes without saying that a publican needs to be a rather special person – a paragon, in fact, patient and equable, tolerant yet firm, personable and hospitable; he needs to like other people's company. It is equally obvious that there are some publicans in the trade who were attracted into it years ago by the thought of being a 'genial mine host' but for whom the geniality has long since worn off. The dream of many is to retire to run a little pub in the country. For those who are unprepared, far from being a happy dream it turns out to be more of a nightmare. On duty and in close customer contact every day, they quickly realize that they are trapped by the long hours and arduous work involved. For others, the pub is a light burden to carry. They find the work enjoyable and by constantly meeting people they feel they are part of their regulars' lives and feel they provide a valuable social service – which indeed they do.

Most pubs offer considerable business possiblities. The majority in Great Britain are still owned by the breweries and leased to tenants – they are called tenanted houses. About a quarter of all pubs are owned and managed by the breweries themselves; the brewery puts in a manager who is responsible for the profitable operation of the establishment. Managed pubs tend to be large multi-bar units with a fairly sophisticated food operation. The brewery has invested heavily in it and it makes a good return, though not all food operations in managed pubs are run by the brewery. It sometimes happens that the manager pays a token 'rent' to the brewery for the catering franchise in the pub — above that, what he takes is his. Tenanted pubs are usually smaller and, in some cases, the food operation is non-existent. It is in this area that the tenant can make a great deal of money.

Pubs, which are the original franchise operation, have traditionally been used only as a retail outlet for the brewer's beer. The tenant pays an 'ingoing' which is the equivalent of a franchise fee and agrees to buy only the brewer's beer, wines and spirits. The brewery is responsible for the exterior and the structure of the building but the tenant is responsible for the interior and for the operation of the pub. He can if he wishes sell food and this has become a major trend. In fact, breweries are now keen to encourage pub food because it helps increase beer sales. They impose no restriction on a publican wanting to serve food and, indeed, usually have a catering adviser to give guidance to the publican. All food revenue and profits go to the tenant and the more food he can sell, the more money he makes. As his wage costs are usually small (most pub food is prepared by the publican's wife) the profit can be considerable. Good food acts as a powerful attraction to many pub regulars, particularly at lunch-time, so the development of pub food is to everyone's advantage. The food is often simple, consisting of sandwiches or rolls and one or two home-made dishes, and the food costing is not difficult. More recent trends, however, reveal that pub food is becoming increasingly sophisticated, and few pubs can now survive without offering a food service.

Apart from tenanted and managed houses there are free houses – pubs which are not tied to any particular brewery. The number of these that are available varies in different regions of the country but, in recent years, more free houses appear to be coming on to the market. Even so, the number of free houses does not compare with the number of tenancies available. People wanting a pub tend to look first for a free house and because of this they are highly prized and rather expensive. In buying a free house, you are buying the equivalent of a hotel without bedrooms. They can be an excellent business but you are obviously committing a much greater degree of capital to the enterprise than for a tenancy and you must be that much more certain of your abilities and interest. It is sound advice to work in a pub for a time to get the feel of the business. In this way, you will get a thorough introduction to the problems and difficulties you will face in a place of your own. If you buy a pub, hotel or restaurant afterwards, you will be basing your decision on a much firmer foundation of experience than you would otherwise.

Your choice

The choice of which sector to enter – hotel, restaurant or pub – is a personal one but there are some final points to make.

First, examine your motives carefully. If you are thinking of retiring in peace to a hotel or restaurant – forget it; better to invest your money in something much safer and less demanding. It won't be so exciting but it will, at least, give you peace of mind. Hotelkeeping and catering is a place for only the most energetic and committed people.

If you want to come into the industry because you like 'meeting people' – think very hard about the consequences. A hotel or restaurant is a public place; anyone can use your facilities and unless they are being a nuisance, there is nothing you can do to stop them. If you are attracted because you like 'throwing parties' remember that you are accustomed to doing this in a controlled environment where you invite those guests whom you wish to invite. This is not the case in a hotel and people you do not like will certainly walk in. How will you be able to cope with them? Think of the person you dislike the most. Would you be willing and able to act the perfect host for him? You should also answer another question honestly. If you want to come into the industry because you like meeting people – do they like meeting you? On the answer to that question will largely depend the success of your business.

Second, if you want to buy a hotel or restaurant 'to get away from it all' be sure you know what you are escaping from and what you are committing yourself to. For many who have made the step it has been a liberating move, giving them an immense amount of personal satisfaction. For others, it has been a step inside a prison of work in which there is no free time and little opportunity to get away from the premises. Even those who have experienced the excitement of building up a business in the early days have eventually found a worrying lack of personal freedom in being unable to get away for any length of time. The problem is compounded if you have young children. Bringing up children in a hotel is one of the most difficult of all achievements. It brings tensions to both parents and children. The hours of work demanded in the hotel make children a complicating factor and both parents (but particularly the mother) are often torn between the needs of the child and that of the hotel. There is little home life in the accepted sense of the word; children cannot be themselves and often feel they are constrained in a hotel. In any large sized hotel, being surrounded by staff can also have a deleterious effect on children in another way, giving them a sense of undue importance. I have known at least three hotelier parents who have felt obliged to move out of their hotel because they discovered that their children were giving orders to the staff. It could be argued that living out, rather than in the hotel, is the right course of action anyway. In a perfect world, this would be true but there are few couples who can afford to buy a hotel and a house of their own at the same time. The attraction of the industry initially is that it provides food and accommodation as well as a business.

Third, if you want to buy a hotel or restaurant 'to try something new' you will be reassured that the industry takes kindly to the inspired amateur – to the person who, without any previous catering experience, can set up a business that exactly fills a need in a market. By offering something new with a menu or an atmosphere that is fresh and imaginative they catch the public's imagination. But for every one of these capable people, there are many more who believe that catering is a soft option and who bring little to catering but their own desire to jump on to what they believe is a successful bandwagon.

These are fundamentally the wrong reasons for wanting to come into hotelkeeping and catering though there are important points about all of them. The main reason for coming into the industry is to make money. If that sounds too obviously commercial it is a point that needs emphasizing, nevertheless. Hotelkeeping and catering is one of the last genuinely entrepreneurial industries left in the British economy that can accommodate the 'inspired amateur' so that he can have a satisfying job and can still make money. At the same time he can provide a service that the public needs. It is easy to talk of the need for service but neither the service nor the product can be supplied without, at the end of the day, a profit being made. Hotelkeeping and catering is a service industry but it is also highly commercial. The rewards are big but the penalties for slipshod control, low standards and poor marketing are all too obvious. The need to provide value for money is paramount.

There are a number of other factors that need to be considered once you know exactly why you want to buy your own business and what you want to buy. Will you run it by yourself? Are you thinking of setting up by yourself or

Customers can be very difficult!

Don't underestimate how difficult customers can be. This is an extract from 'Business at the Bear', a series of real-life articles written by John and Amanda Willmott, then the proprietors of the Bear Hotel, Wantage, Oxfordshire, for a weekly catering industry newspaper.

Every hotelier must have had one of those disastrous days when he believes that things cannot possibly become any worse – and then they do.

We had one such day last Saturday. Our problems began in the evening, at the commencement of our regular Saturday night dinner dance. A party of 22 had booked, wishing to eat early at 7.30 p.m. We had agreed to this and the band were due to begin at 7.30 p.m. However, at 7.45 p.m., as the party were being served with the main course, the band had still not arrived. They eventually turned up at 8 p.m. and spent the next 40 minutes setting up the equipment and establishing that their amplifier was faulty – it was emitting a high pitched buzzing noise at regular intervals.

By this time, our other large party of 15 people had arrived and things began to hot up.

We suggested to this party that they might like to congregate in the bar and we would take their orders there. Their 'organiser' seemed to assume that we were delaying their dinner for some reason and, having seen the party of 22 already seated in the restaurant, complained that it was unfair that his party should be unable to sit down until other people had left. We assured him that this was not the case, and that his table was already prepared.

He accepted this and returned to the bar, although, as we later discovered from our bar staff, he omitted to pass on the information to the other members of his party.

Having successfully served the first course to this group, our next big hitch came with the main course. The same gentleman waited until all the dishes had been silver-served and the vegetables passed round, and then called us over. Without even picking up his knife and fork to taste his food he demanded that all the meals should be returned to the kitchen as they were stone cold (some of his party had already begun to eat their dinner, and with obvious enjoyment).

Chaos reigned for the next few minutes as plates of food were hurtled back into the kitchen, the other large party clamoured for more coffee, the band's amplifier buzzed, and our 'awkward' customer told everyone in the restaurant that his meal had obviously come straight from the freezer.

In order to make amends to those people who had had their meals whisked from under their very noses, we provided the party with additional complimentary wine. The meal was re-served, and despite a number of sarcastic comments to members of our staff, all 15 people ate it.

Comments continued throughout the service of the sweets, although at all stages in the meal no wasted food was returned to the kitchen.

The chain of events was completed by a disastrous mistake over the bill – the complimentary wine was charged for.

Despite our apologies, the atmosphere created by these few unpleasant people permeated the restaurant and the smaller parties were also affected. The 15 left declaring they would not return – a sentiment of which we heartily approved.

We certainly never wish to re-live that night. After a post-mortem of the evening's events, we agreed that we had all learnt some valuable lessons about human nature.

We feel sure that none of these 15 people would have behaved in a similar way in a bank, shop or in their own homes, but good manners are sometimes not preserved for hoteliers.

To make matters worse, when we expressed our dissatisfaction to the band they refused to accept any responsibility for their faulty equipment and the resulting poor performance. We wish we could deal with complaints in a similar fashion – although we should soon be out of business.

We were delighted when one of the smaller parties present that night returned later in the week for dinner – and made a point of telling us how badly behaved they considered the party of 15 had been. We are hoping that others present on that fateful night also thought along those lines!

in partnership with your wife or husband or with some other person? Will you be the sole owner or joint partner?

This is an area full of potential pitfalls. Most couples who consider buying their own business are in early middle age where the husband and perhaps the wife have both worked separately. They hardly know each other in a business environment. The conflicts that can arise when they begin to work together are almost too obvious to need mentioning, yet they are often forgotten. The time to face up to them is before the business is purchased and not afterwards. By then, when everything begins to fall to pieces, it will be too late to find that you cannot work together.

Hotelkeeping and catering can put a strain on the health of people working in it and it can kill a marriage through the stress of long hours, hard work and exhaustion and through the lack of privacy. Working together can add to these strains. Many couples adjust to the new environment and happily prosper; some do not, surviving only long enough to talk to the Divorce Court judge. I suspect that the industry has a high divorce rate not because hoteliers are any more fallible than others but because the industry itself is frequently the marriage partner. Often, there is not much room or time left for anything else.

Individual couples who are successful make their own *modus vivendi* but it is likely that consciously or sub-consciously one of you will eventually emerge as the boss. This is natural, but decisions need to be taken after consultation and by agreement if the partnership is to prosper and develop. Make sure you have well-defined and separate areas of responsibility. One of you may be responsible for the kitchen and cellar. Don't interfere with each other's areas – you have to make your own mistakes. If you want to make comments, do so when you are rational and sensible, not under pressure at the point of service or before staff or customers. A sense of humour is vital. If you have children, make sure you give them some of your time every day.

Husband and wife teams are frequently found in hotels, almost always in public house tenancies but are less common in restaurants. In a pub, the husband and wife work together on the same jobs and there is little chance of separate areas of responsibility though the wife is usually in charge of food. If you are taking a pub you need to be especially convinced that you can work together. It is often said that wives run pubs. They give strength and character, even if it is apparent only behind the scenes. A hotel offers more scope for separate developments being, generally speaking, a larger place and there are many examples of successful husband and wife couples operating hotels. If you are thinking of operating a hotel together try to talk to local hoteliers and their wives to identify from them what problems they faced when they took over.

A restaurant offers the most delineated areas of responsibility. The husband cooks and the wife is in charge of the service (or vice versa) but beware! Anyone who has ever worked in the industry will tell you that the greatest area of friction in a hotel or restaurant is the contact between the kitchen and the restaurant. Like oil and water, the two sides appear incapable of ever mixing happily together.

There are other factors governing your choice of business, the chief of which is how much money you have available. Broadly speaking, hotels and free houses are more expensive but offer better security for a loan; a restaurant is cheaper to buy but its potential is the most difficult to estimate. Raising a loan on a restaurant presents more problems than a hotel because the bricks and mortar of the latter provide more of a solid asset base. Banks and financial institutions look more favourably on hotels as collateral because they are usually property-backed businesses; a café in a rented High Street lock-up does not have the same financial standing. Nevertheless, any financial institution will value your hotel as a business, not as property, and there may be a disparity between the two.

Your success in raising finance depends on how much you want to raise, how much you can invest in the business and your business experience. Most couples can sell their own home and other assets in order to help raise sufficient capital to go into business by themselves. Whatever you can raise yourself it would be reasonable to look for matching capital of at least the same again (more on this in Chapter 6).

In general terms most first-time purchasers will be able to buy a 15-20 bedroom hotel in a resort but not so easily in London or a major provincial city. Hotels are expensive to buy in London because you are paying a premium for the capital being the most successful hotel city in Britain and because property values there are the highest in Britain. Hotels in many provincial cities, particularly those that are well-maintained, are also expensive. Prices in resorts are somewhat discounted because of their more uncertain future and their seasonal trading pattern. But this does not mean that a seaside hotel cannot be profitable. Many of them are. They also present excellent opportunities for untrained hoteliers to gain experience of hotel life and can be used as a stepping stone to bigger things.

Before you begin to look seriously for a hotel, there are three final pieces of advice.

1   Make sure you talk to as many hoteliers as you can beforehand – they are usually happy to give advice to people seriously thinking of entering the industry. Better still, work in the industry for a month or two to get the feel of it. Anyone who has not worked in a hotel or restaurant should do so before he takes the plunge into ownership. In a week behind the scenes you can learn more about the difficulties of hotelkeeping than any book could possibly explain.

2   Second, it is essential that you commit yourself to the process of buying a business. The search is likely to be a long one – six months is an average time – and there will be many times when you will feel like calling a halt. Try not to be deterred. If you look hard enough and if you are determined, you will eventually find the right place.

3   Don't equate your own private standards with commercial standards. A
    hotel or pub may not be as clean as your own home, for example. Many
    couples, when they look over a hotel, are appalled at the dirty little
    corners, the carbonized gas stoves and spotted carpets. The standards of
    many hotels are much lower than most people would tolerate in their
    home. When you take over you will obviously do your best to raise
    standards – a task that will become your top priority.

3 How do I find a place of my own?

Location, location and location

Conrad Hilton once defined the three most important factors in the success of any hotel. They were, he said, 'Location, location and location'. This clever analysis has become the most famous remark in the hotel industry because it provides the recipe for success for any hotelier, whether he owns his own business or whether he is the president of an international hotel corporation.

Hilton was not being merely clever when he made his remark. The success of a hotel, he was saying, depends on the country in which it is located, the area of the country in which it is located and its precise location in that particular area. All three factors are important and all of them are interdependent.

For example, if you are purchasing a hotel in Britain, do Scotland and Wales offer the same potential as England? The answer is yes, broadly speaking, but hotels in some parts of the Highlands and Islands have a lower occupancy than most country hotels in England. On the other hand, Aviemore enjoys year-round occupancy. Certain areas or towns are clearly better than others. Is it better to have a hotel in Glasgow, for example, than in Liverpool which has been more badly hit by the recession, and which, in any case, has too many hotels? The answer is that Glasgow is better. But where in Glasgow? Would you buy a hotel in the city centre or in the suburbs? Most professional hoteliers would prefer to be in the city centre although it is unlikely that a first-time purchaser would be able to afford a city centre hotel, even if one was available. This simple example helps to illustrate the importance of location as the primary consideration in buying a hotel but does not explain it precisely.

One constraint is that a person buying a hotel will have already made up his mind about the part of the country he wants to settle in. That may have been a decision dictated more by his personal preferences than by commercial consideration and there are problems in this area. Do not underestimate the difficulties of a southerner running a hotel or restaurant in the North of England where he may find it difficult to be accepted. Ironically there does not appear to be a similar difficulty in northerners coming south. In the same way a Glaswegian would be able to run a hotel or restaurant in Edinburgh successfully but Edinburgh folk have difficulty in being successful in Glasgow. This is too complex a subject to examine in depth here but the difficulties nevertheless exist and continue through to the type of food customers want and the size of portions.

A more important constraint is that once he has decided on an area there is little a hotelier can do to improve an existing hotel's location. A hotel cannot be physically moved to increase its business. It will therefore have to encourage customers to find their way to it, rather than rely on attracting them in as they pass by. In this situation, the important consideration is whether trade can be developed by a proper marketing strategy and effective sales promotion techniques (see Chapter 9). In many cases, this is possible and the hotel will be able to overcome what appears to be a poor location.

The situation is different with popular, café-style restaurants. Because they rely much more on passing trade and because there are far more restaurants than hotels in a town, precise location is crucial. One side of a street can be acceptable, the other can be disastrous; a few hundred yards up the street the good side can become bad while the bad side can improve. There is no certain formula for success. Much depends on the character and layout of the town. What a popular fast food restaurant needs most of all is good passing residential traffic, preferably in a busy shopping area; a nearby cinema, bingo hall or theatre is often useful in generating trade as is a nearby pedestrian area. A street with many other restaurants in it is usually an advantage to each individual restaurant in the street. The introduction of a nationally known restaurant, such as Wimpy, can encourage more people into the street and consequently into other restaurants. Being the only restaurant may appear to give you a monopoly but it is often not beneficial – a solitary restaurant does not easily encourage people into the eating-out habit. While a popular restaurant benefits from heavy pedestrian traffic on its doorstep, a haute cuisine restaurant selling expensive food may not. That will survive on the quality of its food, service and ambience because people will make a specific journey to get there.

Whether you are buying a hotel or restaurant, you must first make up your mind which part of the country you want to move to and the type of business you are looking for. That is the major decision on location and the various tables and charts in Chapter 1 may help you decide. You then have to look more closely at the area and decide whether there are any particular towns you favour. If there are, get to know them well. Stay for a few days if you can. Walk about the town; drive around the area. Read the local town guide to see what competition there is and find out what is the population of the area and its relative prosperity.

Talk to as many people as you can – hoteliers, restaurateurs, locals and council offices. Get to know what makes the town prosperous, when it is busy and whether there are any plans to expand it. What major industrial companies are there and are they developing? Is the local authority keen to attract new industry? Is the housing market buoyant and are new houses being built?

You should also find out whether the centre of the town is being redeveloped. Popular restaurants are particularly vulnerable to shifting patterns in major cities. New shopping precincts upset the balance of trade, taking shoppers away from traditional shopping streets and moving them to the new area. Make sure you know what developments are being planned – you don't want to buy a busy restaurant which, in a year's time, will be deserted because people have been attracted to a new shopping precinct elsewhere.

The same criteria apply to a hotel though the precise location in a town is not quite so vital. The important question to ask is whether the hotel is convenient for people to find. A hotel in the High Street will pose few problems but a hotel tucked away off the main road will miss all passing traffic. As planning authorities strictly control the erection of directional signs you have to encourage customers to the hotel by other means – which is why you must be sure this can be achieved before you decide to purchase. A hotel on a major trunk road can be as busy as one in a city centre. Many new hotels have been built on roadside sites – Trusthouse Forte's Post Houses, for example. A city centre hotel may pick up passing pedestrian trade but if it does not have convenient car parking facilities car owners will be attracted more to out-of-town hotels, most of which are built on 'green field' sites and have extensive car parking areas.

The most important factor in hotel or restaurant location, therefore, is the ease with which the customer can find the establishment. With the growth of car ownership, this is why many new hotels have been built on prime trunk routes. Passing traffic can be attracted to such hotels and, at the same time, customes can be more easily directed to them than if they were in obscure streets off the city centre. Many of the hotels on trunk routes are near trading estates (an important source of business) and it is usually easier for guests to get away in the morning because they avoid traffic congestion in the city centre. There are economic advantages, too. Green field sites are generally cheaper to develop and provide more space for the future expansion of the hotel.

Location may dictate the ultimate success or failure of a hotel but two hotels in the same town, with similar facilities, can achieve strikingly different profit results. Apart from location the other factor that vitally affects hotel profitability is the marketing strategy. Is the hotel in the right market? In other words, is it trying to find the right kind of customers for its location and facilities? Is the pricing policy correct for its market? A hotel cannot expect to attract the cheap, high volume summer coach trade if its tariffs are high. Is the hotel too dependent on one source of business – tourist or holiday maker, commercial executive or conference delegate? If you are trying to obtain a good mix of business does one source affect another? A hotel filled with a cheap coach party may have no room for commercial traffic for which you can charge a higher tariff. Happily, however, the peak season for coach and holiday traffic, which is June–September, coincides with the time when commercial traffic is at its lowest because of holidays. In some instances different types of clientele may not mix socially and one type may deter another. A small hotel filled with elderly winter residents may not be attractive to commercial guests, for example. On the other hand, a coach party is better than an empty hotel. An accurate assessment of the market is therefore of prime importance to any hotel because this will dictate its profitability.

There are other ingredients to success, one of the most important being the efficiency of the owner or manager to control the enterprise and its staff. A good manager can develop a hotel in the most unpromising location; an ineffective manager can ruin the best-located hotel.

Business potential

In buying a hotel or restaurant you not only purchase the building but also its business potential. There are many hotels where the potential is not yet fully realized. This could be for any number of different reasons – the present owners may be nearing retiring age and are just coasting along; they may have put the business in the hands of a manager who does not care; they may have neglected to maintain the property and its services, thus deterring potential customers; or they may be merely incompetent.

To be able to judge this type of business needs some experience which is why, when you are seeking a hotel, it is better to visit as many as you can. Half an hour sitting in the lobby of almost any hotel indicates whether the place is well-run. The staff will be tidy and attentive to customers; the telephone is answered efficiently; the manager or proprietor will be seen often and staff will be working purposefully; if you order tea or coffee it will come quickly; the hotel will be clean and so will the cutlery and china. All these are pointers to a well-run hotel. A badly-run hotel indicates that the potential is not being fully realized. Don't be put off by such a property – it may be an opportunity for you to grasp. The potential may be considerable providing the location is right. A hotel with poor results is less expensive to purchase than a professionally-run establishment which is already making handsome profits, though you may have greater difficulty in raising matching capital. With the former, you are gambling with your own abilities; with the latter, you are paying for the present owner's past efforts.

Having got as far as inspecting a hotel, you need to talk to the vendor to find out the answers to a large number of essential questions. Don't be fobbed off with vague responses. It is absolutely vital that you know the true position of the business.

The first question to ask is why the hotel is on the market. There are many legitimate reasons. Some hoteliers move from hotel to hotel, climbing the ladder by acquiring bigger properties. Conversely, some want to move to a smaller hotel so that they have fewer commitments. Others are retiring or going abroad or merely want to move to a different part of the country. A reasonable time for a proprietor to develop a hotel is three to five years – a hotelier who is selling more quickly than this to get a bigger hotel is either being too ambitious or may realize that the establishment is not working. You must judge whether, with your own greater efforts and personal commitment, you could make it work better.

The most important next step is to look at the accounts. This is a subject of such complexity that it is difficult to give any advice at all although it is dealt with in greater detail in the next chapter. Ideally you need access to figures for the last three years in order to judge the true performance of the hotel and to assess its growth and profit record. But remember the phrase attributed to Disraeli: 'There are lies, damned lies and statistics'. He was not discussing the hotel industry at the time, but the accounts of many small hotels and catering concerns could fall into one or all of those categories. Hotelkeeping is a highly practical profession and many hoteliers clearly prefer to serve their guests than to spend time keeping their accounts.

The records that you should ask to see (and which do show the whole story) are the hotel reservation and banqueting diaries (if banqueting is applicable), rooming charts and the sales ledger (if one is kept). It is normally safe to assume that the outgoings are fully stated in the accounts, perhaps even exaggerated in some cases.

It used to be the situation, and it might still exist here and there, that resort hoteliers did not know whether they had made a profit until the next season was about to start. Budgeting was unheard of and monthly profit and loss accounts did not exist. Money was received and recorded, bills were paid (eventually) and only later did the hotelier or his accountant work out whether they had made a profit. Customs and Excise, because they demand VAT returns every three months, have done much to tighten up accounting procedures, but the old adage that hoteliers keep three sets of accounts – one for themselves, one for the bank manager and one for the Inland Revenue – may only just be an exaggeration. Treat every set of accounts prepared by a hotelier with some degree of reserve. The industry offers such scope for conflicting opinions and views on the treatment of items that every set of accounts must be carefully analysed before you can judge whether the profit is real or imaginary, understated or overemphasized. Hotelkeeping and catering is a cash business and the scope for cash leakages, whether on purpose or by accident, is considerable. (It should be noted here that both the Inland Revenue and the Customs and Excise appreciate this and will not hesitate to prosecute if they believe that turnover or profit is being flagrantly under-recorded.)

The accounts will, with some reservations, indicate the position of the business as it has been for the past three years and as it is now. They will show whether the growth has been steady or erratic. You also need to examine other areas. What occupancy is experienced by the other hotels in the town and in the area generally? Talk to other local hoteliers. If they are not willing to divulge their occupancy figures, the local tourist board will be able to help. If occupancy is low, where are the problem areas? If no one is staying at the weekends, can you build up the trade? Is there greater potential in food and drink sales? Is the wage ratio at the right level and are the other costs realistic? Is there a possibility of saving money in these crucial areas? Don't forget that profit is not just a question of attracting extra revenue but is also dependent on containing existing costs.

There are many other questions, most of which are explained in detail in the next chapter. At the end of the visit you will come away with the feeling that either the property is definitely not the place for you or that it is your ideal hotel. In one or two cases, you may be uncertain. If that is the case, be clear in your own mind about the factors that attract you to the hotel and the factors that deter you. They have to be balanced out and you should try to avoid the danger of rationalizing the drawbacks and highlighting the advantages – a dangerous exercise in any important commercial decision. If you like a hotel's style and character be sure that it is commercially viable and has potential for development.

You also have to balance the need for urgent action in putting in an offer and the need for caution in not being stampeded into a situation that you may regret later. Before being able to assess the value of the business and how much you believe you should offer for it, you should undertake a simple feasibility study (see Chapter 5). However, if there are several people interested in the property, you may feel it advisable to put in an early offer and work out your feasibility study later. There is still time to withdraw if your figures do not come up to expectations.

Estate agents

Some explanation of the role of the hotel estate agent may be helpful here. It is likely that you will have already been in contact with at least one agent if you are reading this book. In doing so, you will have realized that the most effective way for any inexperienced hotel purchaser to buy a hotel is to get his name on to the list of a reputable agent. Even better, go and talk to him. To save their time and yours, the better agents will ask penetrating questions that will make you think – the sort of questions that we have already covered. What type of business are you looking for? Where should it be located? How much money have you got? The answers to these are important if any agent is going to help you. While you should never forget that he is working for the vendor (and is thus committed to obtaining the best price possible for the property) he has an interest in matching the vendor's aspirations with the purchaser's requirements.

A good estate agent, sympathetic to your requirements, will work hard to create a deal and make it stick. He is being paid by the vendor but as he gets the bulk of his income from completed sales, he is always prepared to work hard to effect a sale that is to the advantage of both vendor and purchaser.

Good estate agents have a sixth sense in sniffing out those inquirers who are not genuinely serious or who have totally insufficient capital. This is why, if you are serious, you should definitely see some agents at the outset so that they appreciate your interests. Too many applicants don't know what they want. You will get on to any agent's books initially at the drop of a letter in the post box (although some are beginning to consider charging a nominal fee for this service) but the particulars will soon start drying up if you subsequently show little or no interest in the details. Postage and stationery costs are too high for an agent to continue sending particulars without any response, so you should appreciate the agent's difficulties and make sure you make your mark early on.

Don't just talk to an agent at the beginning but keep in contact with him at least once every ten days, preferably by telephone. In this way, he knows that you are serious and he will be able to help you. With such constant contact you may well come across a new property on the books before it is generally released. An agent who is convinced of your seriousness will even call you if he believes he has something new that is of interest.

There are, of course, other methods of discovering properties for sale – the columns of the trade press, the local and national papers, and specialized property papers like *Dalton's Weekly* and *London Property Advertiser*. The drawback to these methods is that few, if any, potential purchasers subscribe to the trade press (though they should because it gives them a feel for the industry). Most of the properties advertised are, in any case, in agent's hands.

Don't stick only to national hotel agents, important though they are, if you are seeking a small hotel or restaurant. Make contact with local agents if you know which part of the country you want to settle in. It is unlikely that a local agent will carry a major property without it being on the books of a national agent but the possibility should not be overlooked. Some local agents are likely to be more useful than others – contact those with large commercial premises departments who may well have lock-up shops on their books that can be used as a café or restaurant. One couple I know bought a 25-bedroom hotel through a local agent. This is comparatively rare, but it does happen. Unfortunately, the quality of information from a local agent, unaccustomed to handling a hotel or catering property, may be poor. If you are in doubt, follow the advice given in the next chapter and if you want further advice, talk over the proposition with a reputable hotel agent or licensed valuer. He may charge for his advice but it could be money well spent. One other way of discovering a property is to write to a likely hotel yourself, perhaps through an accountant or a solicitor. You need to be bold to do this, however, and you also need to be absolutely certain of your intentions.

In an ideal world, you should make up your mind about the viability of the business and of its potential before you put in your offer, but time might be against you. You might well have to make an offer and work out the figures later. There are some rule of thumb methods of assessing a hotel's value but they should be used only by professionals. A figure related to the turnover – ranging from £3 for every £1 of turnover for a smaller establishment to £1 for every £1 of turnover for larger establishments – can often apply to free houses. With hotels, it is preferable to calculate the net disposable profit, since the purchase price can be anything between four and eight times that figure.

Some professional hoteliers go on a cost per bedroom – buying an existing hotel they would not pay more than a certain amount per bedroom; but this calculation is often thrown awry by the degree of food and beverage revenue, the quality of the rooms and whether they have private bathrooms, and other factors. In London property values would make these calculations a nonsense anyway. A simple test (more accurate costings are essential) would be to assume that for every £1000 per cost of bedroom you will have to charge at least £1 bedroom tariff. Thus if a hotel had ten bedrooms and you paid £200,000 for the property you would have to charge at least £20 per night. The question that you would need to answer is whether you could charge such a tariff for the hotel.

In the final analysis, the only satisfactory means of working out an offer is to take a long and critical look at the hotel and its location, to examine how it has performed in the past and to pinpoint its weak points. Then you need to show how you can improve its performance in the future. These figures will indicate whether the asking price is reasonable, bearing in mind the investment you will be making and borrowed money that you will have to repay with interest.

The result of this exercise is called, somewhat grandly, a feasibility study – but don't be put off by the jargon because its purpose is simple even if its execution is more difficult. It will show (it cannot prove, but then nothing is certain) that either the business will generate enough profit to pay off the borrowings you require and leave something extra for you; or that the revenue that the hotel can earn will not sustain your financial borrowings. The next two chapters explain in detail how to go about preparing your own feasibility study.

4 Is the business sound ?

Buying a business, particularly a hotel, presents the same problems as buying a house but they are greatly magnified. With a house, you need only to be satisfied that the building itself is sound. Buying a hotel means you not only have to be satisfied that the structure is sound but that the business is on firm foundations, too. Maintaining a hotel is an expensive operation; if you buy a property that needs rewiring, replumbing or a new roof you can incur enormous unbudgeted expense. Since you will be borrowing money on the business potential of the hotel and on the building itself, a financial institution will need to be satisfied on the soundness of both structure and accounts.

After meeting the vendor and seeing the hotel or restaurant, most purchasers know whether or not they like the property. Initial discussions with the vendor will have established the main facts about the business, particularly on turnover and profits. Either at the first meeting or at a later discussion you need to ask the questions that are covered in this chapter. In an ideal world you should go away to think about the hotel for a few days. A couple of days' reflection tends to make a potential purchaser more enthusiastic about the property; alternatively, he might begin to lose interest, the drawbacks and disadvantages overcoming his initially favourable view. For those who continue to be non-committal about the hotel it is probably wise not to pursue the purchase. If you are not enthusiastic when you buy it, what chance is there of becoming more committed afterwards?

Unfortunately, there are times when the opportunity for reflection is just not available because the demand for hotel or catering properties is very strong in some areas. The vendor may have a large number of other potential purchasers knocking on his door (or he may claim he has) and rather than trying to agree a price you may even be faced with being gazumped. So you may have to move very fast. If this is the case put in an offer and, if it is accepted, prepare your feasibility study (see Chapter 5) later.

Before you discuss the business with the vendor, make sure you have some knowledge of the accounts. You could ask an accountant friend (it would be worthwhile to hire an accountant) to go through them with you but most accountants know little about hotel industry and they may try to advise you against the purchase on the basis of the accounts alone. Let them see your feasibility study as well.

The following series of checklists on the main aspects of the business will be helpful to you when you talk to the vendor. These can best be divided into four different sectors – land, property, business, stock and contents. The lists given here are not intended to be completely comprehensive – the hotel and catering industry is too diverse for that – but the questions indicate the areas which you should be probing. Some of the questions are obviously in the province of your surveyor or solicitor. Professional fees can be high but it is better to incur them before you buy the property than to find high unforeseen expenditure afterwards which a professional could have warned you about. Rancorous disputes may be avoided in this way.

Land

These questions affect your fundamental ownership rights and are self-evidently important.

1   Is the land leasehold or freehold?
    If leasehold:
2   Who is the landlord?
3   What is the current rent?
4   What is the length of the lease and is it fully repairing and insuring?
5   How many unexpired years remain?
6   Can you use the lease as a security for a loan?
7   When and how often is the rent subject to review and on what basis?
8   Does the lease contain restrictive clauses concerning such aspects as entertainment, liquor licence, car and coach parking?
9   Are there any rights of way, rights of parking or access, rights of cropping or grazing?
10 Who is responsible for the maintenance of the exits, entrances, boundary walls and fences?

The name of the landlord in the case of a leasehold will, of course, be of interest to you but it will not be critical – don't forget, you are buying the lease only. Most of these questions fall properly within the province of your solicitor. It is helpful if he knows something about the industry so obtain advice – perhaps from your agent – about a suitable person to act for you. If the hotel agent is doing his job properly, he will know the answers to most of these questions anyway.

There are two schools of thought in the hotel industry on the merits and disadvantages of leasehold property. One views the hotel industry as a business primarily concerned with maximizing the use of a property. The structure itself is viewed as the main asset and, because of this, it is important to own the freehold. In this way, the rise in freehold values through inflation and improvements are reflected in the accounts, thus giving the business an ever more solid asset base. With no rent reviews to be implemented, the cost of purchase of a freehold property becomes historically cheap particularly in times of high inflation.

The other school of thought, which is common in the restaurant business where there is much more leasehold property, views property primarily as a tool for a business purpose. The ownership of the building is irrelevant and may even be detrimental because it ties up capital in bricks and mortar which cannot earn money until the building is sold.

A leasehold, therefore, should not be rejected out of hand but it needs careful scrutiny because it has to be made profitable before the lease expires so that you can get your investment back with interest.

Property

The next area to look at closely is the property itself. Here is a checklist:

1 Has a fire certificate been granted and is it up to date? If not, why not? Don't forget, every time an alteration is made to the premises after the date it was granted, approval needs to be obtained from the fire authority for the fire certificate to remain valid.
2 Is the property connected to the main sewers?
3 If the hotel is not connected to the main drainage, how is sewage treated and disposed of and what is the cost, if any, of this operation? Why are main drains not connected? Will pressure be exerted on you by the local authority to connect to the mains?
4 Have any verbal or written warnings been issued to the vendor by any of the following:
   (a)   the fire officer?
   (b)   the environmental health officer?
   (c)   the police, over the liquor licence or any other matter?
   (d)   the landlord?
   (e)   neighbours?
   (f)   local authority surveyor?
5 Is the site subject to flooding or subsidence?
6 Is the property officially listed as being of outstanding architectural or historic importance?
7 What planning and other applications have been submitted for future extensions and improvements? What have been the results of these applications?
8 What is the rateable value? When was the last rates assessment made? Is a new assessment likely because of recent improvements or additions?
9 Has any work been carried out during the last ten years to remedy structural failures or weaknesses, subsidence or rising damp? Are there any guarantees regarding rising damp, woodworm, etc?
10 How old are the boilers and how are they fired? Are the original boilers able to cope satisfactorily with supplying hot water to extra rooms in an extension?

11   How long is it since the property was rewired and has the electrical
     installation been recently tested throughout by a qualified electrician?
     (Normally, a certificate is needed in respect of the electrical installation
     before a fire certificate is issued.)
12   Is the water hard or soft? Has a softener been installed?
13   How many customer car parking spaces are available and where are the
     nearest local authority parks? What is their capacity?
14   Are nearby car parks open until midnight, seven days a week?
15   Are main gas services available in the immediate vicinity?

These questions indicate the main areas of the property that need probing.
The hotel agent will have answers to some of them but it is always wise to
check either yourself or through your surveyor (for questions 2, 3, 5, 9, 10, 11,
12, 15) and your solicitor (for questions 1, 4, 6, 7, 8).

Fire certificate
Any hotel or boarding house that sleeps more than six people (guests or staff)
needs to have applied for a fire certificate. Any establishment, however small,
where sleeping accommodation is provided above the first floor level or below
ground floor must have also applied. The Fire Precautions Act was
introduced in 1971 and the vast majority of hotels have now complied with the
requirements of the Act. Be sure that the hotel you are purchasing has an
up-to-date fire certificate from the local fire authority who is responsible for
enforcing the regulations. The Act has been interpreted in different ways in
different parts of the country (an irritant to many hoteliers) but fireproof and
self-closing doors on bedrooms and corridors, flameproof materials,
emergency lighting, a regularly tested fire alarm system, smoke detectors and
other fire fighting appliances are among the most common demands. The cost
of these in a big hotel can amount to many thousands of pounds and even in a
small hotel proprietors have been known to pay well in excess of £10,000 to
bring their premises up to the standard required.
   Before purchasing you need to know whether a fire certificate has been
granted. If the hotelier has applied but there has been no inspection you
should try to estimate what expenditure, if any, may be incurred after the fire
officer has made his inspection.

Sewers
Some country hotels are not connected to the main sewer. This need not
necessarily be a disadvantage but it is important to know how the cess-tank is
emptied, what the costs are and whether the local authority will eventually put
pressure on you to connect the hotel to the main sewage system. Get your
surveyor to advise you.

Warnings
Warnings by any of the parties mentioned in the checklist need to be

investigated initially through the estate agent though you should always get your solicitor to check if you are in any doubt. The local environmental health officer may have visited the hotel's kitchens (like the fire officer, he has a right of access at all reasonable times) and may have warned the vendor about poor hygiene practices. Local authorities are imposing higher standards of hygiene in commercial catering establishments. There is long-standing legislation, the Food Hygiene (General) Regulations, 1970, in this area as well as the Food and Drugs (Control of Food Premises) Act, 1976, which lays down the legal requirements. The local authority has the power to close down a hotel kitchen or restaurant until it improves its standards of hygiene, though closure normally comes only after a warning. Make sure the environmental health officer is not on the point of closing down the hotel. Make sure, also, that he has not visited the hotel and demanded extensive improvements in kitchen facilities and equipment. These would become your responsibility if you buy the property.

Warnings from the police indicate another possible danger area and complaints from neighbours about noise and other nuisances should be investigated. A large percentage of a hotel's revenue may come from evening functions or a late night disco. Their continuing success must not be endangered by constant complaints from nearby residents about the noise from the music or from people slamming car doors and talking loudly when they leave. This is a matter for your solicitor to investigate.

Listed building

A listed building may sound an attractive proposition but it can be a hotelier's nightmare. Planning regulations on listed buildings (there are various grades) make it difficult and sometimes impossible for a hotelier to extend or adapt the property to suit his needs. Both internal and external alterations need to be approved for some grades of building by the local planning authority.

Some hoteliers have had to abandon much-needed improvements because of planning regulations. The local authority is also responsible for approving all exterior signs. Hotels situated some way off a main road will find it difficult to obtain permission to erect directional signs – especially if none has been erected before – even if the hotelier considers it crucial for business. Do not underestimate the difficulty of obtaining planning permission in this area. Both your surveyor and solicitor should advise you.

Planning applications

A key aspect of any hotel is the possible extension of the premises either in the form of new bedrooms or by the addition of some other facility, such as a conference suite. If the vendor has already made an application which has been rejected, it is important to know why. A revised application may succeed but in some cases the planning authority may not consider the application under any circumstances. Outline planning permission lapses after three years (five years for detailed planning permission). Get your solicitor to check.

Structural weaknesses

A new damp course for a large building is expensive; a roof slipping because the beams are rotten and full of woodworm could ruin you. Few professional hoteliers would be prepared to purchase a hotel without a thorough and proper survey. There have been a number of cases where serious structural defects made it most unwise to buy a property. If you don't have a full structural survey undertaken, which can be expensive (one hotelier spent £2500 on a full survey of a twenty-five room hotel and found to his alarm that a new roof and a new electrical system was required and that one wall suffered from subsidence; he reckoned the money was well spent and he bought another hotel) get a local builder to check the major potential problem areas – the damp course, the roof, the cellar; check for woodworm in the major timbers and get an electrician to inspect the electrical system. The finance company will send a surveyor to the property but this is only to satisfy itself on the mortgage valuation and is no substitute for your own investigation. You must satisfy yourself that the property is structurally sound.

Boilers

A hotel consumes vast amounts of hot water and needs a constant supply of energy. The boiler is the heart of your energy system. If that breaks down the business begins to collapse. With no hot water for the guests or kitchen and with no heating, a hotel can hardly operate. Boilers are expensive and very difficult items of equipment to replace because they are large, bulky and usually sited in inaccessible places. Any boiler and hot water system over thirty years old needs to be inspected carefully, but there are hotels in existence with boilers up to 100 years old. Wherever possible, it is preferable to have a standby boiler, sometimes also used for central heating, which will prevent the hotel being without hot water if the main boiler fails. There are other points to consider. The heat loss through unlagged pipes in any reasonable-sized hotel is enormous. The roof also needs to be insulated and, perhaps, cavity walls filled. Get your surveyor to advise you.

Soft water

Hard water scales hot water pipes and boilers, reduces the pressure and eventually blocks up the system. All hot water if it is not naturally soft needs to be softened with a commercial water softener. Get your surveyor to advise you.

Car parking

Over 85 per cent of the public go on holiday in their car; most business and conference delegates travel by car; almost all your local customers will use cars. The importance of an adequate car park therefore can hardly be overemphasized. Unfortunately not every hotel has a suitable area and local car parks may have to be used. How convenient are these? Are they closed at night when your evening trade will need them to be open? Are you dependent on street car parking and, if so, is this likely to be restricted in the future?

Mains gas
Oil has become an expensive commodity and mains gas is the most acceptable alternative though gas prices tend to move up in line with oil. Gas boilers require less maintenance and gas has another advantage – it demands no storage space or deliveries. If you want to change over, is gas available for the hotel?

The business

The next area that must be investigated is that of the business itself – its accounts, its customers and its staff.

Accounts
1 Are property audited accounts available? If not, why not?
2 Are the sales figures shown inclusive or exclusive of service charge and VAT?
3 Does the owner pay a proper salary and expenses to himself and relatives who help him run the business?
4 Are adequate sums to cover maintenance and depreciation charged into the accounts?
5 What is the annual sales promotion budget?
6 What is the total value of stock normally held?
7 What is the gross profit on food and liquor? Gross profit is revenue less cost of materials, expressed as a percentage – see Chapter 12.
8 What is the growth in turnover per annum over the last three years?
9 What forward bookings have been obtained and at what prices?
10 What deposits are held against forward bookings?

Customers
11 Who are the principal customers of the hotel?
12 What is the bedroom and sleeper occupancy over the last three years?
13 When was the bedroom tariff last increased? By how much?

Staff
14 How many staff live in and on what terms and conditions?
15 What are the wage costs, including staff meals, as a percentage of sales?
16 When were the members of staff last given a wage rise, by how much and on what understanding?
17 How many managers have been employed in the last ten years?

18   Have the staff been informed of the decision to sell?

General
19   What service, maintenance and hire contracts exist?
20   What brewery ties exist and can they be cancelled?

This may appear a formidable list of questions but the answers are necessary to give you an accurate picture of the business, as the following comments make clear.

Accounts
A business should develop logically and steadily. Economic factors may arise which will blow a company off course occasionally but the trend of any successful business should be noticeably upwards through increasing sales and increasing profits. A roller-coaster performance, in which turnover and profits rise and fall in an uneven sequence of events, shows that the business is either out of control or is developing haphazardly. Three years is the minimum period of time to judge the accounts of any business but not all hotels or catering businesses have accurate accounts available for this period. What you are looking for is evidence of a steady increase in sales and profits, rising occupancy due to more successful sales promotion, tighter budgeting and cost procedures. Ideally, you will be looking for a net disposable profit (before owner's salary, interest charges and depreciation) of 25 per cent of revenue. The net profit shown on the accounts presented will, however, probably show nearer 5–10 per cent of revenue after all outgoings, including servicing the capital and, if necessary, depreciating the capital investment. Make sure that the basis of the profit figure is sound and judge whether the accounts understate the true position or whether the business has potential for development – or both.

Owner's salary
This is one way by which the vendor may try to increase the scale of his net profit. An owner operator needs income of two kinds – a regular salary to remunerate him for his work and effort and a profit on his business activities that pays for the capital he has employed and rewards him for the risk he has taken in developing the enterprise. The two should not be confused but often are.

It is true to say that hoteliers (and their families) do not need to pay themselves what may be regarded as an adequate wage because they are living on the premises and do not need substantial income for personal expenses. Although, theoretically, an owner should pay himself a reasonable salary depending on the nature and size of the business, in practice it may not pay him to do so for tax reasons. If this is the case, an allowance should be made for this in interpreting the accounts.

VAT and service charge

Money collected for VAT does not belong to the business but to the Customs and Excise. It should not be incorporated in the sales revenue but should be shown separately. If VAT is included, the revenue is being artificially inflated and needs to be reduced by the amount of VAT.

The situation with service charge is more complicated. The money raised by a service charge legally belongs to the owner of the business. Although the customer pays it in the belief that it goes to the staff in the form of a gratuity, the current legal position is quite clear: the owner can dispose of it as he wishes. He can distribute all of it to his staff or only some of it; he can put it towards staff wages or he can pay it to them in addition to wages. Alternatively, he can keep it all for himself.

A considerable sum of money is involved if a $12\frac{1}{2}$ – 15 per cent charge is imposed. In studying the accounts it must be clear how the vendor has treated the distribution of the service charge. If all of it goes to the staff, then it should not be included in the revenue because it is not going to be retained in the business.

Maintenance and depreciation

No rules can be laid down on the annual amount that is needed for repairs and renewals (see Chapter 13). Every hotel is different but every hotel needs regular maintenance. The longer this is put off, the more expensive it will eventually become. Has regular maintenance taken place and has the depreciation of plant and equipment been realistic during the past five years? Suggesting a figure for maintenance expenditure – it is usually called repairs and renewals – is difficult because no two hotels are alike. A modern hotel may not need so much attention as an older property. A heavily-used city centre hotel restaurant may need completely redecorating every three years partly because of the high incidence of cigarette smoke; a less-busy restaurant may survive twice as long. Public areas will need to be decorated more often than bedrooms.

Most professional hoteliers operating large hotels spend at least four per cent of turnover on repairs and renewals but a small hotel may need much less. Your visual inspection of the hotel and its equipment and the survey of the property will help you form an opinion on whether or not adequate sums have been charged in the accounts for repairs and renewals. If not, then make the necessary adjustments to the figures.

Marketing

Have the marketing activities, if any, been consistent over the years or are they high one year and low the next? Effective sales promotion, whether it is advertising, face-to-face sales calls, telephone interviews, mail shots or brochure production, depends on consistency. An irregular effort will result in a patchy response. What you are looking for is regular sales promotion expenditure because that shows that the hotelier has been developing his business consistently. If he is a member of a marketing consortium (see page 163) it is a sign that he is very serious indeed about promoting his hotel. If no sales promotion is undertaken it may indicate that the hotel is too small to need it or that the hotelier does not care (in which case his occupancy may be low). If the latter is true it may present a good opportunity to develop the business.

Stock

There are still some hotels and restaurants that have a wine cellar representing a five-figure investment. The cost of tying up that amount of capital can only be justified if the establishment has a high wine turnover. If the vendor regards wine as a long-term investment, you need to ask why he is running a hotel.

The level of stock must be realistic. A wine cellar filled with fine wines which are rarely sold may satisfy the proprietor's ego but it does not help his cash flow; over-stocking on food and groceries can lead to spoilage and wastage. On the other hand under-stocking can lead to inefficiencies. Stock includes other areas – chiefly, tablecloths and bedlinen. If the hotel is using its own linen, for example, it needs to stock supplies for four to six times the number of beds and tables – unless it has an in-house laundry, in which case it can make do with rather less.

Before you take over, you will have a full stock-take and an inventory check (see Chapter 7) but before deciding to purchase it is important to know whether stock in hand is going to cost you £2000 or £20,000. Try to agree a fair figure beforehand and stipulate, if you want, that the stock should not exceed a certain figure on the day of the takeover.

Gross profit

Gross profit (GP) on food is the price of the meal less the cost of the food. In most sizeable restaurants, the gross profit is not less than 65 per cent and is as high as 75 per cent in many popular units. In other words, for every meal sold at £1, the food cost is no more than 35 pence. The gross profit has to be as high as this for a restaurant to be viable. Wage costs will add another 30 per cent, overheads (heating, lighting, maintenance) will add up to 25 per cent, leaving a 10 per cent margin for net profit. The food gross profit is an important figure for any restaurant because the cost of food has the most direct bearing on profitability – a restaurant's wages and overheads have to be paid no matter how many customers the restaurant attracts. A small hotel, with its own residents' dining room, may not find the gross profit percentage quite so crucial as it will be offering an all-inclusive tariff. Nevertheless, a notional cost for meals has to be incorporated in the tariff and no hotelier should be unaware of the cost of the food and drink he is serving and of the profit he needs to make.

A good GP will indicate that the vendor is running an efficient business; a poor GP may offer an opportunity to you if you can tighten control. Never underestimate the difficulties of running a commercial restaurant, however, whether it is by itself or as part of a hotel. Even professionals make mistakes in trying to make an establishment profitable. Increasing the GP and maintaining it is a difficult job for any inexperienced caterer. The natural tendency is to give too high a quality or too large portions for the prices charged. Do not, also, be overwhelmed by the necessity of making a fixed GP. Many restaurants mark up wine, for example, by 100 per cent; there is much to be said for marking it up by less to encourage more sales. It is better to sell two bottles at a profit of £4 each than one at a profit of £6. The relationship between price and volume is important and it is often better to reduce your gross profit to achieve higher sales (and profits).

Turnover

If there has been a rise in turnover in the past three years, is it steady? Is it a genuine increase in excess of inflation? A business that increases its turnover from £100,000 to £110,000 in a year when inflation is running at 12 per cent is going backwards. It is possible for a business to increase its turnover and profit in money terms but not in volume (e.g. the number of sleepers) by upgrading its facilities and by charging a higher tariff, but volume is usually the most important factor, whether it is interpreted in the number of sleepers in a hotel or in the number of customers in a restaurant. Establishments that rely merely on price increases to yield greater revenue may be suspect. But if a hotel is operating at near peak occupancy, it may only be possible to generate more profit by further price increases; or by better in-house selling (i.e. persuading the customer to spend more in your hotel on ancillary goods and services); or eventually, by building an extension.

Forward bookings

This is an important point, particularly if the hotel is seasonal. How many bookings are there for the next year and how much has been taken in deposits? All payments in advance should be transferred to you on completion. Forward bookings are a sign of health in resort hotels but lack of them indicates little in those hotels that rely on chance trade. Changing customer trends, however, mean that resort hotels have a pattern of forward bookings similar to many provincial hotels. They now have to rely much more on chance or late bookings, so a seaside hotel, with no summer bookings in the early part of the season, is not necessarily a bad bargain.

Customers

Who are they? The success of every hotel depends on attracting customers – but where do they come from and how much are they willing to spend? These are crucial questions that need answering. Occupancy figures vary from area to area, city to city and resort to resort. Most resort hotels close in October or November, re-open at Easter and are full in the peak months. City centre hotels are mostly full in the week and quiet at weekends all the year round. London hotels are busier in the summer than in the winter.

National occupancy figures are available from the various tourist boards but they can be misleading unless you understand the pattern of local trade. Confusingly, of course, occupancy can vary within hotels in one area because of management expertise. What matters is how many beds (not rooms) the hotel has and how often they are filled. If you have a twin-bedded room and fill it every night with a single person, you are losing half the potential revenue, assuming the double rate is twice the single. This is why sleeper occupancy is so important. A high single occupancy of twin- or double-bedded rooms will indicate that the hotel is attracting weekday businessmen who only need a single room; there is not much you can do about this although it may be possible to convert some of the larger rooms into two singles. If the demand exists, however, a double room may be let as a single at a higher rate than the normal single tariff or even at the full double rate.

Room revenue in a hotel is of primary importance. No matter how high food and liquor sales are, they cannot make up for lost room sales. The profit from one night's accommodation is much greater than that from a meal in a restaurant, even though the price may be the same; a restaurant incurs considerable material and food costs which do not arise in a room sale. It is easy to calculate occupancy and thus the total potential revenue from room sales, but that is a more or less hypothetical figure. A hotel rarely, if ever achieves 100 per cent annual bed occupancy. A realistic estimate should be based on the figure achieved in your locality. Is the present performance of the hotel below the local average? The accounts should show a steady increase in room revenue but, ideally, this should not have been achieved by increasing prices without some increase in the volume of business. What a hotel needs is an increase in the number of customers, which is why sleeper occupancy is so important. Rising occupancy means that the hotel is healthy and attracting a growing share of the market; a declining occupancy means that the hotel is losing out. Why? There could be many reasons: the prices may be too high, standards poor or the location may be bad. Whatever the reasons you should analyse the situation and be convinced that you can rectify it.

There are other pointers. A high level of repeat business (i.e. customers returning regularly to the hotel) means that most customers are satisfied with the hotel and its services. A contrary trend may only indicate, however, that the hotel is in an area of high chance trade with people paying one-off visits. Repeat business may not, in fact, be wholly advantageous, because it could be due to the personality of the present owner. It may disappear when he leaves and you take over.

A useful exercise is to look at the visitors' book and analyse where guests came from and how often they stayed. This will provide a picture of the pattern of the business which will help you when you prepare the feasibility study and when you begin to develop the hotel's potential.

Tariffs

If tariffs are due for a 10 per cent increase the day after you take over, you may well find that there will be customer price resistance with a consequent reduction in trade. The tariff needs to be realistic in relation to the hotel and its services and to the tariffs charged by other hotels in the area. The hotel may have high occupancy at artifically low and unprofitable rates. In that case, a sudden increase in tariffs without increasing standards would create ill-will which would affect the level of business.

Staff

Wages

You will see from the accounts how much the staff are costing the hotel. In large, highly staffed, de-luxe hotels, the figure may be 30-35 per cent; in simpler hotels, the wage percentage may be between 20 per cent and 25 per cent – very occasionally lower. A commercial restaurant is likely to have a wage cost between 30 and 35 per cent unless it works on a self-service principle. A wage percentage may be low because the proprietor has not costed in his own salary or because the owner and his wife are doing too much themselves.

The wage percentage of a hotel may be an indication of the efficiency of the management. Wages comprise the highest single expenditure of any hotel and the management's ability to control it largely influences the profitability of the enterprise. Too high a wage cost indicates slack control; or it may show that the hotelier is providing a higher standard of personal service than the business warrants – in other words, he is employing more staff than is justified. More unlikely, he may be paying them too much. Minimum wages in the industry are controlled by Wages Councils Act, 1979 (see page 174) and while some hoteliers outside London and major provincial cities pay above the minimum rates laid down, many do not.

If the staff were last given a rise a year ago, the purchaser may be faced with a wage demand immediately after he takes over. A 10 per cent increase on an annual wage bill of £20,000 could badly dent the profit forecast of any small hotel. You should ask whether any staff are on a bonus, how many live in and how long they have been employed.

Previous proprietors or managers

A long procession of proprietors or managers implies an unhappy hotel, troublesome staff and disgruntled guests. To have had one owner or manager does not necessarily mean the reverse is true but it is likely to be so. You will have to use your own judgement; but if you do not like what you see and do not want the present manager to stay, you may be responsible for redundancy payments since a new employer is required to observe all the terms and conditions of employment which applied before the transfer. Any fundamental change to the contract made as a result of the transfer could lead to a constructive dismissal claim. Any dismissal arising from such a transfer would be unfair dismissal unless there are sound organizational, economic or technical reasons.

Telling the staff
Most hoteliers are very unwilling to reveal that their hotel is on the market. There are two major reasons for this: they believe that customers will be deterred if they know the hotel is about to be sold and that the staff will also leave.

Unless the personality of the proprietor is such that he acts as a powerful attraction, the danger of staff leaving is more serious than customers staying away. Staff naturally become worried about a change of ownership. They feel their jobs are endangered and fear new working conditions and methods. If you want to talk to the staff, ask the vendor if you can do so.

Can any of them be dismissed if you feel that to be necessary? It is never easy to dismiss staff. If you believe that the hotel is heavily overstaffed and a high proportion are living in, you must be careful about cutting down the numbers because you will be liable for redundancy payments for all those who have been in continuous employment for more than twenty-six weeks, although 41 per cent of the money can be reclaimed from the Department of Employment. In country areas, some living-in staff are essential but most employers prefer not to offer accommodation unless it is absolutely necessary. In many cases, staff bedrooms can be better utilized as guest bedrooms.

When the staff should be told is a matter for the vendor to decide. Left to him, in most cases, it would be no more than an hour before the purchaser takes over but this puts the purchaser in a difficult situation. Some employees may leave immediately, some might stay but will try to cause trouble, others will work normally. As the new owner this will be your introduction to what is any hotelier's greatest and most perplexing problem – the staff.

Ideally, employees should be told as soon as the contracts have been exchanged, not when the sale is completed, and you should arrange to go and meet them. It is probably better to ask the vendor to tell staff formally than to allow the news to leak out which will inevitably lead to rumours and counter-rumours which are much more unsettling than plain facts.

General

Contracts
Regular contracts to service boilers, the kitchen and electrical equipment and other major items are indications that the vendor has looked after the property. The equipment should be in reasonable order. Inspect the kitchen

yourself, preferably with someone who knows about catering equipment, and make sure the equipment is sound.

Brewery ties

A brewery tie is not necessarily unsatisfactory though few professional hoteliers like them. They restrict the supply of beer, wines and spirits and prevent the proprietor from obtaining supplies elsewhere, possibly at a lower price. But a tie often helps the hotelier. The brewery may be willing to help finance the fitting out of a bar and in some cases it may go so far as to help the finance the original purchase of the hotel itself. A tie will therefore affect your purchasing policies.

Stock and contents

We now come to the last of the checklists:

1   Does an accurate inventory exist? When are you entitled to have it?
2   Of all the items of furniture, furnishings, fixtures, fittings – china, glass, cutlery, pictures, antiques – which belong to the vendor and are therefore not part of the property for sale?
3   Is cutlery, china and glassware to be treated as contents or as stock to be paid for?
4   Are any motor vehicles included in the sale?
5   Are linen and blankets in stock or are they hired? What other items are hired or on lease?
6   What items of stock not required for normal day to day trading are in hand?

Always ask for a full inventory of fixtures, fittings, furnishings and effects which are to be included in the sale. Before you take over the hotel, a full stocktaking will take place (see Chapter 7). This will consist primarily of a stocktaking of the food, liquor and other consumables which you will be purchasing on the basis of cost or current valuation, whichever is the lower. You must be sure to know what else is included in the sale. One hotelier bought a hotel believing he was purchasing all the excellent paintings that hung in the hallway and dining room; on taking over, he discovered that they had all been stripped out by the vendor. Subsequent investigations revealed that they were the owner's personal property and were not included in the sale. Detailed questioning at the outset and a close examination of the inventory will prevent such a situation occurring in your purchase.

All these many questions are designed to help you analyse the state of the business and its potential. Presuming you have a three-year set of accounts, you will be in a position to assess the past performance of the hotel. With the key ratios – food cost, staff percentages and other percentages – you can assess how efficiently the business is being run. Before you are able to make an offer, however, you should undertake one more exercise – you must produce a simple feasibility study for the hotel to show how profitable you believe you can make it in the future. The next chapter explains how such a study can be prepared.

5 Looking to the future

The accounts have shown how the hotel has traded during the past three years. The vendor's answers to your questions have given important information about the physical structure of the building and about the business. Now, we have to look at the future. How will the business develop in the first few years of your ownership?

If the hotel is making good profits with high occupancy you need to satisfy yourself that those profits will continue to grow. This is not always so obvious as it seems. The hotel and catering industry is one in which the personality of the owner plays a significant part in the success of any business. The smaller the establishment, the more likely it is that the owner attracts customers by the strength of his personality. This is particularly true of restaurants. You should expect some decline in trade until regular customers have become accustomed to your new style of ownership. A proportion may never do so but, to compensate, you should be able to attract customers of your own.

Even with a profitable hotel, opportunities for future expansion and development should not be overlooked. It is a cliché to say that a business that stands still goes backwards but it is true, nevertheless. In the long term more bathrooms may be required; a new conference room could open new markets; more bedrooms with bathrooms en suite may be needed. The need for such developments may be more urgent if the hotel is making a loss or if the potential of the business is not being fully realized. Whether or not the hotel is making a profit, you have to look to the future rather than the past. In doing this the accounts will show the way; an analysis of them will show where the business is going wrong. You have got to show how you think you can put the business right and how long it will take you.

This is the basis of the feasibility study – and it is not so daunting as it appears. Its benefit to the potential purchaser is that it concentrates his mind wonderfully on the solution to the problems of the business and makes him think of the opportunities that are presented. Like every plan and target, the objectives may not all be reached at the right time but the exercise of putting aims and objectives on paper, of carefully reasoning them through, is a highly beneficial discipline. It is also important if you need to raise finance to buy the hotel. The bank manager or finance house will want to know where you see the future of the business and will be favourably impressed if a reasoned and realistic feasibility study supports the application.

A feasibility study can take several forms. For a large new, multi-storey hotel, it will be a highly sophisticated revenue and cost forecast, which examines every aspect of the business, including international and national business trends, the nature of the local demand, detailed occupancy forecasts, cost forecasts and cash flow projections. All this will have taken place before the foundations of the building are laid. Such a study – often computer-assisted – takes weeks to prepare and demands a high degree of economic and accounting skill.

The feasibility study of your purchase will not be so sophisticated but it will achieve the same results if properly carried out. It will give you a picture of the business in the first year and over a longer period. This, in turn, will confirm that the asking price is realistic.

Feasibility study: an example

The following true feasibility study is based on a sixteen-bedroom hotel in an English market town. The hotel was bought by a professional hotelier whom we shall call Jones and it was prepared for two reasons:

1   To give precise reasoning to back up his initial enthusiasm for the hotel;
2   To help raise finance for the purchase.

The example has necessarily been shortened and some of the details of the hotel have been omitted. For many small hotels, it may be too detailed, but it is the approach that is important.

The study began with a full description of the hotel and its facilities, the number of bedrooms with or without baths, the number of bathrooms, the services and other physical amenities. This information was available from the agent's particulars but they should always be checked on site and Jones did so. The study then explained the geographic area of the town, noting its close proximity to other major centres by road and rail. Jones then examined the town itself, its state of prosperity and its future business and industrial potential. The harder he looked, the more promising the hotel purchase became.

He found that the town was small but expanding – always a good sign for any hotel. A contracting town means that business activity is declining and will produce little new business for its hotels. Plenty of building societies and estate agents had offices in the town centre – another good sign because strong activity in the house market means that a town is popular and growing. It also may mean that there is business to be picked up from people looking for houses in the area. Although farming was the major activity (perhaps a promising source of potential business for dinners) there were a number of well-known national companies with big factories on the outskirts. The town also attracted tourists in the summer because of its historic and scenic connections. Nearby were colleges and a university and, in the town, one or two boarding schools.

Jones wrote in his report: 'Such a profusion of educational establishments suggests a flourishing resident population and also indicates a flow of people into the area, visiting offspring at the various establishments. All must be potential users of the hotel services . . .'

Looking to the future, he found that a national company was building a new office complex scheduled for completion by the end of the following year. This would accommodate 600 new employees, all of whom would be living in the area. There were several major new housing developments and the average price of secondhand houses had risen by 15 per cent since they had been built a year earlier – another good sign that the town was prospering.

Jones then looked at the hotel he was considering buying. It was the only hotel in the town – a fairly unusual situation – which made his business forecast easier. There were the usual number of pubs and some small unlicensed restaurants and guest houses but few of the pubs served real ale or had a strong line in bar snacks. There was only one other restaurant that provided dinner and dancing facilities although the town hall provided space for large functions.

This information was gleaned from visits to all the pubs and restaurants in the town where he talked to the landlords and the locals about the area and about the hotel he wanted to acquire. From all these investigations into the locality he concluded that the town was:

'a thriving market town with a prosperous farming community, rapidly expanding industrial developments and a centre for leisure and sporting facilities.

A number of factors have acted together to produce a great demand for hotel and catering facilities. These include:

1 Increasing population
2 Movement of industry into the town
3 Proximity to other large towns and their easy accessibility
4 Tourist attractions
5 The provision of sports facilities in the town and local sporting events such as horse racing

The lack of any other hotel and the lack of good licensed restaurants means that the hotel, under professional management, could exploit the market for hotel and catering services.'

The hotel was being run by a local brewery under a manager and the figures shown in the accounts revealed the financial position shown in Table 9.
These figures show the importance of analysing accounts. While a business might appear to be prospering, in real terms, it may be declining. Such was the position in this case. When inflation was taken into account, the figures revealed the business to be fundamentally weak.

Table 9   *Turnover for year ending September 30*

	Year 1	Year 2	Year 3
Bars	82,122	94,230	107,140
Catering	52,586	51,704	49,592
Apartments	25,354	31,650	33,236
Sundries	3,986	3,410	4,240
	164,048	180,994	194,208

Bars

Between the first two years, turnover rose by 14.6 per cent and between the second and third years by 14.9 per cent. In other words, turnover in the bars hardly kept pace with inflation which, at the time of the purchase averaged 15 per cent.

Catering

Between the first two years, turnover decreased by 1.5 per cent and by 3.5 per cent between the second and third year. This apparently small fall in catering sales in current terms is infinitely more serious in real terms – a decline of 16.5 per cent and 18.5 per cent between the two accounting periods.

Rooms

Between the first two years, turnover increased by 28.5 per cent and by 5 per cent between the second and third year. Allowing for inflation, there was a real growth in room sales of 13.5 per cent in the first year but a decline of 10 per cent in the following year.

Total turnover

In the first period, turnover increased by 10.4 per cent and in the second period by 7.3 per cent. Again, the increase in turnover had not kept pace with inflation and showed a decline of 4.6 per cent and 7.7 per cent respectively.

This true example emphasizes the need to analyse hotel figures taking into account past and present levels of inflation. Only in this way can the real financial position be revealed. The accounts illustrated a fundamental weakness in the hotel's trading position. For a sixteen-bedroom hotel with one bar, the unit was too dependent on bar and food sales. The rooms, proportionately much more profitable, were producing less than 25 per cent of revenue. Why was this? Were they under-priced or was the occupancy low? Subsequent investigations revealed that the tariff was low but so was occupancy. The estimated number of sleepers per night was seven, giving an average sleeper occupancy of 35 per cent. Many rooms were being sold as singles but in spite of the cheap tariff the hotel was still not attracting customers. In the restaurant the average spend per customer at lunch and dinner was reasonable for the establishment but the number of covers sold was very low and there was no chance business.

A closer examination of the hotel produced the following information:

Commercial accommodation business
Monday to Thursday only; poor occupancy possibly due to poor hygiene, lack of promotion, poor food standards.

Lunch and dinner business
Very low numbers all week; no chance trade.

Bar trade
Quite busy bar trade all week from locals and residents but for a hotel in a prime location in the middle of the town, much of the potential was not being realized; no 'hostmanship' was being displayed.

Bar snacks
Only served Monday to Fridays although Saturday was a market day when bars were very busy. The take-up was poor because portions were small and presentation appalling.

Gaming machines
They were available every weekday evening in a function room that had been converted into a pool hall with fruit machines and a pool table. The room had a bar but produced poor takings and attracted under-age drinkers. At the same time it deterred other locals from using the hotel and made the room unavailable for letting for functions.

In general, the standard of food was poor and so was the standard of housekeeping and cleanliness. The bars lacked supervision and experience indicated that pilferage would be rife. The hotel was overstaffed and little leadership was given. Staff were left to run departments with little or no supervision. There was no promotional literature and no advertising was undertaken. A fire certificate had been obtained and a great deal of expenditure had been incurred to obtain it but there was no regular maintenance programme. Redecoration was necessary in almost all main areas and all the bedrooms.

Jones's summary of the business was:

'The hotel represents a totally unexploited business. It would appear that it has been run as a public house with emphasis placed on earning revenue in the bars and associated outlets such as gaming machines. Little effort has been made in the past to exploit the growing demand for hotel accommodation despite the extensive facilities that the hotel possesses. Advance reservations for rooms and catering are extremely poor. Opportunities for pilferage abound through lack of supervision and security. Very poor opinion with local populace.'

Such a badly run and unprofitable hotel may appear to be a depressing acquisition but it is precisely this kind of establishment that offers some of the most attractive business opportunities. Providing the location of the hotel is right and the potential is unexploited, it is just as profitable in the long term to acquire a hotel in a loss-making situation as it is to acquire an already profitable concern with no significant opportunity for development. There are many hoteliers who have bought unprofitable hotels with unrealized potential. They have built them into highly profitable units by hard work, an ability to see the marketing opportunities, good sales promotion, tight budgetary and cost control and enthusiastic leadership and positive direction.

This was precisely the situation here. Looking at the market opportunities, Jones divided them into a number of different areas and his feasibility study had the following sections:

'Weekday accommodation business: Build up on existing slim trade by offering higher standard of cleanliness, comfort and food. When this has been achieved, increase the tariffs to yield higher revenue. Direct mail local companies and organizations.

Weekend business: Build this up by offering attractive inexpensive packages, similar to those offered by major hotel groups. These could be promoted through the local tourist board, advertising, etc. Before this can be activated, higher standards must be implemented.

Tourist accommodation: Build this up by advertising, use of the local tourist board and national tourist boards.

Chance restaurant trade: Build this up at lunch and dinner by local advertising, word of mouth advertising and by direct mail shots to local businessmen. Before this can be achieved, higher standards of food and presentation have to be introduced.

Increased bar snacks: These can be developed every lunchtime by better food standards and presentation. The hotel's prime trading position on market day – Saturday – needs to be exploited.

Morning coffee and teas: These can be developed through signs outside the hotel and inside.

Functions: These can be promoted by taking out the uneconomic gaming machines and pool table and by using the room for functions – meetings, auctions, dinners, weddings, etc. This facility can be promoted by direct mail shots to local companies and by advertisements in the local press and in the hotel.

Dinner dance: With an average of four covers on a Saturday night, the hotel's restaurant is completely uneconomic. Trade can be developed by putting on dinner dances for local people in the attractive restaurant, which can hold about 90. Advertising will help to promote this kind of function but word of mouth advertising will be better. Areas to develop are: food quality, speed of service and a good band.

Special promotions: It may be possible to develop package promotions to nearby race course, in conjunction with local coach firm.

Rotary: Fortnightly meetings are held. These will be encouraged because they get local people and local businessmen into the hotel. With better standards of food and service, the meetings will act as an effective means of getting the hotel known among an important section of the local community.

Early morning tea: Possible to develop sales here – but the cost of staff will be high. Kettles in the bedrooms may be a better alternative. There will be no direct revenue but the tariff can be increased as a result of improved amenities.'

These plans gave the bare outline of Jones's objectives. What they show is that he had a clear idea of the problems and of the solutions. The aim was to turn the establishment from a bar-orientated hotel into a unit with a much sounder and broader base, with higher bed occupancies and with its proper share of local business entertaining. Equally important, the aim was to make the hotel a centre for social activity in the area. In the longer term, once the demand for rooms had been improved, he could see two major development opportunities:

1　To turn three unused staff bedrooms into guest rooms, all with bath or shower
2　To convert a large, empty barn at the back of the hotel, which fronted on to a back street, into a rustic-themed wine bar

These were however long-term projects and did not form an integral part of the feasibility study though they were mentioned because they were relevant.

Describing a marketing objective is only part of the feasibility study. How are these plans to be achieved? Jones divided his plans into the short-term (up to one year) and medium-termed (the second year). He believed that any plans beyond two years would be meaningless at the present stage of the hotel's development. He decided to set himself some specific marketing objectives for each of the two years with a brief description of how he would achieve these targets.

The short-term targets were:
1　Increase occupancy to 75 per cent
2　Increase weekday lunches to 10 per day
3　Increase Sunday lunches to 30 per day
4　Increase weekday dinners to 12 per night
5　Increase Friday and Saturday dinners to 60 per night
6　Maintain lunch spend at £5.50 per head (Sunday £6 per head)
7　Maintain dinner spend at £6.50 per head
8　Increase wine spend to £1 per head at lunch and dinner
9　Sell £20 worth of snacks in the bar every day
10　Increase function numbers to 40 per month

Targets are useful only if they are achievable. He had to give thought to how these were to be achieved. It is not enough to say that bed occupancy needs to be increased to 75 per cent; the key question is how is this to be achieved? How can lunch trade be developed? The answer, he believed, lay in raising the standards of the hotel – offering better bedrooms by improving décor and hygiene, improving the quality of the food and service and raising morale among the staff. To achieve the ten objectives he would:

1   Provide 'standards of performance' manuals
2   Set up a system of simple training and keep training records
3   Develop training in social skills
4   Find and record all local sales opportunities
5   Improve bar sales through hostmanship

Before introducing training and standards of performance manuals, Jones realized that it was essential to have a clear idea of the standard required in craft skills and social skills.

Looking further ahead, the medium-term plan consisted of twelve additional targets:

1   Increase occupancy to 90 per cent
2   Increase weekday lunches to 40 per day
3   Increase Sunday lunches to 60 per day
4   Increase weekday dinners to 40 per night
5   Increase Friday and Saturday dinners to 80 per night
6   Increase lunch spend to £7 per head (Sunday £10 per head)
7   Increase dinner spend to £11 per head
8   Increase wine spend to £2 per head at lunch and dinner (Saturday dinner £3 per head)
9   Sell £80 worth of bar snacks per day
10   Increase function covers to 160 per month
11   Reduce staff turnover by 10 per cent
12   Increase letting rooms to 18

He set out the following methods by which he would achieve these objectives:

1   Increase sales calls to 10 per week
2   Increase the catchment area from which business is taken
3   Join some kind of marketing consortium or set up marketing arrangements with other hotels
4   Use special promotional events to attract more business, for example: special weekends, gastronomic weekends
5   Promote the hotel to all new businesses moving into the area
6   Convert unused staff accommodation to letting bedrooms

These targets show how Jones was going to develop the business. After improving standards and quality in the first year, the second year would give him the chance to consolidate. Occupancy would be increased by more sales calls. Through higher standards he would be in a position to increase prices for the rooms and the restaurant, thus yielding more revenue per room and per cover. By means of higher quality food and more professional salesmanship, wine sales would be improved either by selling more wine or by selling more expensive wine. A hotel can accommodate a maximum number of people in the restaurant, bar and rooms. Once the maximum numbers have been reached, the only way a hotelier can increase revenue is to raise prices, increase in-house sales, or to undertake structural alterations by splitting large rooms into two singles or converting staff rooms into guest bedrooms (see Chapter 13). Alternatively, a large single room may be turned into a double. Prices can be increased only if there is a strong enough demand and if the standards are right – hence the initial objectives in the first year to improve standards and to generate a greater demand.

Reducing staff turnover was also important. Staff turnover is expensive in time and money and drains morale. Unfortunately, it is a fact of life in the hotel and catering industry. Every hotelier aims to reduce it but this is more easily said than done. Jones believed that with a proper training system, better personnel practices and with his involvement and commitment, staff would be happier with their work and few would want to leave. He estimated that a 10 per cent reduction in staff turnover was a modest objective and could be achieved.

Finally, he set out some general objectives which he realized would not be achieved immediately but which had to be regarded as essential goals. He believed that they were all achievable but over a much longer period of time.

1 To recognize and develop all sales opportunities
2 To maximize profits through the optimization of all sales opportunities
3 To be recognized as giving value for money
4 To achieve recognition by such organizations as Good Food Guide, AA Guide, Michelin and Egon Ronay for culinary achievements.

The most important of these goals was to provide value for money: this must be the primary objective of every hotel and catering enterprise.

Jones added a brief note explaining exactly how he would raise the standards of the hotel:

Food standards   To be improved through correct purchasing, correct storage, correct presentation, good hygiene.
Bar standards   To be improved by correct purchasing, stock control, correct storage, correct presentation, good hygiene, security, hostmanship.
Accommodation standards   To be improved through correct hygiene procedures, rotation of linen stock, training of staff, regular maintenance programme, and improvements in décor and decoration.
Service and staffing standards   To be improved by increased staff motivation, good conditions of employment, discipline and training.

Jones realized that these plans and objectives only took him so far. A sales and costs forecast was also required for the first year of operation and preferably for the second year. This would show how much extra revenue would be produced by the successful implementation of his plans. But extra revenue also implies extra costs – an 80 cover restaurant requires more staff than one serving only four covers. It was necessary, therefore, to look at projected costs and revenue to verify how much profit the hotel would produce. Such a forecast can only assume that he meets the targets he has set out. Some of these might not be achieved, others might be surpassed. In his particular hotel, raising occupancy levels to 75 per cent might not be achieved in the first year but it was an important goal to aim for. On the other hand, it was likely that if he succeeded in attracting sixty covers for Saturday night dinner dances he would quickly attract eighty people. Success breeds success and the difference between sixty and eighty people is marginal in this context.

So Jones worked out a sales analysis which itemized as accurately as possible how much money he would earn in each of the hotel's four main departments. This analysis appears in Table 10.

He prepared a separate assessment of wages and staff costs because they comprise such an important part of any hotel's general cost structure. The assessment is itemized in detail in Table 11. The projected wages and staff costs amounted to 29.6 per cent of revenue – a somewhat high figure for a hotel of this nature but Jones considered that his projected increase in food and beverage operations would mean he would need more staff. However, close attention would have to be paid to the possibility of reducing that figure in the future. He also prepared a profit and loss account with all known and assumed costs and sales, together with the major operating ratios (see Table 12). The accounts show that he expected the hotel to achieve a pre-tax profit of £72,000 before all other charges.

The figures in Jones's projected profit and loss account (Table 12) have been left as they were for the sake of accuracy; even so, experience showed that most of Jones's projections were correct. All the important percentages were more or less achieved in the first year (see Table 13). Bedroom and restaurant revenue more than doubled and takings in the bar increased also, compared with the turnover under the previous owner (see Table 9).

The wage percentage, which Jones recognized as being rather high in the forecast, evened out at 27.8 per cent but oil costs were much higher and there were variations in other costs including electricity, laundry, music and entertainment and rentals.

Jones's successful ability to forecast sales and costs was due largely to his hotel experience; if you are inexperienced, you should use the existing accounts as a base for your projected figures. Be wary of setting such demanding targets as Jones set in his first year. The knowledge you gain in the first year of operation will allow you to revise your forecasts in future years on a more accurate and realistic basis. One word of warning: do not assume that these figures apply to every sixteen-bedroom hotel. Hotels differ and every hotel will produce a different set of accounts. The example shown here is

Table 10 *Sales Analysis*

		Gross	VAT at 15%	Net
Rooms				
75% occ. at av spend of £14.00 (total 5,475 sleepers)		76,650	9,998	66,652
Food				
5,475 breakfasts	at £3	16,425		
75% sleepers/dinners conversion	at £7.50 av apend	30,712		
60 chance dinners over weekends	at £7.50 av spend	23,400		
10 chance lunches per 5 day week	at £5.50 av spend	14,300		
30 chance lunches per Sunday	at £6.00 av spend	9,360		
10 Rotary lunches per fortnight	at £5.00 av spend	1,300		
1 function of 20 covers per month	at £3.50	1,680		
Bar snacks – 20 per day	at £1 per person (6 days)	6,240		
50% take of early morning tea	at 50p.	1,368		
Total Food Sales		104,785	13,668	91,117
Liquor				
4,095 dinners	at £1 (weekdays)	4,106		
3,120 dinners	at £1.40 (weekends)	4,368		
2,600 midweek chance lunches	at £1 av spend	2,600		
1,560 Sunday lunches 50%	at £1 av spend	730		
240 function covers	at £2 per head	480		
Main Bar sales	at £240 per day	101,920		
Cocktail Bar sales 5 nights per week	at £40	10,400		
Total Liquor Sales		124,604	16,253	108,351
Other Sales				
Telephones	at £20 per week	1,040		
Cigarette machine	at £40 per week	2,080		
Gaming machine	at £100 per week	5,200		
		9,320	1,255	8,365
Total Sales				£274,485

Table 11   *Wages and Staff Cost*

	£
Administration	
Directors' salaries	6,000
Reception – 2 at £70	7,280
Clerical Assistant – 15 hrs per wk × £2 per hr	1,560
Rooms	
2 at 4 hrs. per day × 7 days per wk × £2 per hr	5,824
1 Day Porter – 3 hours per day × 5 days per wk	1,560
Food	
Head Chef – £160 per wk	8,320
2nd Chef – £120 per wk	6,240
Part-time Cook – 5 hrs per day × £2 per hr	2,600
Restaurant	
1 Waiter – £120 per wk	6,240
2 Waiters – £80 per wk	8,320
Casual	200
Kitchen Porters	
1 at £60 (live-in)	3,120
2 at £70 (live-out)	7,280
Bars	
Bar 1 at 60 hrs/wk at £2 per hr	6,240
Bar 2 at 20 hrs/wk at £2 per hr	2,080
Total	72,864
On cost at 10%	7,300
Sub total	80,164
Staff feeding	6,000
Total Wages and Staff Cost	86,164

Table 12 *Budgeted profit and loss account for first year of operation*

	%	£	£
Sales			
Rooms	24.3	70,778	
Food	33.4	97,024	
Liquor/tobacco	39.7	115,374	
Other	2.6	7,704	
Total sales			290,880
Less: Cost of sales			
Food	37.0	35,900	
Liquor/tobacco	45.0	51,920	87,820
Gross profit	69.8		203,060
Less: Wages	29.6		86,164
Net margin	40.2		116,896
Less: **Operating expenses**			
Electricity		2,000	
Oil		2,000	
Gas		1,500	
Insurance		1,200	
Rentals		500	
Laundry		5,476	
Advertising, etc.		1,450	
Music and entertainment		6,240	
Postage		1,100	
Print and stationery		2,000	
Rates		4,500	
Telephone		1,630	
Cleaning materials		2,000	
Miscellaneous		3,000	
Total	11.9	34,596	34,596
Operating profit	28.3		82,300
Less: Maintenance and depreciation			10,000
Net profit	24.8		72,300

Table 13   *Actual profit and loss account after first year of operation*

	%	£	£
Sales			
Rooms	23.7	75,720	
Food	38.4	122,836	
Liquor/tobacco	35.7	114,280	
Other	2.2	7,178	
Total sales			320,014
Less: Cost of sales			
Food	37.4	46,004	
Liquor/tobacco	47.4	54,210	100,214
Gross profit	68.7		219,800
Less: Wages	27.8		89,112
Net margin	40.8		130,688
Less: **Operating expenses**			
Electricity		3,268	
Oil		4,594	
Gas		1,734	
Insurance		1,210	
Rentals		2,230	
Laundry		9,076	
Advertising, etc.		990	
Music and entertainment		3,702	
Postage		700	
Printing and stationery		1,466	
Rates		5,236	
Telephone		1,684	
Cleaning materials		1,588	
Flowers/decorations etc.		3,844	
Miscellaneous		2,800	
Total	13.8	44,202	44,202
Operating profit	27		86,486
Less: Maintenance and depreciation			6,246
Net profit	25.1		80,440

merely to illustrate how forecasts should be drawn up and how valuable they are as a management tool.

It must be emphasized that Jones's hotel, though of only sixteen rooms, had considerable bar and restaurant potential. Not every hotel of a similar size has this potential, nor would every purchaser have Jones's skill in reaching his targets. This feasibility study should, therefore, only be used as a guide and as an illustration. The important thing to bear in mind is the approach – you have to analyse the present performance of the business and forecast the future, setting targets that are attainable.

The need for such a detailed exercise arises in almost all hotel purchases – even in those businesses that are so successful that it may be assumed that improvements in room, food and liquor sales are impossible. Improvements are almost always possible. It is important that a purchaser prepares a cost and sales forecast based on his assessment of the business potential. This gives him a plan to work to and objectives to achieve, which are essential for any business. It does not matter too much if a plan is not implemented in every aspect; the benefit arises from compiling it and making the purchaser think about where he wants the business to go in the future.

It should be added that in some cases the purchaser may be quite happy with the present performance of the business (even though it may be poor) because it will give him an adequate return on his investment. He may not want to work harder and seek more business. If this is the case, so be it. It shows how difficult it is to generalize about the hotel and catering industry.

Earlier, it was emphasized how important it is to obtain from the vendor the hotel's accounts, going back three years. The only accounts that Jones received from the vendor before drawing up his projected profit and loss account were the bare sales figures. This is not unusual. The full figures were not available until later. It needs experience of the hotel industry to be able to draw up a set of accounts without historical figures and still make them meaningful but with a knowledge of the common operating ratios it can be done in small hotels. The vendor's accounts will show, however, the true cost of such items as heat, fuel and power and insurance.

With the knowledge that had been gained from the past accounts and from the projected level of income and costs, it was now possible for Jones to assess the future viability of the hotel. For example, although there was a gross operating profit, there had to be enough left to pay the interest charges on the money borrowed and still leave enough to put aside for developing the business and to give enough reward to the owner for the money he invested in the business. In Jones's case, the projected profit was more than adequate to cover his interest charges.

After the feasibility study

If the figures clearly show that the hotel you are considering is not a viable business at the asking price because you would have to borrow too much money to purchase it, you have two alternatives:

1   Forget about it and leave it to someone who has more personal capital to invest.
2   Put in an offer that will give you a viable return on the capital employed. The size of the offer will depend on the projected accounts and could be so far below the asking price that you may not feel it worthwhile putting it forward. But depending on how long the hotel has been on the market and how keen the vendor is to sell, any offer may stand a chance of acceptance. The agent will certainly be able to advise you about this.

If the asking price is realistic, discuss your offer immediately with the agent. Even getting so far, you will have a good idea of how much matching capital you will need to borrow and whether this is realistic. The agent may have already discussed your needs and, in some cases, may even put you in touch with possible sources of finance. You will have to put in an offer before the availability of finance is certain and if the offer is accepted by the vendor, the agent will stipulate that proof of the necessary matching capital must be given within a specific period of time. Depending on the popularity of the hotel the period could be as short as a few days or it could be as long as a month. With a popular hotel, you may have to move very fast indeed – possibly too fast for an inexperienced purchaser and it may be better to drop out of the race unless you are absolutely certain of your decision. Don't make a decision in haste that you may regret later.

On acceptance you will be asked to give a deposit of some substance to prove your interest. This should be given to the agent via your solicitor. The agent will need to know who is acting for you because of the preparation of the contract of sale and he will be able to put you in touch with a solicitor experienced in hotel sales and purchases if you wish. Once that has been settled, you have to begin what may appear to be the most daunting part of the project – raising the money.

Sources of advice

David J. Pinder and Partners,
Hotel and Catering Business Valuers,
Brewery House,
84 High Street,
Newport Pagnell,
Bucks.

Society of Catering and Hotel Management Consultants Ltd.
PO Box 28,
Richmond,
Surrey TW9 1BX
(*Some consultants are not members of the Society*)

British Association of Hotel Accountants,
c/o Howarth and Howarth (UK) Ltd,
13 Southampton Place,
London WC1

Some accounting terms

Assets   These may comprise the property, plant, machinery and stocks of
equipment owned by a business for permanent use; in which case they are
termed fixed assets. In addition, assets may include stocks of goods for
resale, other stocks of materials used, amounts owed to the business
(termed debtors) as well as bank and cash balances; these are termed current
assets. Current assets, which may quickly be converted into cash, are
termed liquid assets.

Balance sheet   A statement of the financial position of a business at a given
point in time, which summarizes the funds employed, as represented by
fixed assets, current assets and liabilities etc. The individual accounts
maintained by a business, from which this statement is prepared, are
together referred to as balance sheet accounts.

Budget   A detailed statement of policy expressed in financial and, for some
items, quantitative terms, prepared in advance for the purpose of attaining
a given objective.

Budgetary control   The continuous comparision of actual with budgeted
results to secure the objectives of the policy set out in the budget, and to
provide a basis for revised policy.

Cash flow   The difference between total cash receipts and total cash
disbursements in an accounting period.

Cost of sales   The cost, to the business, of goods actually sold, such as liquor
and tobacco, and the materials incorporated in prepared food and drink.

Depreciation   The distribution of the cost of a fixed asset over its expected
useful life by the provision of systematic charges against profits.

Liabilities   Amounts which a business owes, for example to suppliers of goods or services, to employees, and in respect of various taxes, interest, dividends to shareholders, etc., are termed liabilities. Amounts currently due or due within one year of the balance sheet date are termed current liabilities. Amounts repayable more than a year after the balance sheet date are termed deferred liabilities.

Operating statement   A management accounts report, covering a specific period of time, which sets out accounting information for the control of a department's income, expenditue and profit or, in the case of a department which has no income, of its expenditure only. A summary operating statement highlights the principal totals of the individual operated departments at the various control levels, and brings in the income and expenditure of the other departments as well as expenditure not allocated to departments, at further control levels, to show finally the net profit of the business before taxation.

Profit and loss account   A financial statement, covering a specific period of time, summarizing the totals of net income and expenditure from all sources appertaining to the business. The difference between the total items of income and expenditure represents the net profit or loss before tax for the period. The statement also shows the amount of taxation to be borne during the period, and indicates how the resulting balance of profit or loss is to be dealt with.

Ratio   The proportion of one item to another, e.g. profit to sales, rooms occupied to rooms available, usually expressed as a percentage.

Working capital   The excess of total current assets over total current liabilities.

Source   Standard System of Hotel Accounts: National Economic Development Office, Millbank Tower, London SW1.

6 Raising the finance

First, some generalizations in a chapter that cannot be totally precise. Raising money for your project may present severe difficulties or it may be a relatively simple exercise but, in every case, it is an individual problem. There is no single solution because each application for finance is different. However, it is possible to make three general observations:

1 Most suitable financial institutions will readily consider a loan of up to 50 per cent of the value of the business. Some will go as high as 60 per cent and a few even higher. The maximum loan will vary but £100,000 will probably be as much as the first-time purchaser with no experience of the industry can expect to borrow.
2 Most loans will be over a 10-15 year period.
3 Loans are least expensive on freehold property or long leasehold (over thirty-five years), although it is possible to borrow on shorter leases at higher rates. Hotels and free houses are favoured. Depending on the amount you want to borrow, restaurants are regarded as doubtful projects for financial backing unless the establishment has a recognized trade and the purchaser has considerable experience in the industry. To purchase the leasehold of a small café, however, may not require a large capital sum so a substantial loan may not be necessary.

If these observations take some of the myth out of raising finance to buy a hotel or catering establishment, that is all to the good. Quite hard-headed businessmen have been known to tremble at the knees at the prospect of seeking matching capital. Providing your requirements are realistic and you are not unfortunate enough to be seeking finance in the middle of an economic recession, you should be able to obtain financial assistance. But because they are moving into an unknown area surrounded by considerable mystique, many purchasers fear the worst in their search for money. This is unnecessary. Be bold enough to tackle a number of sources at the same time to get the best possible deal. If you are borrowing a sum in the region of £80–100,000 you will be a valuable customer to someone.

Before you actively seek finance, check that your feasibility study is sound. It is surprising how many would-be purchasers attempt to raise money without knowing precisely where they are going, how they are going to get there and how much money they will need to borrow to achieve their objectives. In spite of this, some still manage to raise finance, so if your feasibility study is convincing and well-argued, it will help you considerably when you discuss your proposals with your bank or a financial institution.

Approaching your bank manager

Your first discussions must be with your bank manager. While there are differences in their style of operation, many banks will now consider offering finance on a sound hotel project though they will be less enthusiastic about a restaurant which they rightly view as a more difficult sector of the industry and one that offers a much greater risk. The clearing banks used to be reluctant to lend money on long or medium term loan for the purpose of buying a business but they have adopted a much more flexible and understanding approach to start-up finance in the last few years.

You have to decide whether to talk to:

1   Your own bank manager
2   The manager of a bank recommended to you perhaps by the hotel agent or a friend
3   The manager of the vendor's bank
4   The manager of a bank in the town in which you are buying the property

All these alternatives have their various advantages. You may know your own bank manager well, which would be an obvious advantage, but he may not know much about the hotel and catering industry. As many managers are reluctant to lend to hotels or restaurants, you may find that your own manager is dubious about your application. Bank managers, unless they know hotelkeeping and catering well, tend to view the industry with some distrust because they regard it as an unpredictable and difficult area of business. Being by training a cautious rather than an adventurous person, your own manager may well try to deter you. This may not be a problem if you approach the bank recommended by the hotel agent or even the vendor's bank as both, presumably, will be aware of the nature of the industry and will be prepared to lend into it. The advantage of approaching the manager of a bank in the town in which you are buying the property is that he knows the area, knows the nature of the industry and may well know the establishment in question. Bank managers in those towns where there is a heavy concentration of hotels (seaside resorts, for example) know as much about the industry as the hoteliers themselves. Their knowledge can be formidable.

If you approach your own bank manager and he refuses, do not be disheartened. Ask him why he is refusing to help you and take note of his comments. There may be a fundamental reason for his decision and it may not just rest on his prejudice against the industry. You will have to decide whether the reason for his refusal is based on a serious flaw in your application or whether it is the result of his lack of knowledge about the hotel industry. It would be foolish to ignore the former but if you are convinced it is the latter, have faith in your project and look elsewhere. Tell him that you are determined to go ahead and ask him whether it would be possible for him to put you in touch with someone else in the bank's organization to whom you could talk.

When you do approach any lending institution, do it professionally. Whoever lends you money will be judging not only the viability of your feasibility study but your own professionalism – a properly typed and presented study is preferable to a hand-written report, for example. Almost all lending institutions will demand a surveyor's report on the property prior to final approval, because the building will comprise the security of the loan, so it saves time and certainly helps the bank to decide on your application if you include a survey in your feasibility study. Remember, the bank will expect you to put the building in proper order if there are any adverse findings and your loan application must reflect the cost of doing this. This is another good reason why it is better to get the property surveyed before you see the bank. The survey will specify what needs to be done to the building – basic remedial work will be quite common, but beware substantial structural failings such as subsidence, bad drainage, extensive wet and dry rot.

In deciding whether to help you the bank will examine the same factors that you yourself considered in your feasibility study – the location and type of hotel, whether it is freehold or leasehold, its current trading position and its future potential. The lending institution will not necessarily be looking for previous catering experience (though that would be highly desirable for a project involving a major food operation) but it will need to be convinced of your general business ability. As you are asking it to put substantial resources behind you, it must naturally be convinced that you are the right person with the right project to back. It will be looking for enthusiasm and realism and the onus will be on you to convince the institutiuon that your objectives are sensible and achievable. This is why your feasibility study is so important.

A bank will also be concerned about your other source of funds. Is the money you are putting into the business all your own or are you having to borrow additional money from another source? In the past, banks generally did not favour a borrower raising money from a wide variety of different sources and some may still refuse a loan altogether if they are not the sole source of finance apart from your own personal funds. However, they will regard money raised from your family and immediate relations as your own (providing the money is tied in properly to the business and cannot easily be withdrawn). This is called 'topping up' capital. For example, if you raise £50,000 yourself and borrow £10,000 from a near relation most banks will consider the £60,000 to be your own money. Finally, one of you may still be able to bring in another source of regular income. This is particularly true of small guest houses, which can be run by the wife (or the husband) while the other earns a salary elsewhere. Most banks would find this an acceptable situation.

What will the bank manager want to be told? These are the main points:

1   The amount of money that you are seeking and what you want to use it for. This is not such an obvious statement as it may appear. Nothing puts a bank manager off more quickly than a customer asking 'How much will you lend me?' Such a question reveals a basic mistake in your approach because what the bank manager wants is good evidence that you know exactly how much you want and what you want it for. A customer who asks 'How much will you lend me?' betrays the fact that he doesn't know how much he needs.

    The manager will want to know over what period of time you need the loan. A twenty year loan is not exceptional but a more common period is between ten or fifteen years, in the belief that if the loan cannot be repaid within that time, the project is not viable anyway. In your application, it is wise to assume the shortest possible loan repayment period, but be realistic. Too short a time-scale may lead the bank manager to think you are being too optimistic for your own good.

2   Be sure that you have as much information as possible on the trading record of the business you want to purchase. Three years' accounts would be very helpful. In your feasibility study if your projections into the future deviate from the previous trading record, explain why you think you can achieve better results. Again, false optimism is fatal. The bank manager will recognize a realistic growth plan but he will not believe you if your figures are so optimistic that they are unattainable in normal circumstances.

3   Be sure you explain your own personal circumstances and your own experience. This is most important. Many bankers will tell you that they always lend to people, not propositions. The bank will be lending to you and the manager will need to be satisfied that you are the right kind of person to back. Many an application has been turned down because the property was viable but the applicant was considered unsuitable. The manner in which you present your case will help make up the manager's mind but, just as important, will be some evidence of your determination to learn as much about the hotel and catering business as possible before you purchase. If you can show that you and/or your partner have worked in the industry, even if only as a waiter or barman, then any manager will be impressed. It shows that you are approaching the project seriously and practically. Just as helpful would be evidence that you had attended courses, conferences and seminars in the industry. The Hotel and Catering Industry Training Board is very active in this area (see page 178 for details) and a few colleges run short introductory catering courses for people starting their own business. Breweries, too, run training courses.

    A senior manager of Mercantile Credit, the finance house, explained at a conference how he viewed the importance of the interview:

'Obviously the degree of experience required will vary with the nature of the business but we generally like to see applicants who have had a varied experience in all types of hotel, big and small, and can show us a curriculum vitae which shows a steady progression in terms of managerial experience. My advice therefore to applicants is to prepare your ground thoroughly. Write down full details of your career to date and bring along as many testimonials as you possibly can. Ideally we would like to see that you have had experience in the type of hotel you intend purchasing.

'Obviously it is important that you feel relaxed at this interview. We are really trying to assess your personality, the ease with which you can communicate with us, your business acumen and enthusiasm. We want to hear of your ideas and for you to convince us that you have really looked at the hotel in depth and can improve on the present standard and level of business. Let us remember that generally the bank will be putting more into the proposition than you are and they want to be convinced that if they lend you money, then their investment will be safe.

It is up to you therefore to convince the bank that you really do know what you are doing and that your venture will succeed.

4   Allow the bank time to decide on the application. It creates a bad impression if you try to hustle the manager into lending money because you haven't given yourself enough time for the loan to be processed in the normal way. A loan can sometimes be arranged quickly but most bank managers have loan ceilings above which they have to consult their area office. This takes time.

5   Don't arrive at the bank with your application and demand to see the manager immediately. He's probably seeing someone who's taken the trouble to make an appointment. Ring up the manager's clerk to book a meeting and tell him you will send the details of the application in the post so he can see it beforehand. Don't arrive with the details in your hand believing you can persuade him during the interview. This will not work. The manager needs time to study the application and perhaps consult colleagues before he sees you. Try to predict the kind of questions he will want to ask and pre-empt them by covering the points in your application. If there are more than one of you making the application, he will want to see all of you, but bear in mind some managers are very sceptical about the prospects of a partnership succeeding, particularly partnerships involving friends or family. The stresses of business often put too great a strain on such arrangements with the result that the partnership often breaks up with acrimony. If you don't normally bank with him, he will want to know the name of your bank, for reference purposes. Have you given him all the facts and are all your arguments logical and carefully thought out? Is the loan application reasonable? In many cases, he will want to see the property himself if he does not know it personally and he may well want to meet you on site.

The important thing to remember is that most bank managers are human (some more than others!) and that it is important to look at your loan application from their point of view. If you were in your bank manager's shoes, would you lend the money on your project? What safeguards would you require to protect the investment and what aspects of your application would you view favourably and which would you regard with some disfavour?

All the major clearing banks have loan schemes for people wishing to purchase their own business – Barclays has a Business Start loan scheme and a Business Expansion loan scheme (but only limited companies are eligible to apply); Midland has long term (twenty) years and medium term loan terms; Lloyds has an Asset loan scheme (up to five years) and an Enterprise loan scheme (up to ten years); National Westminster has its business development loan scheme. While the National Westminster scheme appears to offer the most appropriate form of finance, all these schemes have a number of points in common:

1   They are aimed at small businesses – the maximum scheme is in the region of £100,000 for medium term loans but bigger loans or a longer repayment period are possible.
2   They are all flexible – the number of years of the loan is agreed between the applicant and the bank and they can be individually tailored to meet particular requirements.
3   Most loans are at a fixed rate of interest so that repayments are known in advance. The rate of interest is usually about three points above base rate but varies according to the size and length of the loan. In most cases, a bank loan of this nature is the cheapest method of raising finance.
4   As the loan is over a fixed period and at a fixed rate of interest, it cannot be recalled (unless you default on payments). Early repayments may cover interest charges only; capital repayments do not commence until later on in the period of the loan when the business is stronger.

Even if your application cannot be covered under one of these schemes by your bank manager, he may offer you finance under some other arrangement. If this is less favourable, there is nothing to stop you approaching other banks, or even other branches of the same bank, so that you get the best possible deal. It is important to remember that there are 10,000 bank managers in the country and they are not all experts in every sector of industry. As we have already emphasized some managers have built up a special expertise in certain activities so that they take a more favourable view of investment in those industries and you will need to find the bank manager with a knowledge of hotelkeeping and catering.

Other sources of finance

If the bank refuses your loan application, all is not lost but you need to ask yourself why no bank will advance the money. There must be good reasons for this. Either the property must be falling down or the business just is not viable. However, assuming that the project is still sound, other sources of finance include the finance house subsidiaries of the clearing banks. Barclays Bank has Mercantile Credit as its subsidiary, Midland has Forward Trust and National Westminster has Lombard North Central. All are members of the Finance Houses Association and a list of members can be obtained from the association (see page 100 for the address).

Finance house loans will generally be several percentage points higher than medium or long term clearing bank loans. It may well be that your bank manager will steer you towards the finance house subsidiary of his own bank, a move which you should resist if at all possible because of the higher interest rate and the fluctuating rates of interest. If base rate moves up then the interest on a finance house loan may move up. In some cases, clearing bank loans are also tied to base rate and fluctuate according to general rates of interest. On occasion a bank may give you the option of a fixed rate or fluctuating rate of interest. Which you choose depends on how you view the future; with a loan on a fluctuating rate you will gain if interest rate goes down; if it goes up you lose. With a fixed rate loan, you will benefit if the interest rate goes up because interest is fixed. If the rate goes down, however, you will still pay at the fixed (higher) rate. For the last five years interest rates have been high and while there is evidence that they are coming down, their rate of fall is difficult to forecast.

There are other sources of finance you may consider. The Council for Small Industries in Rural England (COSIRA) has an interest in hotel and catering development in Government Assisted or Development Commission Special Development Areas in rural England. Not only will COSIRA advise on starting up a business in those areas but may be able to augment private finance to a maximum value of £50,000 which should never be more than half the total outlay and may be no more than one third.

ICFC, a division of Investors in Industry (3i Group), an independent organization set up by the major clearing banks to help the expansion of small business, is also active in the hotel and catering industry. It has already invested substantial sums in the industry and may be willing to consider lending to first time buyers as well as to hoteliers wanting to expand their business. Generally speaking, ICFC finance is with larger enterprises and the Corporation may ask to have an equity stake in the business or even to put a director on the board.

There are other sources of finance which you should also consider. Insurance companies and pension funds are sometimes willing to lend on a property, particularly if you are a long-standing policy holder, while certain building societies will also lend on commercial premises. The same conditions apply to a loan from these sources. It is unlikely they will lend much mor than 50-60 per cent of the value though they may consider lending over a longer period. A building society loan, if it can be obtained, is probably the cheapest way of raising finance but their funds are very limited for this kind of property and the building will need to have a strong residential element for you and your family.

Another contact for finance may be a broker. If you have a good relationship with a mortgage or insurance broker, he may be able to use his contacts to arrange finance through an assurance company, merchant bank, pension fund or clearing bank. A mortgage broker is useful if you have a difficult property on which to raise money or if you need to raise more than 60 per cent of the value. The few specialist brokers who know the industry and the money market may be able to raise money where you have failed or may be able to better the deal you arrange yourself but you do need to ask yourself whether the terms of the loan that a broker can obtain (which will inevitably involve higher interest rates than normal) will be so onerous that the economics of the project are cast in doubt. Before you deal with brokers be sure you understand the cost of their services. Will they charge you a consultation fee? What commission will they charge if they succeed in raising a loan for you? The Corporation of Mortgage Brokers will be able to supply a list of members and the rules by which they operate.

There is another, more unusual source of finance for a hotel with a good bar trade or with bar potential. All brewery companies are anxious to sell more beer and your hotel may be a good investment for one of them, providing the brewery is convinced about your business abilities. Contact the free trade manager of the brewery concerned, enclosing an outline of your proposition and a copy of your feasibility study. You may find the brewery is not willing to help your initial purchase of the hotel but it could be willing to finance subsequent improvements in the bar.

After you have raised the finance, it is a good idea to check back with the hotel agent to ensure that the offer of finance cannot be improved upon by one of his contacts.

If the bank believes that your application is sound, its next step is to have the business valued by a professional valuer. How much it will offer depends on the results of the valuer's report. If the valuation is in line with the asking price (which is usually but not always the case) there are no problems. If the valuation is substantially below the asking price, and you still want to go ahead with the deal, you may be forced to put up more money than you originally intended.

Whenever you take over a new business you never have enough finance. There is always something unexpected that costs more than you estimated. So if, on what may be already a tight budget, the bank tells you that its offer will be less than your requirements, you may be put in a difficult situation. There are a number of courses of action. You may be able to raise a further sum from your family. Alternatively, perhaps you can cut back on your working capital – the amount of money you must set aside to get through the early stages of operating the business. Be careful about doing this. You must be able to pay all the bills that will inevitably land on your desk in the first few months of ownership. Your bank manager will provide a short-term loan or overdraft facilities. You may be able to persuade the vendor to leave some money in the business for you to pay off, with interest, over a fixed, short-term period. For some vendors, this may be an attractive proposition, particularly from the tax point of view, but from the purchaser's point of view it should be avoided if at all possible because it will be an extra debt to repay. Your solicitor should certainly be involved if you consider this. If none of these alternatives work, shop around among other clearing banks. With the incentive of taking over your account, one of them may be sympathetic to your case. The moral is: don't be put off by an unfriendly bank manager and persevere with your case until you succeed. Competition for business by the banks is keen so get the best deal you can, even though you may have been a customer at your present bank for many years.

Because you want to make only one application for loan capital, be sure to raise enough to buy the property and to operate it comfortably in the first few months. This is particularly true of seasonal hotels where you may be taking over in the winter without the prospect of earning any money until the summer. In some cases, the bank will defer the first repayments until your summer cash flow begins. Even if this is allowed, however, you will still require cash in hand as working capital. Work out how much you will need if heavy electricity, gas and telephone bills arrive at the same time, together with a demand for the rates and the insurance. Having paid out your estimated weekly expenses for food, wages and other materials, will you have enough left over to meet these extra items? Don't forget, also, that you will have to pay stamp duty, solicitor's, valuer's, surveyor's and stocktaker's fees and you will also have to purchase the stock at valuation on the day you take over. To protect yourself, you can insert a clause in the contract stipulating that the value of the wet stock (liquor) should not exceed a certain sum of money. If this figure is exceeded, you can insist that the vendor takes away the unwanted stock. The agent can help you in assessing these costs. Estimate them at the time of the loan application and be sure you have enough finance to cope. Even when all these items are taken into account, you should still have enough left over to meet emergencies and contingencies.

Some idea of the amount of money involved in repaying capital loans with interest is given here. With a fixed rate of interest, the loan repayment does not fluctuate on a monthly basis and the bank will tell you exactly what this amount is. For a commercial loan over ten years at 8 per cent annual interest (an effective rate of nearly 13 per cent), the repayments shown in Table 14 would apply. If you take out a loan that fluctuates you will find that monthly repayments can vary dramatically when interest rates rise or fall. As an indication, on a notional loan of £50,000 over ten years at true rates of interest, the monthly repayments are:

13 per cent: £747
14 per cent: £776
15 per cent: £806
16 per cent: £838
17 per cent: £869
18 per cent: £901

Table 14

Amount of loan	Interest at 8 per cent	Total	Monthly repayments
£10,000	£8,000	£18,000	£150
£20,000	£16,000	£36,000	£300
£30,000	£24,000	£54,000	£450
£40,000	£32,000	£72,000	£600
£50,000	£40,000	£90,000	£750

There is an important difference between the true rate of interest and the flat rate. The true rate is calculated on the reducing balance of the loan whereas the flat rate is calculated on the original sum borrowed throughout the period of the loan. Thus, if you borrowed £50,000 with interest charged at a flat rate of 14 per cent over ten years, your monthly payments would be £1000 giving a total payment of £120,000 compared with £93,120 on the true rate (£776 x 120 months) – a difference of nearly £26,000.

The amount of interest charged, which may vary by up to 3 per cent according to your source of finance, is important but may not be crucial because interest on the loan can be charged to the hotel's profit and loss account. Assuming that you are making a profit, the interest that you will be paying will be reduced by the sum allowed against tax. Remember, however, that you are working for yourself, not the bank or the finance house. Don't accept a loan that is so onerous that, no matter how well you succeed, you are always working for the lending source.

One final word of advice. Keep in the closest possible contact with your bank manager and if you see financial problems looming, be sure you tell him about them. He will help you as much as he can beforehand but his ability to help may be severely circumscribed if you approach him too late. Emergency measures to save a business are never viewed with any favour by a bank and it is not wise to put your bank manager in a position in which these measures have to be taken. All the banks, by the way, have business advisory services and it is a good idea to ascertain how they can help you on a regular basis once you have got the business established.

Any lending source will insist that you take out sufficient life assurance cover because the death of you or your partner could create considerable problems for the business. Other insurance may also be necessary. Most banks will need you to take out fire and consequential loss insurance – be sure you insure for full reinstatement value.

Raising finance not only poses problems at the time of purchase. Once you have bought the hotel, your financial arrangements may still be difficult to control, particularly if you want to expand or develop the property. If you have a resort hotel, you may also have a cash flow problem. Alternatively money may need to be spent on redecoration. Compared with your requirements for long-term finance, these projects are of a short-term character and your bank will be the best source of such finance. For a small project a short-term loan will be all that is required. The bank will also consider providing an overdraft facility when it is required which, for many seasonal hoteliers, is an essential part of a bank's service. Unfortunately, an overdraft can be called in at short notice so you should not finance a capital project by means of an overdraft facility. You should secure a short- or medium-term loan if you need to spend money on a major refurbishing scheme. Unless you fall down on the repayments, a loan will not be called in and, as we have seen, the interest rate will be fixed at the time the loan is granted. With an overdraft, interest charged can rise and fall with general interest rates. You should also consider leasing as an economic way of acquiring new typewriters, cash registers, accounting machines, furniture, etc. This releases capital for other purposes; leasing charges are also tax allowable.

If you need to put in hand a substantial expansion programme after a couple of years of ownership, you should consider going back to your original source of finance. With a successful operation behind you, any bank would be willing to consider a further advance for a specific project.

Before you contact them, however, there are various forms of grants and loan schemes available from official sources. The tourist boards for England, Wales and Scotland can give financial assistance under Section 4 of Development of Tourism Act for tourist projects. These funds are discretionary and all applications are individually considered. The conditions of the grants are:

1 That the project attracts tourists from both UK and abroad
2 That the project increases tourist spending and makes the tourist's stay in the area more agreeable
3 That the project creates employment, either directly or indirectly.

The type of scheme that would be considered would be the addition of extra bedrooms, new bathrooms, lifts, new public facilities. Funds are limited.

There are other official sources of finance. In Scotland, the Highlands and Islands Development Board will consider supporting a suitable tourist project in its region.

Developments that would attract this type of aid, of course, lie in the future. The immediate task is to secure your initial finance. Once this is achieved, the purchase of the business will move ahead in much the same way as a house purchase. The vendor's solicitor will prepare the contract, your own solicitor will institute the necessary searches, contracts will be signed and the deal will be completed within twenty-eight days of the exchange of contracts. All this is in the hands of the solicitors with the hotel agent keeping a watching brief.

There is one additional step you have to take, however, before you are able to say the business is yours. You will have to buy the wet and dry stock of the business at valuation on the day you take over. This process is described in the following chapter.

Suggested reading

Financing Tourist Projects; Non-Commercial Sources of Finance; How to Approach a Bank for Finance, three development guides available free from the English Tourist Board, 4 Grosvenor Gardens, London SW1.

Raising Finance; Raising Finance for New Enterprises, two titles in a series published by the Small Firms Information Service, which is part of the Department of Trade and Industry. Offices of the service are located in Newcastle-upon-Tyne, Manchester, Liverpool, Leeds, Nottingham, Birmingham, Luton, Bristol and London (65 Buckingham Palace Road, London SW1).

Addresses for further information

Finance Houses Association
14 Queen Anne's Gate
London SW1

Council for Small Industries in Rural Areas
141 Castle Street
Salisbury
Wiltshire
SP1 3TP

British Bankers Association
10 Lombard Street
London EC3

Corporation of Mortgage Brokers
88 Victoria Road
Aldershot
Hants GU11 1SS

Industrial and Commercial Finance Corporation
91 Waterloo Road
London
SE1 8XP

7 Taking over

The time between the day you exchange contracts and completion day will appear all too short because there is a great deal to be done. The precise length of time will depend on the arrangements you make with the vendor. Normally, it is not more than twenty-eight days but it can be less; it is even possible to exchange and complete on the same day.

As soon as the contracts are exchanged, the business is technically yours and you cannot withdraw from the deal without severe legal complications. In Scotland, you make an offer in writing (through your solicitor) and if this is accepted by the vendor (again in writing) these documents form a legally binding contract. No money changes hands but you cannot withdraw from the purchase without breaking the contract.

Insurance

The first objective is to take steps to insure the property from the day of exchange of contracts. If you are borrowing money from a financial organization, it will have probably made this a condition of the loan but all that it will require is an insurance on the building, so that if it burns down its investment is covered. This is only a minimum requirement. You must also take out insurance on the contents of the building because re-equipping a hotel is an expensive undertaking and one that can ruin you if you are not adequately covered. Insurance against occupier's liability (see page 117) is also essential. You should consider a profit protection policy which will provide you with a regular income based on past profits of the business if the building and its earning capacity is destroyed. It is usual to insure for three years' loss of profits based on the gross figure, but this is entirely up to you.

On a more personal level, you should consider taking out adequate life assurance cover so that sufficient funds are available to repay the capital sum borrowed if you or your wife (if she works in the business) were to die. The need for personal permanent health insurance cover and for cover on key staff should also be investigated. This will provide income if you or your key staff become permanently incapacitated. The precise form of this insurance depends on your personal circumstances and it is possible to get over-insured. On the other hand, the premiums are tax allowable and sensible insurance cover should be regarded as a prudent investment. Many people coming into the industry, particularly if they are young, believe that the worst will not happen to them and fail to take out sufficient insurance cover. They may be fortunate. But occasionally tragedy strikes when it is least expected.

One aspect of personal insurance that should not be overlooked is the need to make suitable pension arrangements. Being self-employed means you cannot rely on company or state schemes; you have to make your own arrangements. There are numerous schemes for the self-employed, most of them with tax advantages, and you should discuss your own situation with a pension expert or insurance broker.

Omitting to take out personal insurance could be considered unwise but failing to take out adequate business insurance cover must be considered a folly. Be sure that you are sufficiently covered so that you can rebuild and refurnish the property on a new-for-old basis. It is likely that the vendor will already have the property insured but you must ensure that the insurance is adequate for your needs.

Licensing

Another task that will have been put in hand at the time of the drawing up of contracts is obtaining the liquor licence. This is not a mere formality. The police will investigate your background and character before they decide whether or not to object to your application. Your solicitor – or, preferably, one specializing in licensing law – will apply on your behalf and most contracts to purchase a hotel or licensed premises depend on the purchaser getting the licence. If the licence is refused, the contract will be considered null and void, which is why an early application is essential. The police will generally indicate if they are going to object to an individual being granted a licence before the court hearing. Even if they do not object, the licensing justices can still refuse a licence on the day of the hearing, though this is rare.

The licensing laws of England and Wales and Scotland vary considerably. In England and Wales there are five main licences:

1　Full on-licence, for the sale of all or some classes of liquor for consumption either on or off the premises
2　Off-licence, for sale for consumption off the premises
3　A residential licence, for sale only to residents and their private friends
4　A restaurant licence, for sale only to persons taking substantial meals on the premises
5　A restaurant and residential licence, which is a combination of both previous licenses

In Scotland there are seven kinds of licences:

1　A hotel licence for residential premises
2　Restricted hotel licence

3   Restaurant licence
4   Public house licence
5   Off-sale licence
6   Refreshment licence
7   Entertainment licence

If the property you are buying does not already have a licence, you will have to apply for one, and this is something which needs to be undertaken by your solicitor. If the property already has a licence you will be applying for its transfer from the vendor to you. For a transfer, the sequence of events is more simple but the police will still investigate your background.

In England and Wales, you have to apply at least twenty-one days before the date of the transfer to the licensing justices – but six weeks is the preferred length of time. Application for transfer of a licence in Scotland must be lodged with the clerk of the licensing board not later than five weeks before the first day of the meeting of the board.

In all cases, notice has to be given to the clerk of the licensing court, the chief officer of the police, the local authority, the local fire authority and the existing licensee (who will be the vendor). Your solicitor will advise about the exact procedure. Licensing justices in England and Wales meet annually in February plus an additional four (minimum) to eight (maximum) transfer sessions throughout the year.

The licensing authority will take account of the view of the police before it grants a transfer of the licence. By the time of the hearing, the police will have already told your solicitor if they are going to object. Generally speaking, the authority will refuse an application if the police object or if it considers that the applicant is not a 'fit and proper' person to hold the licence. This clearly gives considerable scope for different interpretations from one part of the country to another. Any convictions that you have will probably be held against you and some authorities will now use a conviction for driving while under the influence of drink as a good reason for refusing a licence. Both you and the vendor (if he is the licence holder) will have to attend the magistrates' court on the morning you take over and you will be given what is called a Protection Order. You will have to attend the next full meeting of the licensing authority to be granted the full licence.

Inventory

Another activity in the few weeks before the takeover is agreeing the inventory. The vendor will have already drawn up an inventory of the fixtures and fittings of the business before contracts are exchanged. The inventory will include items on hire or lease, and copies will be sent to you, your solicitor, and the vendor's solicitor. This will list all the items in the building that are included in the sale, such as kitchen equipment, bedroom furniture, linen, carpets and curtains. Before this is agreed, you must ensure that all the items you understand to be included in the sale are listed in the inventory. This will save arguments on the day of the takeover when the inventory will be checked. Don't assume that all the paintings and pictures, for example, are included in the sale. Some of them may be the vendor's personal property. If the property is leasehold, there will be two inventories. One will list the fixtures that you are buying from the owner of the freehold – such as fixed seating – and the other will include the fittings that you are buying from the leaseholder. On the day of the takeover, you will have to engage your own valuer to check the inventories as well as the wet and dry stocks.

Be sure that all the items listed in the inventory are still in the establishment and that no important item has been switched. It is not unusual for a purchaser to find that items of a poorer quality have been substituted in the time between the initial inspection and before the inventory is taken, so keep a sharp eye out and pay particular notice to the quality of the bedlinen, cutlery and china.

On takeover day, the wet and dry stock will have to be valued at wholesale prices. In some cases (an exchange of tenancies, for example) both the vendor and the purchaser will employ their own stocktakers who will have to agree on the value of the stock. In many hotel purchases, the vendor and purchaser jointly appoint a stocktaker to act for both parties which saves one set of fees.

Whether you have to pay for the fixtures and fittings separately will depend on the terms of the contract of sale. Most hotels are offered for sale complete with fixtures and fittings though you should check whether any furniture is subject to a hire purchase or leasing agreement. In some contracts, however, fixtures and fittings are not included and have to be purchased at valuation; this applies primarily to a change of tenancy of a public house. In this case, both your valuer and the vendor's have to agree the value of the fittings before completion date. Valuing furniture and fittings is a skilled job but sometimes not even experts can agree. Your valuer will look after your interests and will bargain for you if that is necessary. If the two parties cannot agree, it will go to arbitration. An independent valuer will be brought in who will make a decision that will be binding on both parties. His decision on the value will be kept in a sealed envelope until the time comes to settle up on the day of the takeover.

You will also receive a schedule of existing contracts and a schedule of current staff employed. The former will list all the contracts which have been entered into by the vendor, such as boiler maintenance and linen hire. The latter will list all the staff currently employed by the hotel, giving their name, position, current salary, age and length of service. This will give you a picture of the staff position and will indicate how much they will be entitled to if you do not want to keep them on (see Chapter 11).

On the morning of the takeover, the valuer and stocktakers will move into the hotel. They will measure and value all saleable liquor on the premises at wholesale cost prices; this includes beer, wine and liquor stocks in the cellar, in the optics and on the shelves. Food stocks will also be valued. Usually, the premises are assumed to be yours at 10 a.m. – the time when you are likely to be in court applying for a licence. Depending on the size of the hotel, the stocktaking will probably have finished by lunchtime. In a big hotel, the stocktake could continue into the afternoon. When the value of the stock is agreed, a settlement will have to be made there and then on the premises. While the completion of the purchase is likely to take place in your solicitor's office (only rarely on the premises), the purchase of the stock will be completed in the hotel immediately after the stocktaking. This transaction was traditionally done in cash, in some cases up to £10,000 being passed over in notes, but now cheques are used.

The settlement will comprise not only the purchase of the wet and dry stocks but any necessary adjustments in the general and water rates. The vendor is responsible for the payment of rates and other charges up to the date of completion; thereafter they become the purchaser's responsibility. Make sure that the electricity, gas and telephone meters are read on the morning of the takeover and that the vendor assumes responsibility for these charges.

The settlement will take account of this, the stocktakers' fees and other costs, some of which are rated for VAT purposes (reclaimable later). You will have to pay your own valuer's fee (5 per cent of the value of the stock.) Either at the time of the settlement or previously at the time of the completion of the contract, money that has been accepted by the vendor as deposits for forward bookings will be credited to you.

One final point: after your appearance in the magistrates' court for the liquor licence, obtain sufficient money from the bank for floats for all the tills – £100 in small change should be enough.

Once the appraisement of the stock in trade is signed and you have paid for it, the hotel and all its stock is legally yours. The stocktakers will give you a copy of the appraisement. The vendor should be made aware that the property is now yours and he should be discouraged from stepping behind the bar! He will depart, leaving you as the new owner of the property.

8 Budgeting - and some legal points

Sole trader or limited company?

One factor that you will have already considered is whether you should form a company to run the business or whether you should operate it as a sole trader or as a partnership, possibly with your wife. Your solicitor will explain the full implications of this in the same way that he will have guided you through the legal implications of purchasing the hotel. When you purchase the hotel, for example, he will have made sure that you only purchase the building, not the company owning it – if it is operated by a company. If the Swan Hotel is run by the Swan Hotel Co Ltd, even if it is the company's sole asset, you will have only bought the hotel and not the company. It is an important legal difference, just as there are legal differences between being a sole trader and running a company.

The simplest way of running a business is as a sole trader. The proprietor is solely responsible for the operation of the business, personally owns all the assets and takes all the profits earned. He can add to the business or dispose of it in any way he thinks fit and does not have to consult anyone if he wants to change its nature. But there are legal and tax implications in being a sole trader. The proprietor becomes personally responsible for all the debts incurred and his own personal possessions can be sold to realize sufficient money to pay these debts if the business goes bankrupt. It is by no means unusual for the private home of a sole trader to be sold to raise money to pay his debts. A trader has unlimited liability and while it is a legally uncomplicated form of business in the good times, the legal ramifications are considerable if the business strikes a bad patch.

The same applies to a partnership which is created when two or more people act as sole traders together. The partnership deed (if there is one) will set out the amount of capital each partner contributes to the business and will outline how the profits are to be divided. The same principle of unlimited liability applies and the partners will be responsible for the debts incurred according to the partnership agreement regarding the sharing of profits and losses. A sleeping partner (someone who invests money into the business but who usually takes no part in its operation) will lose his investment but he has no further responsibility for the debts incurred by the other partners.

Both these forms of business provide little protection to a businessman and most hoteliers take the view that it is commercially sound to form their own company or to buy a company that is already registered 'off the shelf'. Your solicitor can advise you which course of action to take.

As the name implies, a limited liability company limits the liability of the directors of the company to the amount each has invested in the business. If the business goes into liquidation, the directors will lose their investment but nothing else; their personal possessions cannot be sold to recover debts. However, if a bank loan is involved, the directors would have had to have given their personal guarantees and these would be called on in the case of insolvency.

A company, therefore, has a legal entity of its own, irrespective of the number of directors. Whereas a sole trader employs people personally, a company, not its directors, enters into a contract to employ staff.

Forming a company may have tax advantages. Basically, the sole trader will be taxed on his net profit as income. If this exceeds a certain amount (£37,600 in the 1983/4 tax year) he would be better off to trade as a limited company and pay corporation tax at the small business rate of 38 per cent, which applies to net profits up to £100,000. The other alternative, which saves tax after £22,000 joint taxable income, is for a husband and wife partnership to split the income equally and opt for separate tax assessments. It only pays them to form a company, as opposed to a husband and wife partnership, after reaching £68,000 joint taxable income. There could be an optimum mix between company tax and directors' fees and you would be well advised to obtain financial advice in this complicated area from a qualified accountant or financial planning and tax adviser.

Your solicitor will help you in the steps that need to be taken to form a company. Broadly speaking, you must apply to the Registrar of Joint Stock Companies, submitting the memorandum and articles of association, the statement of nominal capital and a declaration that you are complying with the Companies Act. The memorandum will give the name of the company, its registered office, the objects of the company and the amount of share capital; the articles deal more with the way the company is run and the duties of the directors. As soon as the registrar accepts the document, the company is in existence as a legal entity – hence the importance of ensuring that the date of incorporation is no later than the date of takeover of the hotel.

A company must have a secretary who is responsible for sending annual accounts to the registrar (in a small company, the secretary is usually one of the directors or perhaps the hotel's solicitor) and an auditor must be appointed to verify the accounts. The auditor cannot be a director or any other officer of the company. The fees involved in forming a company are not great though your solicitor's and accountant's charges will be a cost element.

If you do decide to run your own business as a sole trader and if you do not operate it under your own name, you must have your name on all notepaper and official business literature and on display on the premises.

Having completed the purchase, your immediate task is to operate the establishment. You will be so busy in the first few days that you will not have much time to think but there is a need to plan for the future as well as to operate in the present.

Experience with your stocktaker, for example, will have served to emphasize the size of your financial investment in wet stock and the need to make sure that the investment is properly protected. In a small hotel, the value of the stock can be as much as £10,000; for a small country pub, about £4,000; for a larger hotel, with a cellar full of wines, the value of the stock would be much more. Where bar staff are employed, you should arrange for the stocktaker to come back every 28 days to take a liquor stock. Shortages will be rapidly revealed in this way and the action will have the added benefit of showing employees that you intend to keep a close eye on pilferage and wastage. If the hotel is so small that only you and your wife or family run the bar, the need for regular stocktaking is not so pressing. Even so, a quarterly stocktake is desirable just to check the accounts. Many hoteliers do their own stocktaking. In a small hotel this may not be an onerous task but by employing a professional company you ensure that the job is accurately carried out, leaving you time to do more essential jobs.

A more immediate task is to ensure that you understand the intricacies of VAT. The principle of VAT is simple: for every £1 of revenue you raise the Customs and Excise wants 15p. In practice, it is not quite so simple. You have to charge VAT on customers' accounts but you can claim it back from suppliers who have charged you VAT. In the early days of operating your new business, the VAT office will probably keep a closer eye on you than it will subsequently, but you can expect VAT officials to call every three years to inspect all your books and accounts. Read up the many booklets available from the Customs and Excise before you take over and, if in doubt, talk to VAT officials. You will find them very helpful.

Your accountant will deal with the quarterly VAT returns but his most important job is to prepare regular accounts. In a large hotel, weekly or even daily trading accounts are compiled but in a small business, a monthly profit and loss account should be sufficient. Depending on the size of the business, an accountant may appear to be a luxury but he will be able to do the job properly and quickly and it will enable you to concentrate on other activities.

Monthly accounts are important to any hotel or catering business because there is no point in knowing in July that you made a loss in the previous February. You need the information by early March so that you can take remedial action. By July, it is too late to do anything about the situation and the loss may have got worse. Your accounts should, therefore, simply balance the income and expenditure for the month. In the simplest system, the accounts will show revenue and outgoings, the balance being the gross operating profit. In fact, it is not quite so simple as that. Annual payments, such as rates and insurance, and quarterly charges, such as electricity, gas and telephone, need to be allocated to the accounts on a monthly basis so that a proportion of the total annual expenditure on these items is set against every month's income. This can only be done if you know the annual cost of these items. The vendor's accounts should provide you with the historical costs and you can work on these providing you have not increased consumption dramatically or the charges have not been raised.

Budgets

Your feasibility study will have provided you with a budget for the year but the annual figures need to be refined to a month by month basis. Before you take over you should work out the hotel's projected income and expenditure for the first year on a monthly basis. Some months may be poor – February is usually the worst hotel month – so you cannot take an annual figure and simply divide by twelve. You should look at each month and realistically estimate your income and expenditure for that period. The vendors may be able to help you after the contracts are exchanged. You will find that you are budgeting for a loss in some months because occupancy will be low while your outgoings, such as heat and light, will be high. You may be able to reduce some cost centres (staff for example) but even with a skeleton staff you will still find that you will incur a loss in some months. At the height of the season, however, you will be making a healthy profit and you need to budget for that as well by estimating your occupancy level, your room revenue and other income. Taking the year as a whole, your profitable months will hopefully exceed your loss-making months to give you an overall profit.

A budget provides you with the financial framework in which to operate your business. It sets out your annual expenditure and income on a month-to-month basis. Both sets of figures – income and expenditure – provide you with targets to aim at. If you achieve those figures your business will be on the right course and you should achieve your estimated profit by the end of the year.

Because you want to monitor your financial position regularly, your monthly profit and loss account should relate actual performance to budgeted performance. The simplest way of doing this is to have three sets of figures side by side in the monthly accounts – the previous year's figures, the actual figures achieved and the budgeted figures. In this way, the three sets of figures are easily compared and you will be able to see instantly whether there is any major deviation between budgeted and actual figures and whether business has improved or declined compared with the same month in the previous year. Your first few monthly budgets may be somewhat inaccurate but with experience they will become much more precise. There is no point in having budgets that are completely unattainable; they should be realistic and provide an incentive for you to reach your business objectives. At the same time, they will provide a measurement of your financial success.

Accurate budgets and up-to-date monthly accounts are important in the first few months for another reason. If you take over a hotel that needs major improvements, the temptation will be to spend considerable sums of money on the property immediately. This is understandable and may be fully justified but it is all too easy to overspend on redecoration schemes in the early stages of ownership. If you prepare a redecoration budget, it will act as a realistic brake to your enthusiasm. Unless you have borrowed money specifically for the purpose you will probably not be generating enough cash flow in the first few months of ownership to afford to spend much money on renovation. A budget helps you plan your redecoration schemes and ensures that you undertake only what can be afforded.

Budgets are tiresome to produce and demand considerable time and thought; in addition, forecasting income and expenditure for a year ahead involves a degree of guesswork. Even so, the discipline that is imposed on you by setting a budget will be worthwhile because it forces you to think about the future needs of the business. A budget can be as simple or as sophisticated as you want to make it but the actual process of creating it is almost as worthwhile as the benefits that accrue when you have the figures available for comparison.

As you prepare the budgets, one of the principal economic features of the hotel and catering industry will immediately become apparent. You will find that your costs, spread out over a twelve month period, will hardly rise or fall – in sharp contrast to your income, which will rise in direct proportion to your occupancy level. Hotels have high fixed costs. Before a hotel can accept a single guest, it has to invest large sums of money in the building itself, on furniture and equipment and on the decor. Whether the hotel is full or empty these costs, including the financial charges, still have to be met. Fixed costs do not vary with the amount of trade the hotel enjoys and in many hotels amount to well over half the total costs of the operation. You can work out your own fixed costs – those which have to be met whether or not you have any guests staying – by listing all the costs that will have to be paid for if the hotel is empty. The list will include such items as general rates, insurance, interest charges on your loan capital, a proportion of your heating and lighting charges and some wage costs (because you cannot reduce your staff to nil). If the hotel is full, these costs will still be incurred but you will also incur other costs – called variable costs – which vary in direct proportion to the amount of business that the hotel is enjoying.

Break-even point

Because of the high fixed cost structure, your budget will quickly show that your break-even point in the hotel will be somewhere between 30 and 50 per

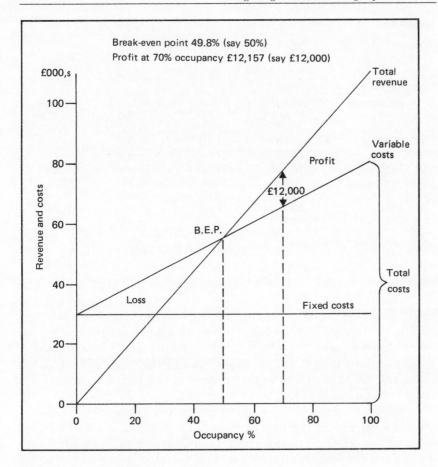

Figure 6   *Break-even point*

cent room occupancy, given a constant income from the bars and restaurant. In certain city centre or de-luxe hotels the break-even point is much higher. If occupancy falls below the break-even point the hotel loses money unless additional income is generated in other areas like the bar. Conversely, once the break-even point is reached and the fixed costs have been covered, almost all the income generated is turned into profit because a hotel's variable costs are slight in comparison to its fixed costs.

The break-even chart (Figure 6) and Table 14 illustrate this point in graphic and tabular form and emphasize the importance of filling those last couple of seats in the restaurant or those few remaining empty bedrooms.

In the example we have assumed a hotel with fifteen single bedrooms which provides bed and breakfast only; there is no food cost other than for

Table 14

Occupancy	Revenue	Variable Costs	Fixed Costs	Profit/ (loss)
%	£	£	£	£
10 (548 sleeper nights(sn))	10,950	4,928	30,000	(23,978)
20 (1,095 sn)	21,900	9,855	30,000	(17,955)
30 (1,643 sn)	32,850	14,783	30,000	(11,933)
40 (2,190 sn)	43,800	19,710	30,000	(5,910)
* 50 (2,738 sn)	54,750	24,638	30,000	112
60 (3,285 sn)	65,700	29,565	30,000	6,135
70 (3,833 sn)	76,650	34.493	30,000	12,157
80 (4,380 sn)	87,600	39,420	30,000	18,180
90 (4,928 sn)	98,550	44,348	30,000	24,202
100 (5,475 sn)	109,500	49,275	30,000	30,225

* Approximate breakeven point

breakfast which we have estimated at £1 per guest per day. Staff feeding costs are included in that figure. The hotel's tariff is £20 per person, bed and breakfast, and as the hotel has only single rooms (for simplicity's sake – in most hotels there would be a mixture of singles, doubles and possibly triples) the maximum revenue that the hotel could earn in a year is: £20 multiplied by 15 people multiplied by 365 days which totals £109,500 for 5475 sleeper (or bed) nights. In reality there would be other income (liquor, cigarettes, for example) but we are ignoring these.

No hotel ever achieves 100 per cent sleeper or even room occupancy and the national average is about 50 per cent room occupancy. This would be achieved in a resort hotel by high occupancy in the summer and low occupancy in the winter; for a provincial hotel occupancy may be high in the weekdays and low at the weekend.

What of the costs? We are assuming the following:

	£
Rates (local authority and water)	4,000
Insurances	1,100
Manager's salary	7,000
Loan interest	900
General overheads	17,000
	30,000

The general overheads include such items as: repairs and maintenance, depreciation, staff expenses, advertising, stationery, guest supplies. The loan repayment is the interest at 15 per cent due on a £6,000 loan.

All these costs are called fixed for a simple reason; no matter how many guests the hotel accommodates – if it is empty or 100 per cent full – it will always have to pay these charges. The interest on the bank loan, for example, will be payable even if the hotel does not have a single guest; similarly, rates, insurances and the manager's salary must be paid. In other words, fixed costs do not vary in relation to the number of guests or the level of business achieved.

What of variable costs? With more guests in the hotel, more bed-linen will be used and so laundry charges will increase in direct proportion to the number of guests accommodated. The same applies to food costs for breakfast; heat, light and power (possibly to a lesser extent) and some wages. These variable costs over a year will add up to a considerable sum of money but to highlight their impact on profit, it is always helpful to break them down on a cost per guest basis. In this way you will know what each guest costs when he stays with you. Some of the items are easily assessed (laundry charges, for example) but others will need to be estimated until you have more accurate figures.

In the illustration we are using, various assumptions have been made so you should not take the figures as realistic for every establishment – each will vary according to individual circumstances. The costs below are, however, sufficiently realistic for the purposes of the example.

Cost per guest	£
Food cost for breakfast	1
Heat, light and power	1
Laundry costs (sheets, towels tableclothes)	1
Wages (cleaning and breakfast staff)	5
Miscellaneous	1
	9

These figures show that each guest costs the hotel £9. The balance of what he pays for a £20 room – £11 – will go towards covering the fixed costs *or* it will contribute to the profit. It cannot do both because, as the table and chart show, before break-even point is reached (in this case 50 per cent room occupancy) all the balance must go towards covering the fixed costs. Once break-even point is passed the fixed costs have been covered and only variable costs will be incurred. In this case, the £11 balance represents profit and every other guest who stays will each contribute a further £11 directly to profit.

If you can prepare your figures in this way, you will obtain a concise picture of the cost of servicing each guest in your hotel. In our example, Table 14 shows exactly what costs will be incurred at any given percentage rate of occupancy, and these can be compared with revenue.

From both the table and the chart, the economic structure of a hotel or catering establishment can be clearly perceived. A hotel or restaurant has high fixed costs in relation to total cost and therefore relatively low variable costs. In our example, the hotel typically needs to be half-full merely to break even but once that point is reached, a considerable portion of revenue goes directly to profit. Needless to say, this also highlights the importance of containing variable costs. The precise point at which an establishment will break even depends entirely on the particular circumstances but the message is clear: no hotelier or caterer can afford to neglect any sales opportunity that will push his revenue as far beyond break-even point as possible. Only then is he making a profit.

Care must be taken in expressing occupancy figures. Many hotels use room occupancy – the number of times a room is let expressed as a percentage of the total rooms available. This is a reasonable rule of thumb but in a hotel with a large number of doubles or triples such a percentage disguises the fact that a double room is frequently let as a single at a single rate. More accurate therefore is the sleeper or bed/night occupancy which shows how many times each bed in the hotel has been let. This percentage is more precise than room occupancy: a hotel with 50 per cent bed occupancy is doing much better than a hotel with 50 per cent room occupancy, providing there is a mixture of doubles and singles.

Even more accurate than either of these two percentages, and one that is the most strongly recommended, is the room revenue percentage. In this calculation, the hotelier estimates the maximum revenue per night that a bedroom can yield. By addition, the maximum room revenue of the hotel can be calculated easily. Each night the hotel assesses its actual revenue and expresses that figure as a percentage of the maximum.

This is really the only true indication of performance, since both room and bed occupancy figures can be misleading if a hotel has to offer heavy discounts to groups. A 100 per cent bed occupancy for the hotel in our illustration would appear to be excellent but if the hotelier had to let half those 15 rooms at, say, £12 a night because they were a bulk booking, his trading position is in reality far less satisfactory. Half of the guests (who pay the full rate) will enable him to cover the fixed costs for each night that they stay, thus allowing the hotel to reach break-even point, but the remaining guests (at the discounted rate of £12) will be making a much smaller contribution to profit than would be the case if they all paid the full rate of £20 per night. In fact, they will be contributing to profit the difference between what they pay (£12) and the variable cost of servicing each one of them (£9) – only £3, instead of the usual £11. This situation would be hidden if the hotel produced bed or room occupancy statistics.

It is true that room revenue figures may be more relevant to a large city centre hotel which deals extensively in group bookings, but they are of no less importance to the independent hotelier who wants to keep track of his financial performance. Coach and travel operators use smaller hotels extensively demanding (and often receiving) substantial discounts. The independent hotelier has to use his judgement about the value of taking a large number of people at a low rate; even £3 per person profit may be better than no profit at all if, by reducing the tariff, it means that the hotel passes its break-even point. It would be foolish, however, to accept any booking below the variable cost – £9 – because the hotelier would make a loss on every booking he accepted. This is why it is vital that the variable cost of servicing your guests is known, so that rooms are not offered at a loss.

If you are buying a resort hotel the relationship between fixed and variable costs will be the crucial factor in deciding whether to close during the winter. The key consideration is whether it will cost you more to stay open in the winter with skeleton staff to serve a few guests or whether you should shoulder the entire burden of fixed costs without any income, close the hotel and dismiss all but the most vital members of staff.

The importance of keeping your eye on the financial results of the business on a regular monthly basis can hardly be overstressed, which is why you need a good accountant to provide you with the figures. An accountant will also keep you within the law, bearing in mind that VAT officials and the Inland Revenue are particularly attentive to small businesses.

Staff wages will be an immediate problem you have to tackle. If this is an unknown area to you, ask the vendor to explain how he keeps the wages books, what forms and system he uses and how PAYE is deducted. Even if you employ a part-time bookkeeper or your accountant takes over the responsibility for wages, you should make sure you can prepare the wages yourself. A couple of weeks' practice after you take over will be highly desirable. There are a number of companies that offer specialist wages systems, the cost of which should be balanced against their speed and efficiency.

Some obligations

Finally, on takeover, some other important points need emphasizing:

1   You must keep a register of guests. This can be in the form of a book or separate sheets and must be retained for twelve months after completion. The information required from guests over sixteen years of age is their name, nationality and date of arrival. If the guest is an alien (i.e. non-British, Irish or Commonwealth passport holder) the passport number must be recorded with the date of departure and the address of the next destination. Legally, the particulars of a husband and wife should be recorded separately so, while it is usual for a husband and wife to sign as 'Mr and Mrs' this is not sufficient. Guests can sign the register personally or you can fill in the details for them. Under The Immigration (Hotel Records) Order, 1972, British people are not required to provide their address though this is normally requested. It is not an offence for British people to sign in under a false name. The register must be available for inspection by a policeman or anyone authorized by the Home Office.

2   You must display your room tariff in a prominent place in reception, and your restaurant menu and prices outside the restaurant. It is not sufficient to display the room tariff on the back of the bedroom door; by the time the

guest has reached the bedroom, he has contracted to book the room. The notice must be brought to his attention before he enters into the contract. This display must give rates for different types of rooms, suites, etc. If the rates vary from room to room, it is sufficient to say 'from £12 to £18'. Rates must include service charge. VAT may be shown separately, if desired, but in any case, the amount of VAT must be indicated. You must make clear whether breakfast is included or not. The restaurant price display must include minimum and additional charges, such as cover and service charge, and all prices must be inclusive of VAT. The legislation affecting the display of restaurant prices does not apply to boarding and guest houses where food is offered only to residents.

3   If the hotel does not have a fire certificate and has not applied for one, you must immediately contact the local fire authority. Application must be made for a certificate though it is not necessary to have a certificate granted in order to trade.

4   If you are a hotel in law, you are under an obligation to serve all travellers, but the sale of liquor in a bar to a person under eighteen is prohibited. A licensee must not knowingly sell liquor to anyone under eighteen or allow the sale on his premises. Under-age drinking poses problems for licensees for they are held responsible if it takes place on their premises. People under the age of eighteen cannot be employed in a bar and children under fourteen are not allowed in a bar during permitted hours (except children of the licensee and children of the residents, or where children are passing through one part of the premises to another and passage through the bar is the only convenient way.) Games of pure skill are allowed in public bars but games of pure chance are restricted to private rooms. Betting on licensed premises is prohibited.

5   Your premises may have to be registered with the local authority under the Offices, Shops and Railway Premises Act, 1963. This legislation, which has been amended by the Health and Safety at Work etc. Act, 1974, is intended to ensure that safe working conditions are provided and both management and staff have an obligation to see that the various provisions are complied with. Your local environmental health officer will be able to advise you on the requirements.

6   You must ensure the safety of your customers. The Occupiers Liability Act, 1957, makes the owner of premises liable for the safety of 'lawful visitors'. You must take reasonable care not only of guests' safety but of other people, such as postmen and suppliers who are lawfully on the premises. The liability can be covered by insurance which should be taken out as soon as you take over the hotel. Not all the rooms in a hotel need be covered because there are some areas which a guest is not reasonably entitled to enter.

7   You must describe your goods and services accurately. The Trade Descriptions Act, 1968, prohibits use of a description that is false or

misleading. The description can be in writing or oral though the latter is more difficult to prove. Be careful about the description of your hotel in brochures. Don't say it is 'a stone's throw from the sea' when it is a mile or so away. Your menu and wine list should also accurately describe the dishes and wines. A guest would have grounds to sue if your description is false 'to a material degree'. The same applies to all other goods and services. Local trading standards officers are responsible for enforcing the Act.

8 The law about accepting hotel bookings is complex. It would be helpful if you referred to a book on hotel and catering law before taking over so that you know the full details. Broadly, a contract to reserve a room can be oral or written and must include a definite offer of accommodation by the hotel and an unconditional acceptance by the customer within a reasonable time. This causes little problem for bookings undertaken weeks in advance. More difficult are telephone bookings where there is not time for a written confirmation. A guest booking a room by telephone should therefore be told that the room will be kept for him only until a certain time, say 6 p.m., after which it will be relet unless he informs the hotel that he will be arriving later. A valid contract can only be cancelled by the agreement of both parties so the guest could claim compensation if he arrived to find that you could not provide a room which he had booked. In this situation, you must make every effort to accommodate him in a hotel of the same standard in the locality. Similarly, if a guest does not arrive you can claim compensation for actual loss though you must make every effort to relet the room before a claim would be considered. For a single night's accommodation, the ill-will created pursuing a claim on a 'no show' is probably not worth the financial recompense. A busy city centre hotel protects itself by overbooking in the certain knowledge that a small percentage of the bookings will not materialize. This is particularly true of London. For a resort hotel, where a family of four has booked a fortnight's accommodation full board, a cancelled booking at short notice is a much greater financial loss because the opportunity for chance bookings is so much less. In this situation, you must still make every effort to relet the room. If you cannot, you are entitled to claim compensation for the loss of accommodation income, less an allowance for food not consumed, and laundry, heating and lighting not used.

9 Be sure you get to know where the technical services of the hotel are before the vendor leaves. One hotelier took over an old hotel only to experience a blown fuse on his first day. He did not know the location of the fuse nor that there were six of them in different parts of the building. Get to know the position of the fuse boxes, the water stopcock and gas inlet pipe; be sure you have a master key to all the bedrooms, that you know how the beer pumps work, that you can handle the switchboard if necessary.

10 It makes sense to join the most appropriate organizations. You should consider registering with the regional tourist board (see page 167) so that

you can take advantage of regional and national tourist promotion. Their officers are always helpful and will be able to advise you on your marketing efforts. You should become a member of the British Hotels, Restaurants and Caterers' Association, 40 Duke Street, London W1, which is the hotel employers' national association. The BHRCA is able to give legal and other advice to its members. You should also consider joining the local hotel association if there is one, which is likely to be affiliated to the BHRCA. The Hotel, Catering and Institutional Management Association is the professional body of the industry. Membership of this association is by qualification only and further details can be obtained from the HCIMA, 191 Trinity Road, London SW17.

11 Some colleges run short courses in various aspects of hotel and catering management. Full details can be obtained from the HCIMA or the Hotel and Catering Industry Training Board, Ramsey House, Central Square, Wembley, Middlesex, which itself offers one day courses on specialist subjects.

Suggested reading

Hotel and Catering Law, by Frank Bull and John Hooper, published by Hutchinson.

Licensing Law, a development guide published free by the English Tourist Board, 4 Grosvenor Gardens, London SW1.

Accounting and Financial Management in the Hotel and Catering Industry: Vol 1 and 2, by Peter Harris and Peter Hazzard, published by Hutchinson.

A Standard System of Catering Accounting, National Economic Development Office, Millbank Tower, London SW1.

Financial Management in Hotel and Catering Operations, by Donald Sutton, published by Heinemann.

Hotel and Catering Costings and Budgets, by R.D. Boardman, published by Heinemann.

Hotel Management Accounting and Control Systems, by John Harrington, published by Northwood Books.

Various VAT booklets, obtainable from your local VAT office.

9 Starting from scratch

Many people consider entering the industry by converting existing premises to hotel and catering use. There are many attractions in this but also many pitfalls.

Country house hotels

One of the most alluring attractions is to buy a large country house with the intention of converting it into a hotel or restaurant. There are a number of understandable reasons for this:

- It may be easier to find a private house of style and character than a hotel.
- A large house is likely to be less expensive to purchase than an established hotel because you are buying only land and buildings, not a business. The price, however, will depend on the size and condition of the property and its grounds.
- In opening a country house hotel or restaurant you don't have to live up to or dispel a previous reputation. You start with a clean slate. You can plan your hotel in your own way, restricted only by the structure of the building, your finance and your marketing objectives.
- A country house property offers a tantalizing glimpse of gracious living.

These are considerable attractions and there are many private houses in both the town and the country that have been successfully turned into hotels or restaurants. Indeed the majority of Britain's hotels, except for those built by the railway companies and those purpose-built since the war, were once private houses. More recently, some notable country properties have been converted for example Inverlochy Castle, Scotland; Eastwell Manor, Kent; Hambledon Hall, Rutland Water, Leicestershire; and Hunstrete House, near Bath. These establishments have been converted to exceptionally high standards and are taking advantage of a small but well-defined group of customers who demand the highest standards of food and accommodation in elegant and spacious surroundings and who are willing to pay for the ambience and facilities provided.

More typical examples of private houses converted to hotels would be Holmwood Park, Bath; Beechfield House, Melksham; and the Riverside at Helston in Cornwall, where the cost of conversion has been contained to a more realistic level so that more modest tariffs can be charged. It is this kind of hotel that most people seek to emulate but before doing so there are some important points which need to be considered here, while some of the factors relating to a town house conversion (see page 127) are also relevant.

Motive

Before you decide to buy anything, question your motives for wanting to run a country house hotel and decide what facilities you want to offer. Be sure you stay in other hotels of the same style and character as the one you want to own. You can learn an enormous amount from their good and bad points. How do they receive guests? What facilities do they offer and which do you believe are the most important? What is the standard of their bedrooms and how are these standards achieved? What little extras are provided? What is the quality of their furniture and fittings. How good is the service? What factors make you feel comfortable?

As you go around take notes so that you can translate as many good ideas as possible into your establishment. This is not copying; it is sensible market research which enables you to assess how high your standards should be and what you have to achieve to be comparable. You get the feel of how a successful country house hotel operates. Such research will be expensive to carry out but, like a building survey, it will be money well spent.

Hard work

While a country house is tempting as a way of life you should remember that it is still hard work. Don't be attracted by the thought of gracious living – you will almost certainly be working so hard that you won't be able to enjoy it! You will be restricted by the availability and cost of skilled staff and much of the work will have to be carried out by you and your wife or partner. Nor should you assume that a country house hotel is highly profitable. This is often not the case because the costs of running and maintaing such properties are high.

Conversion costs

It is possible to buy a large country house in certain areas for a reasonable sum. Because there are few families looking for such properties, they can represent excellent value for money particularly if they have extensive grounds. But the cost of converting the house into a hotel can be high. Not all converted houses need become de-luxe establishments but the expense of conversion can force them into the first class if not the de-luxe category, whether or not that is required. The market for rooms at £60 per night is limited and if the costs of conversion drive your tariff into that category you must be sure of your market.

Every house will have its own individual problems so it is dangerous to generalize but it is safe to say that extensive building work will be necessary to provide sufficient public areas, adequate kitchens and a private bathroom and toilet for every bedroom. In almost every case, the plumbing and electrical systems will need replacing and it is not uncommon for the roof to need attention – perhaps a new roof will be necessary. Check for woodworm and dry rot. Another major item of expenditure lies in the work connected with fire precautions legislation while the cost of equipping the kitchen from scratch should not be underestimated. It should be remembered that the greatest cost is incurred in effecting the structural alterations, particularly the provision of private bathrooms, but furniture and fittings will be no minor expense. Private bathrooms, incidentally, are essential in a country house hotel as most guests would expect them; a shower may save space compared with a bath but is not always in keeping with the image of higher priced hotels.

As an indication only, the 1980 cost of converting one well-known fifteen-bedroom country house into a hotel of de-luxe standard was well over £500,000, but in this case no expense was spared. More typical would be the £80,000 cost incurred by another hotelier who converted his country house into an eight-bedroom hotel and high class restaurant.

Gardening costs

The grounds of large country properties are costly to maintain and initially are often in a poor state of upkeep. It may be expensive to bring them up to standard and there will be continual expenditure in keeping the garden well stocked with plants. A gardener may have to be employed and garden equipment needed – there is no purpose in having an impeccable hotel in untidy grounds.

Planning permission

Many old properties are listed buildings. Even if you can get planning permission to convert such a property into a hotel you may have to retain particular parts of the building at great expense. Never buy a private house with a view to converting it into a hotel without previously obtaining planning permission; alternatively, make your offer conditional on the granting of planning permission. Sometimes the vendor may not wish to wait the three months or so that a detailed planning application may take, in which case you will have to take a gamble on being granted permission. In any case, always have a proper building survey carried out – money spent on a survey may save you thousands later. One hotelier bought a well-known property on the south coast without a survey only to find that the building needed a new roof and new kitchens, which cost £200,000 – expenditure that was totally unexpected and which put the project back two years. Don't be too daunted by a poor survey, however, because surveyors have to tell you about everything that is wrong with a building; sometimes their report reads more like a horror story. What you are looking for are major items of expenditure like retiling the roof or difficult problems like subsidence; every old property has woodworm and many have dry rot but, if these are not too extensive, they can be cured. You have to assume that the plumbing and electrical systems will need attention but the drains should also be checked. Bear in mind that most country houses, particularly Victorian, were solidly built. If they have stood for 150 years it is likely they will stand for another 150 years, given adequate maintenance.

Raising finance
It is more difficult to obtain matching capital for a conversion than it is for the purchase of an existing hotel simply because the property has no track record as a business. You will be seeking a loan based entirely on your own projections without the benefit of any past trading experience. Few banks will consider a loan under these circumstances unless you have considerable hotel, catering or business experience. Anyone determined to go ahead will need a formidably persuasive feasibility study.

Living accommodation
Don't forget that you will need living-in accommodation for yourself, your family and perhaps your staff. A large house may have as many as fifteen bedrooms but you will lose some by installing bathrooms; by providing accommodation for you and your family you will be sacrificing even more letting accommodation which means less revenue for you.

Broadly speaking, it is unlikely that the conversion of a private house into a hotel of six bedrooms or less would yield sufficient income to make the project economic unless you are able to generate a busy restaurant and bar trade. The sums may work out if one of you has another source of income or if you do much of the conversion work yourself, thus cutting down builders' costs, so there can be no hard and fast rules. By providing accommodation for yourself or staff you may come very close to this uneconomic level, in which case you will have to reduce your own requirements to the very minimum. In most small town house conversions it should be unnecessary (and hopelessly uneconomic) to provide living-in quarters for staff but there is often no alternative if you are in an isolated position in the country. This problem can sometimes be overcome by converting outbuildings into staff accommodation but it could be more economic to rent a house nearby. If you have to do this, the cost must be taken into account. In any conversion the absolute need is to maximize your available letting space.

Initial resources
During the period of conversion (which will be hardly less than four months and may be as much as a year) you will receive no income to balance the heavy financial demands being made on you. Sufficient resources will be required to sustain the cost of the conversion including interest charges during this period.

Marketing

A country house hotel presents one of the most difficult of all marketing problems. By its nature and location it will not be able to attract much chance trade. People will have to make a special journey to stay or eat with you so you have to get your name in front of them. Once attracted, they will only come again if your food and/or accommodation satisfy them.

The busiest period for a country house hotel is often the weekend for it is precisely this sort of hotel that people find so appealing for a weekend break; in summer months you should attract tourists and holidaymakers. Unless the hotel is within striking distance of a centre of population or near a main road, where you will be able to pick up weekday commercial business, occupancy in the week may be slack particularly in the winter. The same can be said of lunch-time business in the restaurant while the level of trade for dinner will depend entirely on the quality of your food, service and ambience. With no previous trading experience it will take you time to find customers and probably as much as two years to get your name in the principle guides. For this reason you will have to spend a greater proportion of your time and money on marketing and sales promotion than would be the case if the hotel was situated in a town.

From these comments, it can be seen that each conversion of a house into a hotel needs to be judged on its merits. There are enough examples to show that a conversion can be successful but unfortunately commercial considerations are not always the most important factor – people just fall in love with a property. This is perhaps the most dangerous situation of all.

A conversion scheme may make more sense if the work can be carried out over a few years thus spreading the cost and, at the same time, producing some revenue. Against this, however, is the consideration that continuous building work deters many guests. It is also important to remember that launching a country house hotel is a difficult enough marketing exercise; having a half-completed hotel makes it that much more difficult. Ideally, when you do open the hotel, it is important that everything is running as you want it, that the rooms are available and can be inspected by interested visitors and that the hotel looks attractive and complete.

Whatever your particular circumstances prepare your feasibility study with care and assess precisely the cost of the conversion; remember, once you start, you will find more work to do than you bargained for, so budget for an over-run on costs of at least 10 per cent and assume that the builder will take longer to complete the project than he estimates. Converting old houses always raises problems. Under-estimate revenue in the first few years: don't be over-confident just to convince the bank manager. Make sure you understand your break-even point – see page 110.

Apart from these general observations there are a number of more specific points that should be mentioned to help those who wish to progress with their own conversion scheme.

Location remains a vitally important factor. It is true that customers who use country house hotels will travel to the most obscure places to find them but there still has to be a reason for them to do so. What is that reason and is it powerful enough? What would your hotel offer – peace and quiet – large rooms – gracious living – superb food – impeccable service? Is it one or all of these qualities or will you have some other attraction?

Your house needs to be in an area where there are plenty of activities that attract people. It has to be unique to attract customers from a long distance but surveys show that people going on a weekend break to a hotel do not travel much more than fifty miles to get to the hotel of their choice. Be near a town because you will need to draw lunch and dinner trade from it, and don't be too far off a main road so that passing traffic misses you; even a mile down a country lane can be too much of a deterrent for chance customers, even if they know your hotel is at the end of it. Don't rely on getting permission to erect directional signs to your hotel – it is often impossible to obtain. In general, the further you are away from a centre of civilization, the more difficult it will be for you to generate business. Without question, the most difficult problem you will have in the first few years will be to attract customers; don't make that problem more difficult by poor location.

Try to buy a house in an area which you know; alternatively, get to know the area. It is more important to bear this in mind if you are buying a house for conversion than if you are buying an existing hotel because a hotel has (or should have) an established trade.

Consider carefully your mix of business. Try to attract people into your restaurant by good food and service and into your rooms by a high standard of accommodation. Poor food can ruin your bedroom business (and vice versa) because people demand consistent standards throughout a hotel. Most country hotels need a good restaurant because that is what the customer expects of them but there is an even more important reason from the hotelier's point of view. Good food will attract local people who will then recommend it to others. Eventually this will benefit not only restaurant sales but the bedroom business as well. Local people will recommend your accommodation to visiting friends and business people almost on the quality of the food alone.

A country house hotel without a good restaurant would be excessively difficult to establish so it is important that you or your partner are interested in cooking and can prepare food to a high enough standard to encourage trade. That is quite a daunting thought. You can of course employ a chef but a person of real talent will demand a salary running into five figures and the wage bill is one cost area you must keep to a minimum in the early years at least. One of you, therefore, should be capable of taking control of the kitchen and if neither is able or willing you need to think carefully before embarking on the conversion of a country house into a hotel or purchasing an existing one. Serve the food you enjoy cooking and which you can cook well. Keep your menu simple with a small choice of interesting dishes.

You will want to generate a good restaurant trade as well as a demand for rooms but in the early years it is likely that one department will be more successful and yield more income than the other. In fact, depending on the nature of the hotel and the number of rooms, this situation may continue indefinitely. Your objective will be to maximize the revenue from your rooms and the restaurant and to make sure that each contributes as much as possible to the success of the enterprise. A good mix of business does not necessarily mean an *equal* contribution from both the restaurant and the rooms, however. Your room sales will always be more profitable than your food because there are fewer variable costs involved in the sale of a bedroom (see page 110) while at least 40 per cent and maybe 50 per cent of your restaurant revenue will go directly towards covering the cost of the food alone. What you need to remember is that both departments are equally important, that food sales encourage bar sales, generate cash flow and produce activity in a hotel.

In the first year it would be sanguine to budget for more than 40 per cent room occupancy (the UK national average is only 52 per cent). There are too many unknown factors to give sensible advice on restaurant occupancy: everything will depend on your location and competition, the quality of your food and service, the atmosphere you are able to create, the promotion you undertake – and good luck.

It will take two years or so for you to build up trade to a sufficient level that you can consider the hotel as established. It is vital that any country house hotel gets into all the hotel and food guides including the local tourist board guide. The AA and RAC, Egon Ronay and the tourist board will rate your hotel according to specific criteria but because of the long publishing lead time it will be eighteen months before your entry appears in their guides. Free editorial mentions in any guide including the local and national newspapers are much more valuable than paid-for advertising. Don't spend too much money at once on advertising. Even if you spend £5000 in your first year (this is just an example, not a recommended figure) the money will be insufficient to make any kind of national impact. You must be very selective in planning your advertisements and there are other effective ways of marketing your hotel (see Chapter 10).

A final word about pricing. Your pricing policy must not only be consistent (don't operate an expensive restaurant with cheap rooms or vice versa) but it must bear a relation to the price charged by competitive establishments in your area. This is why you need to have stayed in nearby hotels and eaten in their restaurants – in that way you get a good idea of what price they charge and what value they provide (see page 129 for more information on the relationship between price and value). In a country house hotel you will be introducing a room tariff that bears little relation to the variable cost of servicing that room (see page 107). The fixed costs of course are very much higher. The tariff must be set at the right point in relation to other hotels in the area, initially a few pounds per room under your best competitive hotel because a small price advantage at the outset may be very useful. In budgeting your revenue for the year you will have to assume a certain degree of occupancy and this will tell you whether your income will cover your high fixed costs as well as your variable costs. But setting the exact level of tariff when a hotel first opens is more an exercise of marketing than of costing. The question is: what will the market bear? rather than: what do I need to charge to cover my costs? Incidentally, one common problem met by operators of new hotels is the difficulty they experience in assessing the uptake of double and single rooms. Before the pattern of trade is established you cannot know whether you will be successful in selling your rooms as doubles (thus maximizing bed revenue) or whether you will have to let some double rooms as singles. Don't assume that you can let a double as a double every night. You must remember this in your first year's budget as the shortfall over a twelve month period could be significant. The arguments that have to be considered on the relative number of doubles/twins and singles in a hotel are discussed below.

The cost of conversion can be contained providing you are able to plan the work yourself but with a major project it is unlikely you would save much by carrying out many of the jobs yourself. By employing a builder direct and by dispensing with the services of an architect you can certainly cut costs. The local authority will not demand an architect's plan for conversions or additions so with the help of your builder and a draughtsman it is quite possible to submit plans yourself which will be acceptable to the planning department. Whether you are able to dispense with an architect's services will depend on the complexity of the conversion. If there is much reconstruction an architect will be necessary but a good local builder with skilled electricians and plumbers can plan and execute many conversion schemes. You and the builder must know what you want done and you must be available constantly to sort out the many problems that inevitably arise in this kind of work. If you do this you have much greater control over expenditure. Little things can produce great savings. It is for example expensive to tile bathroom walls to the ceiling: half or quarter tiled walls are no less effective, providing shower units are not installed, though it is still possible to have shower heads on a shorter hose so that guests can wash their hair. A saving of, say, only £100 per bathroom may not sound much but it is considerable when multiplied by the total number of bathrooms in a hotel. Similar savings can be made in other areas without significantly affecting the standard of comfort.

One of the most difficult decisions to make is whether you put single, double or twin beds in the bedrooms. The size of the room may dictate the use of a single bed but it is tempting to put a double bed in a room that is really only big enough for a single (see page 202 for the English Tourist Board minimum criteria). Guests in a country house hotel will expect spacious rooms of character so it would be a mistake to have rooms that are basically too small. That would soon lead to guest complaints. The question is whether to equip your double rooms with a double bed or twin beds. The size of the room may be one factor (two single beds take up more space) but in the final analysis you will have to assess how many of your guests prefer a double and how many prefer a twin bedded room. It is possible to get single beds that zip together but you will then require specially large sheets and blankets for what will be a king-size bed. The best solution is to compromise and to have an equal number of double and twin bedded rooms, hoping that this will suffice; a couple of rooms with zip-beds would provide a degree of flexibility in your sleeping arrangements. If you expect to have a large number of weekday single lets that may encourage you to have more twin bedded rooms; on the other hand, there are few objections when a single person is asked to sleep in a double bed.

Town house conversions

Many of the difficulties posed by a country house conversion are duplicated when you decide to convert a large private house in a town but there are some important differences. Few town houses have extensive grounds so their upkeep will not be a problem. In addition, it may be simpler to market your hotel; people come to the town anyway so your objective will be to obtain a fair share of that traffic. You will not have to create a special reason for people to stay with you, which a country hotel has to do.

Business for a small town house hotel will also be different, falling into the usual commercial pattern – busy weekdays and quieter weekends. Saturday and Sunday occupancy will be difficult to build up and small hotel or guest house dining rooms (unless they are of the highest standard or have some other unique feature) very rarely succeed in establishing themselves as restaurants in their own right. Indeed, some resident guests may not even want to eat in the hotel at all, preferring to eat out in an established restaurant in the town. Under these circumstances, the majority of hoteliers or guest house owners only offer bed and breakfast, believing that the problems of providing lunch and dinner far outweigh the advantages. In this case, the tariff you will be able to charge for such limited services will be reduced to your advantage.

Nearby competition allows a town house hotel to have much less flexibility in its pricing than a country house hotel, however. The latter may have little competition in the immediate vicinity and its character may enable a higher tariff to be charged; comparisons with nearby hotels are not possible. But a town hotel will be easily comparable with other hotels in the area. A new hotel or guest house coming into an established market thus has to be careful in its pricing strategy. Unless it is of a higher standard or has a unique feature it cannot charge more than the competition but if it charges considerably less, potential customers who equate low prices with low value may be put off.

It is for this reason that a feasibility study is again essential for any conversion, answering the following kind of questions: Is there room in the town for a new hotel? What type of customers will it seek to attract and what price are they willing to pay? Are there enough customers to go around – in other words, is the market big enough? What unique factor will your hotel have that will attract customers to your establishment and away from rival hotels? How easily can you give potential customers your sales message? Can you generate enough revenue, even when full, to pay off the costs of conversion (including interest charges) and still leave enough for you to live on and to reinvest in the business?

Depending on your ambitions and finance, a town hotel could be as small as a six-room guest house or as large as a twenty-room mansion. In most cases a newcomer to the industry would convert a property into a guest house or small private hotel of between six to ten rooms because that may be the limit of his financial resources. The differences between a hotel and a private hotel are explained on page 16. Legally, there is no difference between a private hotel and guest house though the former may have more facilities and is more likely to have a liquor licence. There is nothing to stop a guest house obtaining a licence providing you can persuade the justices of the need. The term 'guest house' has a slightly pejorative connotation which you may want to try to avoid by using the term 'private hotel'.

Costs
In undertaking a project of this nature it is important not to underestimate the expense. The cost of purchasing a sufficiently large house will be anything between £50,000 and £150,000 depending on its location, character and state of repair. A property in a provincial city, London or London suburbs would be more expensive than one in a resort. The cost of converting the house by employing a professional builder will be high and the cost of furnishing and equipping each bedroom to a reasonable standard is not likely to be less than £1,200. The conversion of a house even to a small guest house could be prohibitive unless you have considerable finance to invest at the outset; it is unlikely that you could finance such a project out of earnings from the establishment. Another source of income – perhaps one of you may continue working – may be essential.

The costs of conversion can be reduced if you are able to undertake much of the work yourself. This will take longer and, while you are carrying out the work you will not earn income but it will reduce your initial demand for capital.

Facilities
In working out your finances avoid the trap of pretending that a guest house is a hotel. In other words, don't try to provide the range of facilities of a hotel. A hotel charges more because it has to employ staff and provide extensive public areas and private facilities for which its customers are willing to pay. The guest house market is very price-conscious and customers are generally not willing

to pay for such facilities as private bathrooms, colour television and private telephones all of which are a standard feature in most hotels but which cost a considerable sum of money to provide. Private bathrooms or showers and toilets are helpful to a guest from a sales point of view if they already exist or can be provided easily, but a bathroom and toilet en suite, professionally installed, will not cost less than £2000 per room and may be much more. Similarly, a guest house will employ no staff except the owner and his wife and perhaps part-time help. If you add all the extras that you find in a hotel you will price yourself out of the market by having to charge too high a tariff.

Revenue

Unlike a hotel, which earns revenue from a variety of areas – bar and restaurant, for example – a guest house is totally dependent on room revenue. In the early years when you are building up trade, room occupancy is likely to be in the 30 per cent range; even in an average year, room occupancy will not be much more than 50 per cent and bed occupancy less. You will have to finance your interest and capital charges out of income, so prepare your sums carefully.

Local authority

Work as closely as possible with local authority officials such as the environmental health officer, who will be very helpful, but question every decision that goes against you. If planning permission is refused initially, try again and again. Contact the local planning officials personally and, if you make no progress, contact your local councillor so that he or she can bring his or her influence to bear. Question the rates assessment and be sure that the authorities grant proper recognition of the element of private accommodation in your property. If you are not satisfied, contact your local MP. Persevere with any loan arrangements you wish to make. If your usual bank manager refuses to help you go to another bank. Don't accept any official decision that goes against you – it's your money that you will be paying out. An extra £250 on the rates bill may be the equivalent of letting a double bedroom for fifteen nights. You cannot afford to lose that kind of money.

VAT

It may be important not to exceed the level of income above which you have to impose VAT – currently £17,500 per year. A guest house competes with a local hotel by offering a simpler product at a lower price. As soon as VAT has to be imposed on guests' bills, the price rises by 15 per cent – not too important for business travellers who can reclaim the tax, but it may deter many private customers. It is important that a guest house does not lose its competitive price edge over nearby hotels so the imposition of VAT is something to be avoided if possible.

Image

One drawback about setting up a guest house is the poor image of this sector of the market. The seaside boarding house with the martinet landlady, who closes the door on the guests during the day and who shuts them out at night, is the standard target of every music hall comedian. The image deters many people from staying in a guest house. There is no quick or easy solution to this problem and the only way that a guest house can overcome it is to be professional in its approach and to build up the all-important repeat visitor business. The guest house proprietor should offer a real welcome and provide a good quality home-cooked breakfast, a comfortable, clean room and free access to the room at any time of day or night by means of individual front door keys. The guest house owner's unique advantage is that he is capable of offering a home from home and he should capitalize on that. It is warmth and hospitality that will encourage visitors to return and more important, to tell their friends and colleagues about your establishment. You must aim to make every guest so satisfied that he or she becomes your personal sales representative.

Listing in the AA, RAC and the tourist board guides will also do much to help create an image of professionalism. Be sure that the local authority knows about you and maintain good relations with the local police station – the amount of business that can be recommended to you locally can be considerable.

Tariff

Fix your tariff carefully. This exercise is not easy when starting any sort of hotel or catering establishment from scratch but it is easier with a guest house because there is only one source of income – the rooms. In simple terms, you have to list all those items of expenditure that you will have to meet during the course of the year – your fixed costs (see page 110). This includes mortgage repayments, rates, heat, light and power, insurance, telephone, stationery and printing and maintenance. Don't forget your own food and expenses. You will also have to estimate your variable charges – chiefly food and laundry and cleaning costs. When these sums are added up you will have an accurate picture of the total outgoings.

You know how many bedrooms you can let so your maximum daily revenue is the number of rooms multiplied by the room rate. If you extrapolate that figure for a year, you will have your total maximum annual income. Of course, no hotel ever earns its maximum income. If you are starting from scratch it would be wise to assume an occupancy in the 30-40 per cent range in the first year at least, but even that may be too high.

If you assume 40 per cent occupancy for the first year you can fix a tariff that yields the necessary income to cover your expenses. Don't forget your own salary and the profit you require so that money can be ploughed back into the business. When the calculations are complete you will be able to set the tariff for a single and double room. Remember, a double room tariff is normally between 50 and 75 per cent more than a single room and that a room with a bathroom can be let for between £3 and £9 more than one without; you may let children under fourteen stay free in a family room.

Your own costs, however, are not the only consideration. What is the competition charging? You must be competitive, so do not introduce a tariff that is substantially out of line with similar establishments in the area. On the other hand, don't underprice – one of the easiest mistakes that a newcomer to the industry can make. No guest will ever thank you for charging too little and nor will your bank manager. Aim to give good value at a fair price and increase prices with inflation and improvements. If you need to increase the tariff above the rate of inflation try to provide an extra facility that the regular guest will notice so that he recognizes you are trying to maintain – even enhance – the value you provide. Such a facility could be relatively cheap to provide – better soap, for example, or a free newspaper or a welcoming miniature of sherry in each bedroom for regular guests – but its value to the customer far outweighs the cost. Of course, the cost of these additional benefits is priced into the tariff (a fact that the customer may or may not realize) but the impression he or she will gain is that he or she is getting something for nothing, and everyone likes that. Remember, however, that the most valuable free benefit any proprietor or hotelier can provide is his own welcome and friendliness. This is genuinely free and is always appreciated.

Research

Before you start any conversion scheme, stay at the other small hotels. Notice what makes them successful or unsuccessful. Try to analyse how they satisfy their market and note what facilities they provide for the price they charge. Do you consider the price represents good value? If not, why not? If so, why? In the final analysis, you must try to attract customers to stay in your guest house because your facilities are as good as those which the customer experiences at home. So your rooms must be comfortable with a standard of décor and furnishing that bears good comparison with those of home. They must also be clean. No room in a guest house or hotel should be anything other than spotlessly clean; a guest will notice dirt more quickly than anything else.

Price and value in hotels

These are the most important general factors that need to be considered carefully before you commit yourself to any country or town house conversion project, but before we leave the subject we need to look more closely at the question of price and value.

Customers will always try a new hotel or restaurance once out of curiosity but they will not come again unless it provides value for money. Like beauty, value lies in the eye of the beholder so it is difficult to define but a customer decides whether a hotel provides value for money by asking himself a simple question: was the room worth what I paid for it?

The difference between price and value is important. It is quite possible for something inexpensive to represent poor value; at the same time, something expensive can represent good value – like a Rolls Royce car, for example. People who stay in luxury accommodation are not concerned so much with what it costs because normally they can easily afford it. They are concerned that it is worth the money they paid and if it is, they may well return; if they decide it is not, they will never come back.

Building up repeat business, as we see in the chapter on marketing, is essential for any hotel or restaurant and the importance of understanding the connection between price and value is particularly important for the operator of any hotel, guest house or restaurant. Broadly speaking, the higher the tariff the greater should be the value that a hotel provides but it must also be remembered that the higher the tariff, the smaller is the market. A high tariff hotel or restaurant, therefore, has to balance a number of important factors in setting its prices and it would not be correct to assume that price alone dictates the success of a business. There are many expensive hotels that achieve high occupancy levels; equally, there are many inexpensive hotels that suffer low occupancy. The key factor is value. The hotelier or restaurateur has to decide exactly what the customer needs; he must then make sure that those needs are fully satisfied in a way that ensures he makes sufficient profit.

Restaurants

Converting a private house into a restaurant poses similar problems to those presented by a hotel except that the conversion costs will be lower because no accommodation will be needed, except for you and your family. A feasibility study is still necessary and you will have to answer similar questions to those you would pose in a hotel: Who are your customers? Where will they come from? What do they need and what are they willing to pay for? Can you satisfy that need at a profit?

A high price, high quality restaurant in the country is one of the most difficult establishments for a newcomer to the industry to open and operate successfully. While there are many examples of success, as a glance at the food guides will show, there are a greater number of unreported failures, even by experienced caterers. It is also one of the most difficult of all projects on which to raise matching capital. A high price restaurant inspires high expectations of value and any deterioration in quality and standard will lead to a rapid decline in business; just as important, if the standard or ambiance is not right at the outset it will be impossible to build up the restaurant in the first place.

Nevertheless, there is scope in the restaurant industry for those with flair, imagination and skill whether they are based in the country or the town. The key factor, apart from value, is location which will not only dictate, to a large extent, how successful you are but the type of restaurant that you run. A country house restaurant demands a certain type and quality of food – mainly high class or unusual dishes served at a leisurely pace in attractive surroundings. A restaurant of similar style and standard may also be situated in a town. Many town restaurants however provide simpler food and a more limited menu at a cheaper price and their market is the passing customer who is attracted on impulse. The menu of these restaurants may comprise little more than sandwiches and snack items. A high class restaurant can succeed in a town centre but a location in a busy shopping area may lead you to the conclusion that it would be more profitable to offer cheaper items and thus aim to attract the high volume/low price market rather than the high price/low volume market. Much will depend on your own inclinations. If you do want to open a high class restaurant, you will have to make sure that you have something different to offer customers. You must also remember that the restaurant business is more fickle than that of hotels – fashions change quickly and the popularity of a restaurant tends to decline over the years unless the restaurateur can bring new life to it. In some cases, the restaurant will have to be renovated completely every five years or so. There are, of course, many successful restaurants that have remained the same for years but don't assume that a restaurant will stay successful for ever.

Opening a new restaurant demands careful planning and, in doing so, it is important that you look at the whole operation of the unit. A high class restaurant succeeds for a number of reasons; it is not just food, nor the service, nor the ambience, nor the comfort, nor the location alone. It is almost always a combination of these factors, plus luck. Take away one of these factors and the restaurant will not be quite so attractive as it was before. In other words, you may provide the best food in town but you may still not be successful because you are in the wrong location, or you have the wrong kind of service or ambience.

Many newcomers are tempted to open a restaurant by converting a retail shopping unit. The cost depends on the size and complexity of the design but would range from £20,000 upwards. Popular price snack restaurants need to be in locations where there is a high pedestrian traffic count; restaurants serving more interesting and expensive food can trade successfully in a side street. A High Street position is not necessarily a guarantee of success when opening a restaurant or tea room but it certainly helps. Unfortunately, rents for these units (few are available freehold) are often high. The busier the shopping area the higher will be the rent which will also be reviewed normally every three or five years. Beware of buying premises on a sub-lease where the rent has not been adjusted for some years. The rent of one small main street coffee lounge was increased from £9,000 per year to £27,000 in one leap. The business had to close as a coffee lounge and the premises subsequently reopened as a carpet and bedding centre. This situation is common in many towns where landlords are able to increase rents dramatically because there is a demand for shopping units from national retail chains.

The economics of running a restaurant in this type of location must be well understood. You may well attract custom but can you do so profitably? Even in a busy High Street you may not succeed in building up sufficient business to make a realistic profit. Rents for properties in these sites vary from £50 to £500 a week for premises suitable for a small café or tea room with a rate burden of some £3,000 per annum plus sewage and water rates of about £750. These expenses are incurred before you have served a single customer but they can only be financed by your customers – so any business taking less than about £70,000 in these circumstances is hardly an attractive proposition. It may be better to search for empty premises just off the main street of a town; if the property is situated near a bus or coach station or car park, cinema, theatre or some other activity, so much the better. These sites can carry more reasonable rents and rates while passing pedestrian traffic can be just as dense and lucrative as those in main High Streets.

If you are opening a restaurant in a town, there are a few basic points to remember:

Market
Study the competition in the area and notice how busy it is. When are the busiest times and how many people do they have to turn away? Is there much queueing which may indicate a strong demand? What type of food are they serving? There is little point in opening a restaurant of the same type as the competition unless there is an unsatisfied demand in a large catchment area. What type of food will you be serving and will it be good enough or sufficiently different to attract people away from other restaurants? Will it encourage new customers to eat with you?

Local authority regulations
Is the shop big enough for your purposes? Many retail premises have limited facilities and converting a shop to a restaurant poses problems. You will need planning permission for change of use and the local authority and the local residents may object on a number of grounds including smell, noise and litter. Most cafés are unlicenced but if you need a licence make the purchase of the lease conditional upon the granting of the licence. You must talk to the local fire officer who will explain his or her requirements; similarly, the environmental health officer will explain the hygiene regulations. After complying with all the necessary regulations, you have then got to design a restaurant in such a way that it is economic to staff and profitable to run.

Size
As your income will depend on the number of customers you can serve and seat it is important that you use as much space as possible in the front of house and as little as you can get away with in the kitchen. In some kinds of

establishments tables can be situated very close together but generally you need to provide at least 14 sq ft per person and to be able to seat at least twenty-four persons. The business is unlikely to be viable below that number. This allowance on space should allow comfortable seating, adequate gangways with space for refrigerated display counter and cash register point.

Kitchen space need not be so generous – indeed, a small, properly designed kitchen can be a highly efficient unit while a large badly designed kitchen can be tiring to work in and extremely inefficient. Size is not the most important factor in the successful operation of any restaurant kitchen; what matters is the way the kitchen is designed. A rough rule of thumb is 8 sq ft per diner, plus storage and washing up area. The amount of kitchen equipment needed depends entirely on the size and complexity of your menu. Don't equip the kitchen first and then devise the menu for, if your restaurant does not serve full or complete meals, the range of kitchen equipment need not be extensive.

Menu
The type of food offered in a new restaurant is all-important. You must experiment with items to see how popular they become and try to establish your own unique character – don't forget there are thousands of restaurants and cafés in the country. What special attraction will you offer to make people come to you? Frozen foods can of course save labour and are in many ways attractive but most caterers use them and there is a market for those customers seeking something different to the eternal Black Forest gâteau. Try to ensure that you present frozen foods in your own way but better still, customers value home-cooked food providing it is well cooked and presented, and there is usually a better profit on home produced foods. It is best not to skimp on the quality of tea or coffee – use the best ingredients for the price you charge. Keep foods fresh and don't offer yesterday's products – selling stale food will give you a bad name very quickly indeed. Most important of all – be sure that you keep the restaurant clean.

Staff
Keep the number of staff to the minimum and design the restaurant with this in mind. Never employ staff unless you have no other option – the longer you put off the day you employ staff the more profit you will make.

Standard
Once you have successfully determined the standard of your restaurant, maintain it. Letting standards slip is always a mistake. It is dangerous to seek a new market by reducing the quality of your product; doing this will only give you a bad name for poor quality. Redesign your menu and presentation entirely if you want to move down-marked or up-market. Generally speaking, it is better to increase prices and to maintain value than to maintain prices by cutting costs (and thereby reducing quality).

Competition

Finally, keep your eye on the competition. Eat in their restaurants regularly so that you know what is going on in the area. Remember no High Street site is a sure-fire success for a restaurant. Experienced caterers can get their sums wrong even after the most sophisticated market research and pedestrian traffic counts, as has happened on a number of occasions in expensive sites in London's West End. Opening a new restaurant is not, therefore, a business in which the newcomer would be well-advised to invest his life savings without rigorous investigations and the most careful planning and budgeting, but it is a way into the industry for those who have confidence and finance. If the purchase and fitting-out costs can be kept down, success may well be possible particularly at the simpler end of the catering market. Coffee and tea shops which serve light lunches can be profitable in the right location providing staff costs are minimal; restaurants serving more ambitious menus can be highly profitable in the right location if they are properly designed and marketed.

Franchising

There is one other avenue for the would-be restaurateur – the franchise. It may be said that taking up a franchise is an expensive way of getting into the industry but that it offers a much greater chance of success. There are no hotel franchises that would be of interest to the inexperienced newcomer but there are a number of restaurant franchisors including Trusthouse Forte (Little Chef and Kardomah); United Biscuits (Wimpy); Kentucky Fried Chicken; Burger King; Pizza Hut and Pizza Express; and Spud-U-Like.

The advantage of taking up a reputable successful franchise is that you buy expertise and technical help from a skilled operator as well as marketing expertise and a well-known name. The initial fee may be substantial but for that investment, the franchisee receives advice on location, technical help and national exposure through advertising.

To many people a franchise may not be too attractive because the essential element in any franchise is standardization; many people come into catering to do their own thing. The advantage of a franchised restaurant is that it enables the franchisee to provide an established product which is well-known and well-liked by the public. There is little or no problem of public acceptability which is something that a restaurateur may face with his own restaurant. One other advantage: it will be easier to raise matching capital for a franchise operation than for an individual restaurant.

Anyone interested in taking out a franchise should contact individual franchise companies.

10 Building up the business

Aims and objectives

A hotelier needs to establish long-term objectives and short-term aims. The objectives are concerned with the coherent development of the hotel so that its business potential can be fully realized over a reasonable span of time – up to five years, say. The short-term aims are mainly concerned with ensuring that the hotel immediately trades profitably, that sales opportunities are maximized and costs contained. This is the basic difference between marketing and selling.

A simple definition of marketing is 'To identify what the customer needs, to produce a product or service that satisfies that need and to sell that product or service for a profit'.

Because a hotel is a small, individually-owned unit, it does not mean that long-term objectives are unnecessary although there are hotels that survive from year to year without any plans for development or expansion. Every businessman needs to know where he is going and how he wants to develop but there are many who believe that further development is either impossible or unnecessary. Generally, this is a conscious decision. Most purchasers, however, have definite ideas about the future of their acquisition. Some of these may be long-term, for example the construction of extra rooms so that more customers or a different market can be attracted. Other ideas may be more short-term, for example to make sure that existing rooms have a much higher occupancy.

Marketing is concerned with long-term objectives while short-term aims are generally achieved by sales promotion techniques. A marketing plan will be the blueprint for the business development of the hotel and will show what kind of customers the hotel can best attract, what their needs are and how the hotel is going to satisfy those needs over a specific period of time. Sales promotion techniques will be used to implement this plan. Before a hotelier can promote his hotel, therefore, he needs to be sure he is promoting it to the right market. Without taking this precaution he could be wasting much of his sales promotion effort. If, for example, a hotelier believes that his future lies in the conference and banquet market rather than in the holiday market on which it has relied in the past, he needs to direct his sales promotion activities specifically to conference organizers rather than holiday makers. Any further sales effort in the holiday market would be wasted. But the decision to develop conference business may involve the construction of a new conference suite and the employment of a conference sales manager. The marketing plan would show why the hotelier believed the conference market was worth exploiting, what facilities would be needed to maximize the market's potential, what the cost and revenue would be and how long it would take to achieve the objectives.

In a large hotel, the plan would be a sophisticated document but for a small establishment this need not be the case. However detailed and lengthy it is, it must answer two basic questions:

1   Has the potential of the business been realized as the business stands now?
2   Once the present potential has been realized, how can the business expand in the future?

The occupancy figures and the accounts will have already shown how successful the hotel has been in attracting customers and how profitably it operates. A hotel with high occupancy figures, rising turnover and growing profits has probably already discovered its best markets and is exploiting them to the full. If the hotel you are purchasing falls into this category, be careful not to make needless changes in this successful marketing strategy. Every new hotelier wants to stamp his own personality on his hotel; to achieve this, he may be tempted to make a violent change in the hotel's direction which could upset the established clientele. Unless new and more profitable customers replace those who are driven away, the hotel will lose business. In a prosperous and successful hotel it is advisable to leave well alone until you have sound reasons for making changes.

The vast majority of hotels do not fall into this category and pose more difficult problems. A hotel may be reasonably profitable but may have shown little growth in the volume of business during the last three years; the rooms may be busy but the restaurant and bars empty, or vice versa. Alternatively, a hotel may be in an area where the holiday trade is declining and where there is no other potential source of revenue. Or a hotel may be busy in the week but empty at weekends.

All these situations pose classic hotel marketing problems and there is no single answer to any of them.

The initial exercise is to define exactly what is the problem. This may not be easy. A hotel may be suffering from declining occupancy, but is the area itself declining in popularity or is the hotel losing out to other hotels in the area? If the latter, why are the other hotels more successful?

A hotelier I knew once bought a problem hotel of great charm and character. Occupancy was declining and the standard of service and food was poor. The hotelier initially believed that the fall in occupancy was due to poor standards and he assumed that by improving them he would be able to attract back those customers who had visited the hotel once but who had not returned. More important, he believed that he could attract new customers through aggressive advertising and sales promotion. Raising standards of performance would not involve a major financial expenditure but in terms of his own time and effort it would involve a considerable commitment.

The hotelier realized that this approach was based only on hunch. He decided to undertake some simple on-the-spot research. Many people who take over an hotel believe that, by an enormous personal effort, they can substantially improve business. This often is the case but sometimes there are more fundamental problems to overcome. The hotelier looked critically at his own hotel and the two competitor hotels in the town. Standards were not much higher yet they were experiencing higher occupancies. He telephoned them to try to book a room and found that they were fully booked during the week and one of them at the weekends, too.

One receptionist, believing him to be a potential customer, mentioned that all their customers were businessmen and encouraged him to book earlier next time. The hotelier asked himself the obvious question. Why did all the businessmen go to the rival establishments and not to his hotel? He stayed a night in one of them. The bedroom was pleasant but no bigger or better than his. However, there was one major difference: it had a private bathroom. None of his bedrooms had a bathroom en suite. The room was considerably more expensive than those in his hotel. At the bar, he started chatting to some of the regulars – all of them businesmen. He eventually got around to asking why they chose this particular hotel. One of them said that the standards were high, another liked the staff and the food. Another mentioned the bathrooms: 'I always come here because all the rooms have bathrooms. Not like the George down the road,' he added, mentioning the hotelier's own hotel. 'I would never go there unless I had to. Most people want bathrooms nowadays.'

The simple investigation had revealed a different reason from the one which our hotelier had decided was the prime cause of his declining occupancy. It was also a more serious problem to be faced because it did not relate to the quality of food and service but the quality of his basic product – the bedroom. Installing bathrooms into hotel bedrooms is a far more expensive exercise than improving standards of food and service. Improved standards would help to attract new customers but the underlying problem would never be tackled until he could offer more bedrooms with bathrooms. So he made plans to convert the rooms over a five year period. In the meantime, he believed he could still improve occupancy by emphasizing the George's character – the two other hotels were modern and rather impersonal – and by improving the quality of his food and service. His initial aim, therefore, was to develop more business by friendly staff, value-for-money accommodation and good food and service. He decided to improve the George's old world atmosphere immediately standards had improved, realizing that to have more bedrooms with bathroom en suite was a firm long-term objective.

This is a simple but real-life example. The lesson is not that every hotel bedroom needs a bathroom; there are many successful hotels of character which still do not have many bathrooms en suite. What is important to realize is that the obvious problem may not be the fundamental one. The George needed bathrooms so that it could exploit its commercial market because businessmen are normally willing to pay a premium tariff for a bedroom with bathroom. In most cases the higher price that can be charged for a room with a bathroom amply repays the investment necessary to install the facility, even allowing for the fact that some letting rooms may have to be lost to provide space for the new bathrooms. The other lesson to be learnt from this is that it is impossible to overestimate the value of competitor research not only before you purchase but on a continual basis.

Marketing, therefore, is concerned with discovering the real needs of a hotel's customers and how best the hotel can satisfy them. A marketing plan is a document prepared for a specific hotel and depends on the hotel's individual characteristics, but the hotel market generally falls into four broad segments: holiday, business, conference and overseas tourist.

Holiday market

Hotels in holiday areas are dealing with people whose needs are quite different from those of any other sector of the market. Even in this market there are different sectors. In general terms, holiday makers are more concerned about price and value for money than the businessman on an expense account. They are often willing to sacrifice some personal comforts (say a bathroom en suite or a wide choice of menu) if by doing so the price can be contained. A child in a parent's room at little or no extra cost will be accepted but keen pricing may not be entirely the deciding factor in every case. A hotel with children's play and games facilities, a swimming pool and regular entertainment will be able to charge a higher price than one without these amenities.

The potential of any holiday hotel can never be fully realized if it has to close for the winter season, which is why few national groups favour hotels in seaside resorts. Those that do are now committed to broadening their market by trying to attract other types of customers – conference delegates, for example.

There is no doubt, however, that a resort hotel often provides the most appropriate entry to the industry for the first-time hotel purchaser. It will provide an establishment at a price that he can afford. At the same time, it will give him some valuable experience in running a hotel. Sometimes, the hotel is so small that a couple can buy it and the husband will continue working in his own job, leaving his wife to operate the hotel in the day time. If only dinner, bed and breakfast is provided, the wife can probably cope with this by herself with, perhaps, some part-time help. This can be a satisfactory arrangement and for very small establishments is one that may be favoured by the institution providing the financial backing.

Some areas and resorts are growing in popularity while others are declining. For this reason, you should never buy a hotel only on its historical reputation or buy into a resort before you have made sure that its market is as strong as you think it is. The thousands of people on the prom may be day-trippers or staying in self-catering accommodation. As it is clearly easier to generate business for a hotel in a popular area than in an unpopular area, it follows that the hotels in successful resorts tend to be more expensive to purchase and are in greater demand than those in other areas. A hotelier in a declining resort has to persuade people to come to the resort as well as to his hotel. If you are purchasing a holiday hotel, location will be of the utmost importance. You must also consider whether you can develop the business. Can the season be extended at either end of the year – the 'shoulder' months of April, May, September and October? Are there others who are spending time and effort extending the season? How active is the local tourist office? Is it possible to generate winter income, possibly with residents at special terms? They will contribute to the profits of the hotel just by covering the major overheads which would otherwise be a drain on high season profitability. Is there scope for developing conferences and meetings and what improvements or additions would have to be made to cope adequately with this sector of the market?

The answers to all these questions depend on the individual hotel. Most resort hotels shut for the winter and reopen in the spring, recruiting new staff every season. If that is the case with your hotel then the scope for long-term development is limited. Any increase in profitability must come from four sources – increasing occupancy when the hotel is open; better in-house selling; cost savings; and price increases. The latter must be in excess of the level of inflation if you are to gain in real terms. As resorts are in a price sensitive market, the opportunity for raising tariffs may be limited so new income may have to be generated from extra business when the hotel is open. This can only be achieved by knowing precisely what market the hotel is in, giving the customer exactly what he or she wants and then promoting the hotel aggressively. To help in this area, most resorts have active tourism departments and local hoteliers are now pooling their resources with the local authority to attract a greater share of the holiday market. Nevertheless, marketing and promoting a resort hotel can be a difficult undertaking because the hotel is dependent on only one type of customer. Because of this, the hotel is particularly vulnerable to shifts in customer tastes and preferences and long-term trends are unfavourable (see Chapter 1). A resort that loses popularity will create difficulties for its hotels; however much promotion its hoteliers undertake, it will be difficult for them to attract new customers because the resort itself is not attracting holiday makers. Hotels may then be forced to look at other markets. Some resort hotels have been converted into self-catering flats because the traditional market has so fundamentally changed.

Business market

Although vulnerable to an economic recession, hotels in the business market do not generally suffer the winter occupancy problems experienced by resort hotels. On the other hand, most business hotels experience a drop in weekend occupancy which often makes their annual occupancy little higher than that of a busy resort hotel which enjoys high occupancy for seven days a week over a short summer season. If your hotel is full Monday to Thursday night, that means you are full only four nights out of seven; in other words, you are only just over 50 per cent full. Don't underestimate the amount of effort needed to fill the remaining three days because every other hotel in your area will be trying to do the same. The market is highly competitive. If you do succeed in increasing occupancy, however, it will be more than worthwhile because the relationship between your fixed and variable costs means that every £1 earned over your break-even point will be almost all profit (see page 110).

Most businessmen using hotels are on expenses and price for them may not be quite such a sensitive factor as it is for the holiday maker. But the large number of hotels that have been built since 1970 which specialize in the business market have raised standards and given rise to many new customer expectations. For example, all businessmen now expect a bathroom with the bedroom. They also need services that other guests may not require: a telephone in their room to make business calls; a writing area, either in the bedroom or elsewhere, where they can prepare reports; television and radio in the bedroom – even in-house movies are becoming expected in large city centre properties; good quality food in the restaurant and fast service at breakfast. Other facilities may attract but may not be crucial, such as an indoor swimming pool. There are many successful small hotels that do not offer these facilities but, increasingly, the trend will be towards providing such amenities and the wise hotelier will take note of these developments.

In this market, whether a room is £15 or £20 a night may not matter too much as the customer is not paying out of his own pocket. The difference between £20 and £45 would be much more significant but still may not be critical for some business executives using bigger hotels. In other words, hotels in the business market have a greater degree of flexibility in pricing than a resort hotel. Providing it gives value for money (essential for any hotel) a business hotel generally provides a solid base on which to build up weekend or conference business and has the advantage of operating in a less price sensitive market than a hotel dependent on the domestic or foreign tourist.

Conference market

Many hotels in the business market also attract residential meetings, seminars and conferences. The needs of the businessman and the conference delegate are usually similar, the extra requirement lying in the provision of conference facilities, which may or may not be a specially constructed suite of conference rooms. It should be remembered that not only major hotels with large conference rooms successfully exploit the conference market. The number of very large conferences is small; the average sized conference comprises twenty to sixty people.

The location of a hotel looking to the conference market is not so important as that of a hotel tackling the business market. Businessmen go to a town for a specific reason – to do business in the town. This is not the case with a conference. Indeed, companies hold conferences and seminars in a hotel to get away from their own business environment and to be in one that is conducive to learning, thinking or decision-making. Price, however, is a more important factor than may appear on the surface. There are a large number of hotels specializing in residential conferences and courses, so competition is stiff. If it does not matter where the conference is held, price can often become the determining factor in a company's choice of venue. But conferences and courses not only come from far away; local industry needs to hold them, too.

Whether a hotel is able to exploit the conference market depends on its total facilities and the nature of its business. A twenty-bedroom hotel full of businessmen from Monday to Thursday night would not need to develop residential conferences even if a meeting room was available. There is no point in replacing full tariff commercial business with conferences which expect a discount. There would be scope for attracting non-residential meetings, however (particularly from local companies) and, in the long term, for building extra rooms to cope with residential conference accommodation requirements.

Overseas tourist market

The question facing every independent hotelier is how he can attract a bigger share of the overseas tourist market. The expense of selling directly to overseas countries is high and unless a hotel is part of a marketing consortium (see page 163) or unless local hoteliers co-operate in promoting their area overseas, few independent hoteliers can get directly to the market. It is possible to advertise in specific overseas newspapers and magazines, but this needs careful attention and follow-up. Some advertisements can be highly effective, others a waste of money. Experience may be your best guide here, though the British Tourist Authority or local tourist board would be able to advise you.

Location again is the key factor for tourists. The well-known tourist 'milk-run' of Oxford, Stratford, York and Edinburgh explains a great deal. Tourists are interested in Britain's historical and cultural past but they do not necessarily stay overnight in all these towns. Over 80 per cent of tourists stay in London and visit Oxford and Stratford in day trips by coach. It is only when they travel further afield that they need to have overnight accommodation. But, as London hotel prices increase at a faster rate than those of hotels in the provinces more tourists, particularly those on return visits to Britain, will probably want to stay out of London. Tourists now travel to the south west of England, Wales and to other holiday areas. This has been helped by the introduction of sea and air links from the Continent to major provincial centres. Ferries into Portsmouth, Plymouth, Harwich and Newcastle, for example, bring visitors directly into the provinces thus by-passing London. Many hoteliers in these areas have capitalized on these services by promoting directly to the countries served by the ferries and air links. Much of this promotion has been successful and these areas are now becoming popular with many overseas visitors.

Whether your hotel can take a bigger slice of the competitive overseas tourist market is something that you must investigate. The local tourist board will be able to tell you how many overseas visitors are attracted to the area, why they are coming, where they stay, how much they are willing to spend and what they want. The major hotel groups have close contacts with overseas tour operators and travel companies and attract the major share of the tourist market but what is left is a profitable segment – the individual overseas visitor who travels by car or train and who needs good quality hotel accommodation.

Other sources of business

Apart from the four major accommodation markets there are many individual segments. Coach tours, for example, constitute an important part of the British holiday market. It is extremely price conscious, however, and profit comes from high turnover at cheap rates with very efficient catering. It is also a high risk area. Coach companies will book up blocks of rooms early in the season in contracts that have late cancellation clauses – in some cases only two weeks before the arrival of the coach party. That fifty-person coach tour which you expected may turn out to consist of only twenty people and you may not be able to fill the thirty vacancies with chance customers.

The problem faced by most business hotels in summer and winter is the drop in occupancy at the weekend. It may be possible to attract conferences to fill the bedrooms at weekends but a major growth area is the trend to create weekend holiday packages. Success in this market hinges almost entirely on location. Weekend business can be built up in a hotel in London or in a popular holiday destination but it is much harder to generate new weekend traffic into an industrial town. Some extra attraction is needed – industrial archaeology weekends are one example. Unfortunately, these packages can create high promotional costs and take time to become popular and profitable though much can be achieved through good public relations, a little selective advertising in some national newspapers and magazines and with the help of the tourist boards. In the same way that residents may keep a resort hotel ticking over in winter, weekend packages can keep occupancy up, albeit at a lower level of profitability, and thus generate turnover that would otherwise be lost. Cheap weekend packages are much better than empty rooms and as guests will spend money in the bar and restaurant, extra revenue will be produced.

Weekend packages can become an essential part of a hotel's total business mix and, in some cases, they can be very profitable. Because of its popularity, a hotel may be able to charge full rate for weekends and may thus achieve high week-long, year-round occupancy. Such hotels are generally well-placed establishments in the country and have built up a high reputation for good food and accommodation. As more people are now taking their holidays in short breaks – particularly the third and fourth weeks – the weekend off-season break markets is expanding. But success primarily depends on the location of the hotel and the effort put into the promotion of the weekends.

Most hotels will aim to satisfy a number of markets at the same time, building up a good mix of business so that they are not entirely dependent on any one type of visitor. In this way they are not so vulnerable if there is an economic recession or if the tourist market declines. A critical look at the hotel you are purchasing will show what type of customer it is attracting at present and whether you will be able to attract more business from new sources. The key question you need to ask is: What does the visitor need and how can I satisfy that need?

There are other sources of potential business that a hotelier must examine, the eating-out market being one. A hotel may be able to produce a high turnover in its food and beverage operation. A small resort hotel, unless it is in the centre of the town, could find this difficult to achieve and so would most small commercial hotels. But there are many hotels in a town or country location which generate trade in their restaurant and in their function rooms. A purchaser should closely examine the possibilities in this area. If your hotel is not already exploiting this market but has the facilities for doing so you should investigate whether it is possible to build up restaurant trade. What other restaurants exist in the area? What type of food do they serve? How much do they charge? How late do they stay open? Is there a noticeable gap in the market that you can fill? For example, are there only cheap cafés and, at the other end of the market, an expensive haute cuisine restaurant? Would your hotel with the right menu be able to fill the gap as an interesting, value-for-money restaurant? What type of food could you serve most effectively? Would a 'good food' reputation help you to fill more bedrooms? In many cases, the answer to these questions is in the affirmative; if this is so the restaurant could become an important part of your marketing strategy. Not only would it produce revenue and profit of its own but by creating and maintaining the right standard it would get the hotel talked about locally. This is important because most hotels outside London depend on local trade for the broad base of the business. Don't, however, overestimate the amount of business from chance trade. It will take time to build up.

There are dangers and problems in this area because a hotel offering cheap and simple accommodation is unlikely to be successful in offering high quality, expensive food – the markets clash. Customer expectations are too divided; a customer would not expect a cheap hotel to have an haute cuisine restaurant. So while a hotel can successfully mix its market in terms of types of customer – business, conference, tourist and holiday makers – it can only rarely mix it in terms of price and standard.

One further potential source of business needs to be investigated – banquets and other functions. They can be highly profitable and can develop enormous customer goodwill (or ill-will if carried out badly). They can also result in extra bedroom business. Don't assume that every banquet needs to seat 200 people. There are far more dinner parties held for twenty people than large banquets and they are very lucrative, too. A prerequisite in this market is planning. Once the party has sat down everything depends on the timing of the operation. This depends on the skills and capacity of the kitchen and waiting staff and the planning that has gone into the organization beforehand.

Some hotels do not have the space to seat even a small dinner party but many resort and country hotels have large rooms which are ideal for banquets, wedding parties and other social gatherings. Some initial research will be necessary to discover if any other hotel in the area has already developed banquet business. If one has, this may be a good sign because it shows that there is a demand for such a service. One more hotel may be welcomed, giving customers a choice of venue. Even if he or she is satisfied by an existing hotel a banquet organizer can usually be persuaded to use another once, if only to offer a change of scene. After that, you stand or fall on your standard of food and service.

If you have a banqueting room, the question to ask is whether your own hotel, offering a similar or perhaps different standard, would succeed. One hotel may be successful in banqueting because it provides cheap but cheerful food; a high quality but much more costly menu may not attract people away because the market for expensive banquets may not exist in some towns. A much higher quality menu, on the other hand, could be welcomed by some customers who may be getting tired of the cheaper, plainer food.

If there is no banqueting facility in the town it doesn't necessarily follow that there is unlimited scope for developing your own. The town may not be keen to support you because people have got used to travelling to hotels in nearby towns. If this is the case, you will have to persuade the banqueting organizers to a new way of thinking. The town might also be too small to build up a regular banqueting business. These questions need to be answered before you can decide whether your hotel can develop in this area.

Sales promotion

After deciding on your marketing strategy, you need to look at sales promotion techniques. Sales promotion is not just a question of getting customers to use your hotel – it is knowing where to look for them in the first place. If you know that – in other words, if you know where your markets are – then your sales promotion efforts will be effective. If you do not know the markets, much of your sales effort will be wasted.

Many independent hoteliers rely on one basic method of sales promotion – their brochure – aided, they hope, by word of mouth advertising. The latter can be highly effective if it is complimentary (and ruinous if it is derogatory). Brochures are often far less effective than most hoteliers imagine, if only because they are usually poorly written and badly produced. A brochure is a useful sales tool but there are many other methods of selling which are more effective.

The fundamental point to recognize is that sales promotion is an essential part of any hotelier's job. No one else will do it for you unless you pay them; certainly no one else will do it better than you because you know your hotel, its capacity, its strengths and its weaknesses. Customers identify you with the hotel. But your staff are an essential part of your sales promotion effort. An able receptionist is your front line sales person as she sees all the guests and all the correspondence. She can also maximize occupancy by her skill in letting the available rooms to the best advantage so that doubles are not let as singles. The waiter, by his skill in selling a sweet course or a bottle of wine or a liqueur, can increase food and beverage revenue significantly. The room maid, through her contact with the guests, can encourage guests to return. The barman can develop regular trade by his personality. Basically, a hotel is nothing but a series of interdependent sales areas that all need constant promotion if the unit as a whole is to exploit its true potential. Selling is not just a question of getting people into the hotel in the first place – vital though that is. Its real success lies in generating the maximum possible revenue from every customer who uses the hotel's facilities in such a way that the customer is happy and satisfied when he or she leaves. There are many sales courses run in the industry – particularly by the Hotel and Catering Industry Training Board – and a number of excellent books (see page 166) which any new owner should read.

Any promotional effort needs to start at home – with your existing customers and with the locals. Most commercial hotels depend on the people who live in the town and the local residents must be encouraged to use the hotel's facilities.

If the hotel already enjoys a high reputation, then initially you may feel it advisable not to emphasize your new ownership too stridently. This will enable regulars to become accustomed to your style of operation. If the hotel is not highly regarded you may feel that you should announce your presence immediately. Don't do this before you begin to make determined efforts to improve the hotel's reputation. Begin to establish your standards on the day you move in and never compromise. Maintaining your standards, at whatever level you decide, must be your prime business objective.

A personally signed letter to all the important companies in the area and to nearby shops and offices is one good method of getting your story across. Give some positive information on the improvements or extra facilities that you have introduced or intend to introduce, and briefly explain your background. Address your letter to someone specific, the managing director or chairman, for example, and find out his name. A personally addressed and signed letter has a much better chance of being read than an unsigned duplicated letter addressed to an unnamed person. This highlights a fundamental point of sales promotion. In any sales effort ensure you make contact with the person who makes the decision to use your facilities. This may not be the most obvious person. The chairman's secretary, for example, may make all hotel bookings for the company – indeed, in a large company, individual secretaries make reservations for their bosses. In one factory of a company, for example, it was discovered that seventy-two secretaries each made hotel bookings for their own boss, so if you don't get to the decision-maker you can waste an enormous amount of time and effort. Particularly important companies should be sent individually typed letters, suggesting that the recipient visits the hotel for a drink so that you can introduce yourself. If you haven't got the typing facilities in the hotel it is well worth the expense of getting them well typed by an agency; too many letters from hotels contain bad typing, bad spelling and grammatical howlers. Make sure that *your* letter is well written and well typed – otherwise it will get thrown into the wastepaper bin. The way a letter is presented says as much about the sender as its content.

An advertisement in the local paper is another way of letting the public know of your new ownership but an advertisement that simply says 'Under new ownership' means little. Again, try to get the story across in a more positive manner by, for example, publicizing the Saturday night dinner-dance which you are introducing. It is often difficult to quantify the efforts of advertising precisely but it is very easy to spend money on advertisements – so beware. The success of restaurant advertising is particularly difficult to measure but it is important that you try to assess any increase in business, if only to work out the cost benefits of the advertisement. If, for example, an insertion in a local paper cost £50, then it will have to generate at least £100 worth of business to pay for itself, taking a crude 50 per cent food cost. If the average spend is £5 per head, the advertisement will have to attract 20 customers just to break even. The question you have to ask is whether the advertisement will pick up that number of customers or whether a smaller and cheaper advertisement would be equally effective. The same analysis must be made of your room promotion advertising.

Letters and advertising can be effective but everything depends on the style and content of the letter and the way the recipient reacts to it – you have no control over the fate of the letter. The most effective sales method is the face-to-face sales call although a telephone interview can be equally successful if properly conducted and it has the advantage of taking less time. Major hotel companies make extensive use of both these techniques but many independent hoteliers believe that they do not need to use such Americanized sales methods. Selling is regarded as something slightly infra-dig. Nothing could be further from the truth. The public is not going to beat a path to any hotelier's door; he has to attract customers and personal sales calls have been found to be by far the most effective method of attracting business.

The principal advantage of a face-to-face sales call or a telephone call is that you can actually discuss the customer's real needs. During such a discussion, what you believed were his or her requirements may turn out to be something quite different. You may, for example, know that a local company needs regular overnight accommodation for its important visitors without realizing that every week it holds a seminar for twenty people (all of whom need accommodation) and that the chairman gives regular monthly dinner parties for important clients. If this business is going elsewhere, the value of the sales calls will be much greater than you initially appreciated. A sales letter could not have elicited this information. You will also be able to find out what the company thinks of your hotel from past experience and you will be able to correct misunderstandings and misconceptions.

Getting to know important people in local industry and commerce is a primary objective to any hotelier. They may not require your facilities at present but they could in the future and will think of you then because you bothered to contact them. Most people feel flattered if a local hotelier invites them for a drink – not all face-to-face sales calls take place in the office. This is part of the process of getting yourself across to the local people as the new owner. Once the initial contact is made, make sure it is followed up at a reasonable interval, depending on each client's needs. A chairman who says he will contact you in a month's time may just be trying to put you off. Don't let him. If you think there is business there, invite him and his wife to join you for lunch or dinner one day so that you can show them the hotel and the standards you are trying to achieve. Entertaining in this fashion can be a sound investment but never, never try to impress potential customers by over-indulging them. During the meal make sure you discover their needs. Don't waste their and your time by trying to sell them something that they will never need. Get to know, also, the local vicars and clergymen. If you want to develop wedding party business, they have all the information on future weddings. People may also have to stay overnight for funerals, so make contact with local undertakers. Keep an eye on the engagement columns of the local paper and write a personal letter to each couple, offering your hotel's services for the wedding reception.

A systematic filing system goes with any effective sales effort. In this way you can check the success of your sales promotion and keep on producing more business.

There are other sales activities you must undertake. The notepaper of the hotel needs to establish a 'house style' so that it is recognizable; your brochures need to be written so that they invite people to the hotel but they must not be exorbitantly expensive to produce. Full colour photographs are always costly to print and can reproduce badly; it may be better to use a good black and white photograph or line drawing than a poor colour picture, although, in this age of colour, black and white photographs can be unexciting and uninviting. Avoid the use of such pedestrian words as 'superb', 'magnificent', 'luxurious' – they have become meaningless. It is better to give plain facts than try to impress with such phrases as 'superb cuisine' and 'intimate atmosphere'.

Examine the brochures and the advertisements of other hotels, particularly the major groups. If they are effective, analyse why. Generally speaking, a great deal of hotel advertising and brochure copy is ineffective and dull. Resort hotels especially should generate an air of excitement about their facilities and service.

Too often, brochures sell the positive virtues of a hotel without alluding to the beneficial effect they have on the customer. Hoteliers aiming at the holiday or weekend break market are not so much selling beds but holiday dreams and brochures should reflect this important fact – as the brochures of Holiday Inns and Ladbroke Hotels illustrate with great success. The Holiday Inn full colour cover (Figure 7) shows a happy picture of a youngster being looked after by the Weekender hostess. It does not show a hotel, because the brochure is trying to get across a major benefit obtained by the customer when he or she takes a Weekender break. In other words, the effect of the hotel is being emphasized, not the hotel itself. The Ladbroke brochure (Figure 8) tries to illustrate other benefits – the scenery and the excitement of touring.

The difference between the brochures of overseas tour operators and British holiday hotels is quite marked. Overseas tour brochures are exciting and attractive, filled with people and activity; British hotel brochures usually consist of photographs of empty bedrooms and dining rooms and people are noticeably absent. Yet a hotel does not exist without people. Brochures full of empty bedrooms and dining rooms tell the prospective customer nothing – indeed, they may pose a damaging question: why are these areas empty? The customer needs to be able to identify with the hotel and we can only do this if the brochure tries to explain subtly the effect of the hotel on its guests. People give life to pictures: a barman mixing a drink says more than a picture of a bar counter; a close-up of an attractive dish tells the reader more than a picture of a dining room. Brochures need to put over the atmosphere of the hotel and the benefits of staying in it.

The overseas hotels are selling dreams; the British hotels are selling bedrooms. The difference is significant. Figure 9 shows a set of promotional material from Woodlands, a small country guest house in North Yorkshire. Printed in house colours, the literature has a specific purpose: it aims to inform guests of the hotel's services and of various hotel activities as well as providing useful information on the locality. The style of the literature also

Figure 7   *Holiday Inn's Winter Weekender brochure*

says something about the style of the hotel. If the proprietors, Roger and Margaret Callen, can take so much care in producing such well-designed and attractive print, will they not take as much care over their guests?

The lesson to be learnt is not to spend large sums of money on ineffective advertising and brochure production but to employ a good local graphic designer to help you create the image you want to put over. The cost of this service will be more than recouped by the extra business your print will attract. Too few small hotels take care over their print so, if you do, you could stand out as an establishment of character and individuality – highly desirable attributes for any hotel. But don't assume that 'pretty-pretty' design is necessarily effective. Good design is only effective if it says something about

Figure 8   *Ladbroke Hotels' Weekaway Holidays brochure*

your hotel and gets over the message you want to communicate. Print the tariff on a separate sheet and reprint it (and the menu) every time there are tariff increases; many hoteliers only draw attention to increases by crossing out the old prices and inserting higher ones.

Don't forget that your telephonist and receptionist are front line sales people – many telephonists have a manner more calculated to deter people than to attract. Bad customer contact in front of house can lose a hotel a great deal of money by putting people off. Letters to potential guests should be friendly and helpful – never 'Dear Sir' or 'Dear Madam', but 'Dear Mr Smith'. Sign them all personally with your full name, 'John Brown' – J. Brown is too formal and impersonal. All these little points amount to one thing – a hotelier has to create a welcoming and friendly atmosphere in his hotel if he is to succeed. Customers need to be attracted specifically to your hotel – perhaps because the accommodation or the food is particularly good, because the staff

Figure 9   *Woodlands' promotional material*

and atmosphere are welcoming or because they like you as the proprietor. In marketing terms, this specific attraction is called the Unique Selling Proposition. Your USP is something that you have which no other hotel in the area can offer. Once gained, it needs to be cherished and developed because it is your most powerful sales tool.

In addition to your own personal sales efforts on the telephone or face to face, your letters and brochures, there are organizations that can help you. The local tourist board (see the list at the end of this chapter) will be glad to advise you and it is always worthwhile to become a member. Your hotel then appears in the local tourist board guide and you will have the opportunity to undertake further sales activities through the board's regional promotional programmes. In addition, the national tourist boards publish an annual guide to weekend bargain packages, the best-known being the English Tourist Board's *Let's Go* guide. All the boards publish an annual register of hotel accommodation.

If it is appropriate you may also consider small advertisements on the local radio station. You should also think about joining a marketing consortium (see page 163). For hotels in the right location and of the right size, they can generate additional business through centrally organized marketing and sales activities. Some of them also offer very advantageous purchasing schemes and much can be learned from fellow hoteliers who collectively have a wealth of experience and are often prepared to share it in the club-like atmosphere of a consortium.

In many resort areas, the local authority produces a hotel guide in conjunction with the hotel association. These guides may be their only publicity medium though many of them are frequently criticized for being unimaginatively produced and having a poor standard of hotel advertising. If you do advertise, particularly in a national newspaper for weekend packages, make sure the design of the advertisement is carried out by a local artist or graphic designer and is not left to the printer. A high standard of print, which need not be expensive, can work wonders for a hotel's image. The house style that was established with the notepaper should be carried through on all printed matter, including advertisements for both customers and staff.

This chapter only briefly touches on the most important initial problems that you will face in marketing and promoting your hotel – for a more complete picture, read the books listed at the end of this chapter. But two further points need to be made.

A hotelier should never view his marketing and sales promotion effort as a one-off activity. Marketing and selling need constant attention. The hotelier must understand what his market is and how it is reacting to his hotel. Is it altering and what new market opportunities are presenting themselves? He must also promote his hotel at every available opportunity. The results of your promotional effort can only be cumulative. Your initial sales campaign will be aimed at getting your hotel off the ground but you need a regular effort to make sure sales are kept up to the desired level.

Second, avoid selling 'a mile wide and an inch deep', as one of the industry's leading consultants, Melvyn Greene, puts it (and explains further in his book *Marketing Hotels into the 90s*). Make sure that your sales effort penetrates each area sufficiently so that the potential is fully exploited before you move on to develop new sources of business. Money can be wasted, particularly with advertisements, by spreading your sales resources too thinly over too wide an area. To ensure that this does not happen plan the year's marketing effort well in advance and prepare a budget for it. This will act as a valuable discipline for the marketing and sales activities.

Case studies

The following two case studies, entirely factual, show how a hotelier can establish a marketing strategy. Both are based on entries submitted by competitors to the Cavendish Cup Award Scheme – Mrs Voss-Bark won the 1978 award with her entry. Not all hotels can offer the potential of the Arundell Arms or the Moor Hall Hotel, but every hotelier should be clear about his marketing objectives. The two examples show the step-by-step approach adopted and may help readers to establish their own marketing plan.

Arundell Arms, Lifton, Devon
by Ann Voss-Bark

In 1961 I bought an ailing fishing hotel between Dartmoor and Bodmin which had trout and salmon fishing rights on twenty miles of moorland-fed rivers. The hotel's turnover, virtually static, was £20,000 a year and it was making a loss. Although on a main road it was 27 miles from the nearest big town, the local trade was negligible, and the sea coast was too far away to attract the usual holiday crowds. The problem was how to make this remote fishing hotel viable.

I knew nothing about hotels or fishing but family circumstances had forced me to leave my job as an account executive with a London advertising agency to take over the ownership and management. I had three months' training in the kitchens, bars and offices of a friend's hotel near London and then started out for Devon.

The hotel was dreary, the central heating inadequate and the furnishings threadbare. Only one of the sixteen bedrooms had a private bathroom. The cooking was reasonably good but unimaginative, the wine list was poor; there was only a small dispense bar for guests and the public bar was rudimentary. The fishing was a great asset but the rivers had been badly neglected.

Figure 10   *Ann Voss-Bark, proprietor of the Arundell Arms*

Figure 11   *Arundell Arms, Lifton, Devon*

Fishermen came to stay in the hotel from mid-March until the end of September but that was about all and for the rest of the year the hotel was half empty. Most of the fishermen were elderly gentlemen of the old school and very few brought their wives. There was a club atmosphere among the ex-Indian Army colonels and brigadiers who dominated the sitting room and trade was falling.

I knew from various sources that fly fishing was rapidly expanding as a leisure market. I believed that it was possible to attract the new and younger generation of fishermen and their wives to come and stay at the hotel providing I could do two things.

The first was to promote the fishing, to get it better organized and properly promoted. The second: to make substantial improvements in the comfort and welcome provided by the hotel. It had to be a real fishermen's hotel and not just a hotel with fishing, but it also had to be a hotel where non-fishing wives would be delighted to stay.

I put in efficient central heating, made a hotel bar where fishermen and others could meet and talk in a warm friendly atmosphere, and replaced the worst of the furnishings. As well as improving the menu and the wine list I provided a special packed lunch menu for fishermen.

I employed mainly local staff who would identify with the hotel and give guests a real welcome and I made sure I was there all the time to do the same myself.

I produced new and informative hotel and fishing brochures and worked out advertising schedules. The advertising was restricted to specialist fishing and country magazines to avoid readership wastage, and I kept the editors informed of the many improvements in our fishery. They were very helpful and news about our rivers began to be widely published.

I took on a young and expert fisherman as a bailiff. He made sure that fishing guests had everything they needed, organized the beats and fishing rotas and made enormous improvements in clearing the badly overgrown rivers and in developing the fishery. We opened a tackle shop, a rod room and a drying room. We started residential fly fishing courses for beginners – the first fishing hotel to do so – and this gained more publicity. Many of the men and women who learned to fish at the hotel became regular visitors.

I added as many bathrooms to existing bedrooms as was structurally possible and, in 1970, with the help of a development grant from the English Tourist Board, converted an adjoining stable block into seven new double rooms with private bathrooms. Radios, intercoms and tea-and-coffee-making equipment went into all the bedrooms.

This, nine years after I started, was a turning point. The hotel was now lively and friendly, the food and wines were good, and the fishing provided had become nationally known. An ever-increasing number of fly-fishermen and their wives were coming to stay and, even more important, were becoming 'regulars'. The added comfort of the hotel was also attracting people who came to Devon and Cornwall on business. By now we were in the leading food guides.

I started to explore the overseas fishing market and found great interest, though little knowledge, of English fishing potential. With the help of one or two overseas visitors I found out which were the best European and American fly fishing journals and started advertising. Today my overseas advertising budget equals that for the home market.

I made several visits to Europe to contact specialist sporting agencies and invited leading foreign fishing writers to stay. I was greatly helped in all this by the British Tourist Authority and the West Country Tourist Board.

Our fishing package combined with the informality but comfort of an English fishing hotel was immensely saleable.

There was a significant increase in overseas visitors which was fortunate because this came at a time when the home market was being hit by inflation. Also, their length of stay averaged two to three weeks and they usually came with their families or friends.

In 1973 I joined the Interchange marketing consortium (now Best Western) to help fill the occupancy gaps that remained. In 1977 I again took advantage of an English Tourist Board grant to provide a self-catering flat for fishermen and their families. Work is now in progress on further improvements and expansion to the hotel.

Most of the renovations and improvements have had to be financed out of income which means that the ultimate profit is low in relation to turnover. Winter occupancy under the shadow of Dartmoor will always be a problem but we now remain open all year and the local and business trade has been greatly expanded. Winter shoots which were started three years ago have also helped.

The hotel increased its turnover from £20,000 in 1961 to £300,000 in 1983 and is now profitable. It employs a staff of thirty including two full-time fishing bailiffs, and it is recognized internationally as one of England's premier fishing hotels. Of course, during this period we had temporary setbacks, particularly during the recession years of 1980 and 1981 when the overseas markets declined, but we fared better than most. Despite the recession, people still come to fish and shoot. During this period we made various housekeeping economies and held our tariffs but increased our promotional budget so that trade improved greatly in 1982 and 1983 was a record year.

Recent developments have included the creation of a conference centre and engaging a talented French chef to take charge of the kitchens. Both have proved highly successful and the conference centre in particular has increased our winter trade. In 1983 we received our third AA star plus a merit award for hospitality.

In 1983, we celebrated the fiftieth anniversary of the Arundell Arms as a fishing hotel and my own twenty-one years' of involvement. I also edited a

Figure 12 *Jean Webb, marketing manager, Moor Hall Hotel*

Figure 13 *Moor Hall Hotel, Sutton Coldfield, Warwickshire*

book *West Country Fly Fishing* which was published by Batsford. The celebrations and my book received wide press coverage both at home and overseas.

Moor Hall Hotel, Sutton Coldfield, West Midlands
by Jean Webb

Moor Hall is a fifty-five-bedroom hotel in the Midlands. Because my husband had other business commitments, it was run by a general manager up to 1976, when a combination of circumstances, culminating in two poor managers, put the company in desperate financial straits. In March, 1976, my husband decided to assume the role of general manager and asked me to act as marketing manager. This is the plan I put into operation to help put the company back on its feet.

Define the market

Moor Hall had previously divided its marketing effort between conferences, dining out and club activities. I felt that with very limited resources we should concentrate on promoting one aspect at a time. My prime object had to be to fill bedrooms, preferably with conference customers because:

(a)   Our geographical location, in the middle of the country, made us a preferred location for delegates travelling from any area.
(b)   Being in the heart of the industrial Midlands meant that we were surrounded by companies likely to organize meetings.
(c)   The 'Spaghetti Junction' motorway link was only ten minutes away and, therefore, communications were good.
(d)   The National Exhibition Centre gave Birmingham a new image – it was beginning to be regarded as a conference centre.
(e)   24-hour conference business was more profitable than simple overnight stays.

Get the product right

Bedrooms   Fifty of the fifty-five bedrooms already had private bath, colour TV and tea-and-coffee-making equipment. In 1976/77 only urgent redecoration was undertaken, but in 1978 I felt most bedrooms should be given a complete facelift to enable us to raise the tariff.
Conference rooms   These were redecorated and the lighting revised.
Equipment   Visual aids equipment was updated.
Additional meeting rooms   Two rooms, originally occupied by the manager, were converted to additional conference/syndicate rooms.
Local competition: Literature from local hotels was obtained to make sure that we were competitive both from the point of view of price and facilities.
Uniforms   Uniforms were organized for the staff.

Employ a salesman

That was to be my job.

Produce a sales plan

I ought to have made out a five-year plan, but when you might literally be out of business tomorrow every effort has to go into filling that night's room. My one-year plan incorporated advertising, direct mail, personal selling and in-house marketing.

Advertising

To be really effective a campaign needed professional handling and was too expensive for my budget. I therefore confined the advertising to:

(a)   Best Western Conference Manual
(b)   Conference Blue Book
(c)   *Exhibitions and Conferences* Yearbook
(d)   NEC Hotel Pack produced by Expotel
(e)   As a country club, we have 2000 members, many of whom are local businessmen. Living close by, they were probably well aware of the eating and drinking facilities but had never seen the accommodation or conference rooms, so I invited them to an open day.

Direct Mail

I wanted to get in touch with as many people as possible as quickly and as cheaply as possible. I like a punchy direct mail shot because it is:

(a)   Selective
(b)   Personal
(c)   Difficult to ignore
(d)   Easy to measure results

Examples of mail shots:

1   The first people to contact were past customers. I sent a colour postcard of the hotel to every overnight stay for the previous twelve months.
2   A letter saying that the hotel was being run on a much more personal basis and that service and attention to detail would be paramount was sent to everyone who had organized a meeting of any sort over the past twelve months. I enclosed a list of NEC dates for the following year suggesting that conferences be organized in between these times or booked early.
3   We attended all Best Western conference workshops from which we kept valuable mailing lists. We sent these potential customers up-to-date details of the hotel and then invited key people from this list and from our customer records to join us for dinner on various Friday evenings.

Personal selling

For every customer or potential customer, an index card was made out with the company name, address and telephone number, the contact's name and his position in the firm, the type of meeting he was interested in, what approaches were made and what business resulted.

1   A series of Martini evenings was organized where drinks were subsidized by Martini and Moor Hall provided a finger buffet. An average of forty to fifty local people attended each evening and they were shown round the hotel in groups of ten. Everyone was asked to complete a questionnaire before they left to show us who were the most likely companies to use our facilities. Again, we know precisely how many of these companies are still using us.

2   Cocktail parties for residents during NEC periods were held to ensure they booked for the following years before leaving (in addition to softly selling them conference facilities).

3   Cold calling: I visited local trading estates and simply knocked on every door. Although no appointments were made, in 90 per cent of cases I saw the person responsible for arranging conferences and meetings. Even if the conference organizer was not available, I had a contact name and the opportunity of talking to secretaries and receptionists who were often involved in booking overnight stays.

4   Telephone sales: the Birmingham Information Office produced a list of larger local companies which I telephoned and then sent literature to.

In-house marketing

Every member of staff is part of the sales team and the turnover can, therefore, be increased even though there may be no more bedrooms available. I tried:

1   Sales training
2   Drinks in bedrooms
3   Happy hour
4   Attractive à la carte menu to tempt people away from the table d'hôte
5   Conference brochures in all bedrooms.
6   Video welcome. Personal contact is the essence of hotelkeeping, but it is simply not possible to welcome every guest. We therefore made a film in which we welcomed the visitor and took him or her on a short tour of the hotel. This is played on every TV in the house.

The best way of selling a hotel is by the recommendation of satisfied customers. I employed a conference co-ordinator to do nothing but take bookings, ensure that we knew what the customer wanted, prepare a detailed function sheet and distribute it to every section of the hotel. Out of 400 conferences in the first six months of 1978, 375 were repeat business.

We printed two booking forms, one for conferences and one for wedding receptions and banquets giving every detail of the function. The office is now so busy that the conference co-ordinator has a secretary and approximately 25 per cent of enquiries have to be refused.

The financial results of this activity have been marked. A static turnover and an operating loss was turned into a 262 per cent rise in profits on a 25 per cent rise in turnover in the first year. In the following year turnover rose by another 26 per cent but profits by 70 per cent.

From the moment the product is right, it starts to deteriorate. Not only do fabrics and furniture begin to wear but also fashions change.

Moor Hall has subsequently made two changes.

Restaurant

The French Restaurant was always elegant, with its oak panelling and log fires, and served good food. However, the restaurant and adjoining bar tended to be unfashionable. Service in particular had not kept pace with modern trends. Certainly clients appreciate elegant surroundings, and the French Restaurant is more delightful now than ever before, but that does not mean that the menu and service should be stuffy. Today's guests want a more relaxed, informal atmosphere with an interesting menu that does not cost them a fortune.

Therefore, elegantly relaxed, coupled with value for money, was the formula for the new development.

Fitness Centre

Conference delegates and other businessmen are more and more looking for some form of leisure facility in hotels. Fitness is a present day cult, and saunas and spa baths will be the norm rather than the exception in hotels.

We have, therefore, installed a Fitness Centre at Moor Hall incorporating a well equipped gymnasium, saunas, spa bath and (as important as anything) a well-appointed relaxing area.

The difference with our fitness centre is that it is run by professional staff under the auspices of Tony Ford (Commonwealth Games Gold Medal Weight Lifter) who also has a successful club in Burton-upon-Trent.

We feel that this will encourage overnight stays and conferences as well as much needed weekend business.

Furthermore, 'Family Fitness' is to be a speciality at weekends. The motto here is not 'keep up with the Joneses' but keep one step ahead of them.

Marketing consortia

With all the marketing consortia, individual hotels retain their own identity and operating and financial independence but, through their membership fees, they pool their marketing, sales and purchasing resources. Marketing and sales programmes are devised that benefit all member hotels at a fraction of the cost that it would take an individual hotel to tackle the same market effectively. All operate an inspection scheme for new members to assess their suitability and to ensure that they fulfil the consortium's criteria.

Best Western Hotels
26 Kew Road, Richmond, Surrey TW9 2NA

Best Western has traded in Britain since 1967 as Interchange Hotels but changed its name in 1979 to Best Western Hotels when it merged with an American marketing consortium, Best Western Hotels Inc. It now represents 1800 member hotels in the USA and a total of 2800 independent hotels in twenty-five countries worldwide.

Best Western now has over 170 members in England, Wales and Scotland, most of them three-star establishments, although there are some two-star and four-star hotels. It has thirty-five staff in its Richmond headquarters and runs a full marketing, sales and advisory service for members, a central reservations unit and a purchasing company. The consortium now enjoys a fully computerized reservation service which is linked by satellite to most of its affiliated offices overseas for worldwide reservations. It is possible to take out membership of the purchasing company without being a member of the marketing company. A regional structure has been established and regular meetings are held at both national and local level.

The consortium seeks independent hotels with at least forty bedrooms in London and other major cities. Smaller country hotels in areas where it is not represented will also be considered for membership. Cost of membership varies, depending on the number of bedrooms and at July 1983 a fifty-bedroom hotel would pay around £5,000 per annum.

Best Western International promotes common marketing, advertising and sales activities, and is at present the largest hotel marketing consortium in the world.

Inter-Hotel
35 Hogarth Road, London SW5 0QH

Inter-Hotel is a consortium with similar aims to Best Western and it has links with another American consortium – Downtomer-Passport International. It has a small head office staff but a similar number of hotels as Best Western UK. Much of the sales and promotion work is done by member hoteliers as well as by full-time staff.

Inter-Hotel offers a full marketing and sales and advisory service to members and also operates a purchasing company. Cost of membership is kept at the lowest possible level and, at August 1983, ranged from £750 for the smallest hotel to £3100 for the largest. Inter-Hotel says that a smaller hotel can generally recover the cost of membership from savings made through the purchasing company (this is the case with all the consortia).

Inter-Hotel is now looking for members in certain areas – provincial cities or well-known tourist and holiday areas where there are no existing members. New members must have at least 50 per cent private baths or showers and a proven managerial reputation. Hotels presently in membership have as few as eight bedrooms but it is likely that new members will need to have more than this number of bedrooms.

Consort hotels
Ryedale Building, Piccadilly, York

Formed in 1981, Consort has ninety hotels as members in the two- and three-star, middle tariff bracket. Annual membership fee is £75 per room per year. A purchasing scheme is offered.

Exec Hotels
190 Church Road, Hove, East Sussex

Formed in 1981, Exec has forty-one hotels as members in the two- and three-star, middle tariff bracket. There is a flat membership fee of £280 per year. A purchasing scheme is offered.

Comfort Associate Hotels
167 Queensway, London W2 4XG

Comfort Associate Hotels are part of the expanding chain of Comfort Hotels International, which incorporates thirty-seven hotels within the United Kingdom and overseas, including hotels in France, Holland and Denmark.

Comfort Associate Hotels was established by Comfort Hotels International to increase the spread of hotels on offer throughout the UK and particularly in destinations where there are no Comfort hotels.

Particular benefits include the sales and marketing expertise offered by Comfort Hotels and its purchasing powers, as well as Comfort Hotels' inclusion in World Hotel Reservations, a free international reservations service operated by leading hotel companies and hotel consortia throughout the world.

Minotels
11 Palmeira Mansions, Church Road, Hove, East Sussex BN3 2GA

This is a consortium of smaller, owner-managed, moderately-priced hotels charging around £12 per night double occupancy including full breakfast, service charge and VAT. Fees range from £250 for a ten-room hotel to £700 for a hotel with forty bedrooms. A purchasing scheme is offered.

Guestaccom
190 Church Road, Hove, East Sussex

Formed in 1980, this is a consortium of eighty-seven small, budget-priced hotels – the average number has eight bedrooms and all members have fewer than sixteen, based mainly in the country. Membership charge is £8.50 per bed per annum (minimum £200). A purchasing scheme is offered.

Prestige Hotels
13-14 Golden Square, London W1R 3AG

Prestige Hotels consists of some twenty-eight hotels in Britain and three overseas. Membership is limited to those hotels of only the highest standard and suitable size (generally no more than 100 rooms); inspection criteria are rigorous. It is unlikely that a first-time purchaser would be considered for membership, unless he had considerable experience of the hotel industry and was acquiring an established, first-class hotel.

Hotel Industry Marketing Group of the Institute of Marketing
Moor Hall, Cookham, Nr Maidenhead, Berks

This is not a consortium of hotels but an association of marketing and sales executives and hotel managers and proprietors. Regular monthly meetings are held which are aimed at increasing members' knowledge of sales and marketing matters, new trends and opportunities.

Suggested reading

How to Sell Banquets, by Derek Taylor, published by Hutchinson.
Marketing Hotels into the 90s – a systematic approach to increasing sales, by Melvyn Greene, published by Heinemann.
Marketing for Publicans, Hotel and Catering Industry Training Board, £2.75 (plus 25p p&p).
Marketing for Independent Hoteliers, Hotel and Catering Industry Training Board, £2.75 (plus 25p p&p).
Small Business Information Pack, Hotel and Catering Industry Training Board, £1 (plus 35p p&p).
Marketing the Meal Experience, by Graham Campbell-Smith, New University Education.
A Guide to Conference Marketing, published by BTA.
The Independent Hotel: a guide to overseas marketing, published by BTA.

Organizations to help

British Tourist Authority,
64 St James's Street, London SW1A 1NF

English Tourist Board,
4 Grosvenor Gardens, London SW1W 0DH

Scottish Tourist Board,
23 Ravelston Terrace, Edinburgh EH4 3EU

Wales Tourist Board,
Welcome House, High Street, Llandaff, Cardiff CF5 2YZ

Northern Ireland Tourist Board,
River House, 48 High Street, Belfast BT1 2DS

Cumbria Tourist Board,
Ellerthwaite, Windermere, Cumbria
(County of Cumbria)

East Anglia Tourist Board,
14 Museum Street, Ipswich, Suffolk
(Counties of Norfolk, Suffolk, Essex and Cambridgeshire)

East Midlands Tourist Board,
Bailgate, Lincoln, Lincolnshire
(Counties of Derbyshire, Leicestershire, Lincolnshire, Northamptonshire,
Nottinghamshire and South Humberside)

Heart of England Tourist Board,
65 High Street, Worcester, Hereford and Worcester
(Counties of Shropshire, Hereford and Worcester, Staffordshire,
Warwickshire, Gloucestershire and West Midlands)

London Tourist Board,
26 Grosvenor Gardens, London SW1W 0DU
(Greater London Area)

Northumbria Tourist Board,
Prudential Building, 140-150 Pilgrim Street, Newcastle upon Tyne
(Counties of Cleveland, Durham, Northumberland, Tyne and Wear)

North West Tourist Board,
The Last Drop Village, Bromley Cross, Bolton, Lancs.
(Counties of Cheshire, Greater Manchester, Lancashire, Merseyside and High
Peak district of Derbyshire)

South East Tourist Board,
Cheviot House, 4-6 Monson Road, Tunbridge Wells, Kent
(Counties of East Sussex, Kent, Surrey and West Sussex).

Southern Tourist Board,
Tourist Information Centre, Canute Road, Southampton, Hants. (Counties
of Hampshire, part of Dorset and the Isle of Wight).

Thames and Chilterns Tourist Board,
PO Box 10, 8 The Market Place, Abingdon, Oxon.

(Counties of Bedfordshire, Berkshire, Buckinghamshire, Hertfordshire and Oxfordshire).

West Country Tourist Board,
Trinity Court, 37 Southernhay East, Exeter, Devon
(Counties of Avon, Cornwall, Devon, part of Dorset, Somerset, Wiltshire and the Isles of Scilly)

Yorkshire and Humberside Tourist Board,
312 Tadcaster Road, York, North Yorkshire
(Counties of North, West and South Yorkshire and Humberside).

11 You and your staff

Staff present the biggest problem for any hotelier or restauranteur. This is probably the case for all businessmen but recruiting, employing and developing hotel and catering staff pose special problems for five main reasons:

1 A hotel or restaurant has to rely on its staff to a far greater extent than most other industries. A hotel without staff exists only as a building – it is people who provide the services that generate the turnover and profits. Hotel and restaurant workers are in face-to-face contact with customers all the time, unlike those in manufacturing industry, and the demands made on them are complex. All workers in the hotel and catering industry need to have the technical skill to carry out their job, but front of house staff require social skills, too – the ability to deal with customers in a way that encourages them to return.

2 The industry has a poor employment image which is not helpful to recruitment. Conditions of work are now improving, but because it is a service industry, staff need to be on duty when other people are not – at night, weekends and public holidays. The so-called unsocial hours present a real problem to hoteliers and caterers who require staff at these periods.

3 The industry experiences high labour turnover – noticeably higher than in most other industries. In large establishments, it can be as high as 200 per cent but more normally it is in the range of 60 per cent to 80 per cent. Those job categories that suffer the worst turnover are kitchen porters, room-maids and waiters. Significantly, perhaps, these are jobs with the fewest craft skills. Occupations that demand greater skills, such as cooking, generally experience lower turnover.

There is no single cause of such high labour turnover. As the industry employs so many women, one reason is that a high proportion leave to get married or to have children. Employees move to get better job opportunities elsewhere. In some cases, employees move on to acquire experience in a different kind of establishment. But there is a tendency for catering workers to change jobs for no reason other than to find a different place of employment. It is not easy to define what they are looking for and why they become dissatisfied with their present job but the consequences of this dissatisfaction affect every employer. A study carried out by the Hotel and

Catering Economic Development Committee some time ago suggested that the underlying reason was poor management. Too often, it said, customer-contact staff were left to cope with difficult situations without management support. The report laid much of the blame for high labour turnover on what it termed 'management abrogation'.

This may go a long way towards explaining the constant movement of staff from one employer to another, for when they do move few of them find substantially higher wages or markedly better working and living conditions. In these cases, what has happened is that the proprietor or manager has not succeeded in making his staff identify with his hotel or restaurant. Management skills in the hotel and catering industry are of prime importance, particularly in industrial relations. It is usually the case that hotels with the lowest rate of staff turnover are those with the strongest managers, though even the most successful hotel will probably experience an aggravatingly high turnover among the waiting staff. Location and ownership often affect labour turnover, too. A country hotel, employing local staff, is unlikely to suffer as badly as a hotel in a large town or city. A smaller, independently-owned hotel will usually fare better than a large, chain-operated establishment because it is easier for staff to identify with the proprietor.

4   As the industry employs a high proportion of female staff (over 60 per cent of all staff are female) and an even higher percentage of part-time labour, it inevitably faces special problems. An industry with a predominantly full-time work force with long-term career development prospects is going to inculcate a more stable environment than an industry whose workers regard employment more or less as a source of casual earnings. With women and part timers, absenteeism can be high when there is a crisis at home. For this reason, a hotelier quickly has to learn to operate with a staff at less than full strength.

5   Union activity in the hotel and restaurant sectors of the industry is weak. Many large hotels in London have union members (belonging either to the Hotel and Catering Workers' Union, which is the biggest in the industry, or the Transport and General Workers' Union) and almost all the major hotel and catering groups have signed recognition agreements with one of these two unions. But the large number of small units makes union recruitment in hotelkeeping and catering difficult and few independent hoteliers need to deal with a union. This has a major advantage because it has traditionally given employers great flexibility in moving staff from one job to another and there are no job demarcation disputes. But there are disadvantages. Without a union to represent hotel and catering workers, levels of pay and conditions of work have fallen behind those of most other (unionized) industries. Employers have been happy to accept this because many front-of-house staff earn tips while other staff are often granted subsidized living-in accommodation. However, because staff do not have

a union to look after their interests, they have traditionally voted with their feet — which is one further reason for the industry's high labour turnover. With no union to work out the solution to a problem, catering staff think nothing of walking out on their employer in a sudden burst of anger or frustration.

Motivation

It might be argued that high wages and good working and living conditions will ensure that staff are happy and will keep them in satisfied employment. Even that will not succeed, however, if the manager of a hotel does not lead his staff so that they are motivated and encouraged to believe that they are important members of a team. Staff need to be made aware of the fact that on their efforts will depend the ultimate success of the enterprise. This is true of any business, but particularly so of one in a service industry.

In a large hotel instilling this belief is difficult. In a small hotel, with twenty or so staff, the task is easier. The owner or manager is frequently seen in all the departments of the hotel and almost certainly knows every member of the staff by name. He can develop a relationship that motivates them and enables them to identify with the establishment. If the owner himself displays an unwavering commitment to the hotel, that will rub off on to the staff. If he does not, how can he expect the staff to be committed?

No one with any experience of human or industrial relations will deny that employees can be highly individual and totally unpredictable. They will often let you down, frequently quarrel among themselves, constantly cut corners in doing their job and will always need supervising and controlling. They will also try to fiddle you either in cash or with stocks in the bar and kitchen. In the face of this, you will have to encourage honesty and loyalty.

You will have to motivate them and ensure a high standard of performance, encouraging them to put all they have into their jobs. They will need to keep cool with an irate customer and be polite to an over-friendly guest. They must stay cheerful when events go awry and keep their heads when the hotel is busy. They need to be alert when they are exhausted at the end of the day and happy at 6 a.m. In other words, they must possess all the devotion, commitment and determination that you must have yourself. This is a tall order indeed. As the owner of the enterprise you are motivated by the fact that you are building up your own business. The staff cannot have the same motivation. Even so, you will expect them to be as committed to the hotel as you are. Little wonder hoteliers sometimes expect too much from their staff!

As proprietor or manager, your major objective must be to create conditions of work that make the employee's job satisfying and rewarding. If this is achieved, the employee will be able to identify both with you and your hotel in a way that encourages him or her to believe he or she is an essential part of the enterprise. How you communicate this enthusiasm and commitment depends on your own style of management but achieving this major objective will not be easy. It is important for you to get to know staff as individuals and to understand how they can identify with you and the enterprise. In doing this, you may have to adopt a different approach to different members of staff.

A useful step in getting to know a small number of staff is to hold informal interviews within the first week with each employee to find out their background, their current perception of their job, their attitude to the enterprise and any problems and grievances that may be outstanding. Speedy reconciliation of an outstanding grievance (without creating precedent) is an ideal way of attracting staff loyalty.

Staffing levels

If this gives a general impression of the difficulties you will face in recruiting and retaining staff, there are some particular problems that need your immediate attention as you take over. How many staff are you going to keep? How many want to stay? If you want to ask some to leave, will you be involved in redundancy payments?

It is impossible to generalize about how many employees a hotel or restaurant needs. Staffing ratios depend on the style of establishment, its age and type of business. An old property will probably need more staff than a modern hotel because the rooms will be bigger and the hotel will be less efficiently planned. A hotel which has bedrooms without private bathrooms will require fewer staff than a hotel which has all its rooms with bathrooms. The former will need one room-maid for every fifteen or so rooms, the latter one maid for about every twelve rooms. In an efficiently designed modern hotel, with well-planned, easy-clean bedrooms, a maid may be able to service up to twenty rooms. Other staff numbers are affected by the size of the public areas. A hotel with extensive ground floor facilities will require more cleaning staff than one with a smaller public area. Occasionally, contract cleaners can be quite competitive for public areas and window cleaning. A hotel with a large garden will need gardeners.

The food and beverage department is the most labour intensive in any hotel and can provide the lowest percentage of profits, which is why the control of wage and material costs in the kitchen and restaurant is so important. A restaurant with an extensive à la carte menu will need a highly skilled and expensive kitchen brigade with restaurant staff to match. If the restaurant specializes in silver service or lamp work even more staff will be needed. A hotel dining room with plate service will need fewer staff.

In the traditional à la carte restaurant, there is a hierarchy of staff which comprises a restaurant manager, head waiter, wine waiter, chefs de rang and commis waiters. In this system, the room is divided into stations (or areas) of three or four tables, depending on their size; each station is the responsibility of a chef de rang. One or two commis (apprentice) waiters work for each chef de rang, fetching and taking away the plates and dishes, while the chef de rang will be responsible for serving the customer at the table. The commis will also take part in the service. The head waiter will take the order and the wine waiter will take the order for the wine and serve it.

This is the most common way of organizing a large restaurant and provides specific areas of responsibility for staff. But such a structure is inappropriate and too costly for many smaller and less formal restaurants. In these, there may be a number of waiters or waitresses who either have their own tables or, less frequently, work on any table that needs service at a particular time. The head waiter who takes the order may be the restaurant proprietor or his wife and it is likely he or she will also take the wine order.

Working out staff numbers for your hotel will be a matter of experience. Generally speaking, it is better to have too few than too many. Staff are happier when they are busy and have less idle time on their hands. Most important of all, it costs less. Your initial problem may be to decide which staff if any, you want to stay and which you want to ask to leave. You may be altering the operation of the hotel and thus find you are overstaffed. If you decide to get rid of them, don't forget that you will be declaring them redundant. The Redundancy Payments Act, 1965, lays down payments which must be made for those employees who have more than 104 continuous weeks' service and who normally work for sixteen hours or more per week (or eight hours or more for a period of five years or more).

You may find that some of the staff you want to dismiss qualify for redundancy payments. If that is the case, you must dismiss them with the appropriate notice and redundancy pay but don't forget that just over 40 per cent of the redundancy payment may be recovered from the Redundancy Fund via the Department of Employment.

Statutory rights

The employment area has now become a legal minefield for employers and it is important that a proprietor quickly understands the main provisions of the most important employment laws, which are: Employment Protection (Consolidation) Act, 1978; Trade Union and Labour Relations Acts, 1974 and 1976; Sex Discrimination Act, 1975; Health and Safety at Work, Etc, Act, 1974; Equal Pay Act, 1970; the Race Relations Act, 1976; and statutory sick pay regulations. The relationship between the employee and employer is covered by over 140 separate pieces of legislation. Obviously, no proprietor or manager will be perfectly familiar with all these requirements but when the maximum award for unfair dismissal can run into many thousands of pounds, it illustrates how important it is for you to understand the main legislation quickly.

Leaflets on all these Acts are available from the local office of the

Department of Employment. Briefly, the aim of the legislation is to give protection to workers during their employment and against their dismissal but it is the latter that causes the greatest problems to employers. All full-time staff working sixteen or more hours a week with more than fifty-weeks' continuous service are protected by the Employment Protection Act against unfair dismissal. Part-time employees with five years' continuous service and who work eight hours or more a week are also protected. Guidance on the manner of dismissal has been laid down which specifies at least two oral and one written warnings. If the employee believes he or she has been unfairly dismissed, he or she can take his or her employer to an industrial tribunal which can make an award if it decides the member of staff has been unfairly dismissed. It is possible to take out insurance against action under the Employment Protection Act.

There are other legislative points you should immediately understand. The Employment Protection Act gives maternity rights – an important subject bearing in mind the high number of female employees in the hotel and catering industry. In most circumstances you cannot dismiss a woman for being pregnant unless she cannot do her job properly because of her pregnancy at the date of dismissal. If a suitable alternative job is available, she must be offered it. A woman absent because of pregnancy has the right to nine-tenths of a normal week's pay (less the maternity allowance) for six weeks provided she has worked for her employer for 104 continuous weeks. If she has had two years' continuous employment, she can return at any time during the twenty-nine weeks after the confinement date, whether or not her contract is still in existence. The employer must re-employ her in a similar job with seniority, pension and other rights intact.

There are other legal obligations specifically related to the hotel and catering industry. Because employees in the industry have traditionally been poorly represented by trade unions the Government set up five wages councils in the 1940s to introduce minimum wages and conditions of work in the industry. One council, the Unlicensed Residential, which would have covered unlicensed hotels and guest houses, never operated. Another council, set up to regulate minimum wages in industrial staff canteens, was disbanded in 1976. There are now three in existence: the Licensed Restaurant and Residential (all licensed hotels and licensed restaurants); the Licensed Non-Residential (mainly public houses); and the Unlicensed Place of Refreshment (mainly cafés). Each wages council consists of an equal number of employer and employee representatives together with three independent members, one of whom acts as chairman.

Each council meets every year to set minimum rates of pay for its section of workers. When the new rates have been established, they are published in pamphlet form and distributed as an Order directly to employers. They are also available from any Department of Employment office, which can give advice on the interpretation of each annual Order. The Order establishes minimum rates for all staff, either living in or living out, and covers such areas as the length of the week worked, amount of extra pay for Sunday overtime and spreadover working and holiday entitlement. The important point to remember about wages council rates is that they are the minimum – an employer must not pay below them but of course he can pay above them if he wishes. Naturally, the rates paid by an individual hotel will depend on local conditions. When you take over, your pay scale will also depend on what the previous proprietor was paying.

Employers must keep records to show that they have complied with the wages council regulations and the wages council inspectorate has power to investigate employers' records. One recent investigation showed that up to 25 per cent of staff were being under-paid either through ignorance or on purpose. Back payments to staff were ordered in all cases. The Licensed Restaurant and Residential Wages Council is the one with which most hoteliers are familiar and its new wage rates come into effect on October 31 every year although occasionally they are not published until after that date. In this case, employees need to be given back pay if appropriate from the date of the Order's implementation.

It is crucial that you establish what your 'remuneration package' is. Wages form only a part of this. Other elements include tips, service charges, bonus, overtime, number of hours worked, set days off, holidays. Despite the fact that contracts detailing the conditions of employment (see page 177) are required by law, some employers never get round to drawing them up or changes occur which are not formalized. An employee's perception of his or her contract, and of the parts of the remuneration package that are important to him or her, may differ from the manager's view. Be sure, therefore, that you understand what each employee expects, reconcile any differences and record the understanding in writing.

In spite of poor union penetration in the industry, there can be little doubt that wages council awards in the future will increase. The upward pressure on wages has become one of the most difficult problems for hoteliers to deal with. Compared with most other industries, official wage rates are low in the hotel and catering industry because of historical precedence, high incidence of female labour, lack of union activity and because some front-of-house staff receive tips and gratuities, meals and living-in accommodation. Nevertheless, the actual earnings are usually far above the minimum wage rates, as official government earnings surveys show.

Being such a labour intensive industry, it is difficult for a hotelier to reduce staff numbers but there is scope in some areas. A degree of self-service, particularly at breakfast and lunchtime, can reduce the need for some service staff. Tea and coffee-making facilities in the bedrooms mean that room-maids do not need to be on duty so early in the morning. Direct dial-out telephones reduce the need for a large manual switchboard (automatic switchboards for up to 100 extensions can be provided by British Telecom for a reasonable rental). Buffet lunches reduce the number of lunchtime waiting staff and can, at the same time, attract new customers. Vending machines on the bedroom floors may provide a simple form of room service, if there is sufficient demand, when the traditional method is uneconomic. The need for porters has been greatly reduced and most guests now expect to carry their luggage, unless they are unwell or infirm.

These are some of the ways of reducing staff costs in the long term. In many cases you are replacing labour with capital and you will have to calculate whether the capital expense is justified by the saving in staff costs. In some instances (e.g. kettles in bedrooms) it almost certainly is worthwhile. In other cases (e.g. vending machines on floors) it may not be.

Standards

In the face of ever rising staff costs you may be forced to cut back on service to maintain tariffs. This is not such a simple question to face as it may appear. Would you be justified in doing this? Some hotels are in a market that demands a low price, no frills service; other hotels are in a more flexible market, where the standard of the food, the room and the service is more important than price. It may be a better marketing strategy to increase prices and improve standards than to maintain the price and reduce standards. Unless you are experienced in either hotelkeeping or marketing (or both) don't come to hurried conclusions in this area until you have had some experience of ownership and know your customers' needs better.

All this is in the long term. Your immediate problem relates to the control of staff. When you take over, you will be faced with one of three problems. You will have to establish standards, maintain them or improve them. Only in exceptional cases would you want to reduce them. Standards can be established only if the new proprietor knows exactly what he wants. Staff cannot be expected to work well if nobody has told them what is required from them. The sooner you do this, the better will be the changeover to your ownership. When you take over, you should tell the staff that you will be taking a much closer interest in their work than they would normally expect.

If the bedrooms are not serviced properly, you must show exactly how you want them cleaned. You may need to write down what you want so that it is clear in your own mind before you tell your staff. If you do this, it could act as a simple work manual that tells staff how they should work, the order in which they should carry out their duties and the standards you expect. Don't assume that because you tell staff to do a job it is necessarily carried out. Check constantly in the first few weeks and give specific directions to specific people.

In many areas you will have to work through people. Unless you are a skilled chef and you are going to take over the kitchens yourself, you will have to tell the chef what you want and encourage him to impose your standards. The same situation exists with other department heads like the head waiter and head housekeeper. If standards don't improve you will have to find out. Does the department head understand what you want? If so, is he or she capable of achieving those standards? If not, why not? Does he or she need retraining or replacing?

If the establishment is so small that there are no department heads, as is likely to be the case, then you will have to communicate with all the staff direct. One hotelier took over a hotel with appallingly low standards – the bedrooms were dirty, the wash basins limed, the carpets shabby and the bedlinen old and worn. He realized that it was impossible to make staff take a pride in their work as the basic facilities and amenities needed improving. The staff were already demoralized and could hardly care less. The first thing that he did was to shut some of the rooms, get in the decorators and replace the linen and curtains – an action that showed he meant business. The staff immediately began to take a greater interest in their work as they saw that the new proprietor was serious about raising standards. A new work scheme that he introduced meant that the staff were able to clean the rooms more quickly. New vacuum cleaners were purchased and more efficient cleaning materials obtained. The hotelier frequently accompanied staff in the early stages, explaining exactly how he wanted the work carried out and why he wanted changes to be made (reasons are important because most staff resent change in their working routine).

He took the same approach in the kitchen. He was fortunate because the existing chef left before he took over and he brought in a new chef. The state of cleanliness was poor so a firm of industrial cleaners was brought in to clean accumulated grease from the kitchen canopies; the stoves were decarbonized and a safety-tile floor was laid. Much of this was carried out with the advice of the local environment health officer who suggested that the work surfaces be replaced with laminated plastic or stainless steel. A cold room with separate fridges for raw and cooked foods was installed. By these positive actions the hotelier set the kind of standards he was looking for almost before he and the chef had discussed food quality and portion control. While the physical improvements were being undertaken they got together to discuss the menu, the kind of recipes to be used and how the dishes were to be prepared and presented. The action had a dynamic effect on those staff who had worked with the previous owner.

Even if such dramatic improvements cannot be made, it is always necessary to make clear at the beginning that you intend to impose your own standards and to maintain them. The standards you introduce must be attainable and credible and you need to ensure that, once established, they are always maintained. Once standards start slipping because of lack of management control, it is difficult to revive them.

Training

Other staffing problems will arise. More training for the staff and for yourself may be necessary, in which case the local adviser of the Hotel and Catering Industry Training Board may be able to help you. The local catering college may also help. Recruitment and selection will be a problem for you, especially if you have no experience in this area. The relevant chapters in the books listed on page 183 will be helpful but the training board adviser may be able to get you a place on a suitable short course, which will give you some basic skills. Choosing the right staff is a difficult and complex undertaking and you will need all the skills you can acquire. Similarly, don't forget that, once selected, the most difficult period in any worker's employment is the first few weeks. More employees leave in this delicate period that at any other time. Make sure that new employees fit smoothly into the routine of the establishment by simple induction training. Introduce them to their fellow workers, ensure they know their way around the establishment, make certain they understand exactly what their jobs are and what is expected of them, who they report to and their conditions of employment. Ensure they are comfortable and satisfied with their accommodation. Induction training is always essential but it is often neglected.

There are other problems, such as ensuring that the wage bill stays in line with budget; at the same time, your rates of pay must not fall behind wages in other industries in the area so that staff are attracted away. A long-term aim may be to introduce a bonus or profit-sharing scheme which will help to motivate key staff and ensure their continued interest.

All these objectives highlight the need for simple job descriptions, staff training and development plans and the preparation of simple operating manuals. Large hotels need a sophisticated system of training and personnel control; in a small hotel, because the owner is present all the time and constantly perceives standards in all departments himself, the need for written controls is not so urgent. But it is important that each member of staff knows exactly what his or her job comprises, how it is to be performed and what is expected of him or her. Every member of staff needs to know how his or her performance will be judged and what are the rewards for good performance.

The problem of the hotel and catering industry is that management needs to work through staff to a far greater extent than in most other industries. The drive, quality of leadership and personality of the owner or his manager – and his ability to communicate these to his staff – will dictate the success of a catering enterprise but it will be the staff who provide the means by which the success will be achieved.

Guide to engagement and dismissal of staff

Engagement

It was estimated that labour turnover in 1973 cost the industry over £22 million and that every person leaving cost between £50 and £150 to replace. No more recent estimate has been published but, even with inflation those figures should be doubled. Think of that in current terms and estimate how much revenue you need to generate to make £100 profit – effort that is immediately wasted by unnecessary turnover. Labour turnover doesn't just cost cash – it also means that valuable know-how is lost. The first few weeks of employment are a vital period in retaining staff. Check the following:

1 Is your induction programme effective?
2 Within thirteen weeks of commencing work with you, staff working sixteen hours a week or more (or eight hours a week if they have five or more years' service) are entitled by law to a 'written statement of terms and conditions of employment'.

This written statement must contain:

1 Job title (to preserve flexibility it may be useful to add 'and other duties normally associated with this position' to the title)
2 Date of commencement
3 Scale of remuneration or method of calculating remuneration
4 Intervals at which remuneration is paid (monthly, weekly, etc)
5 Any terms and conditions relating to hours of work (including normal working hours)
6 Terms and conditions relating to holidays and holiday pay, incapacity for work due to sickness/injury, sick pay arrangements, pensions and pension schemes
7 Details of disciplinary and grievance rules, and to whom such matters may be referred
8 Any previous service that counts for continuity purposes and when continuity began
9 The length of notice which the employee is obliged to give and entitled to received to terminate his or her contract of employment. (Minimum statutory periods of notice are shown in Table 15.)

In addition to this information, which you are obliged to specify, you should decide whether you need to include other matters relating to your business. It is important to be as clear as possible about all of the terms and conditions under which your staff are employed. Matters commonly giving rise to misunderstanding, and which should therefore be made as clear as possible, include:

1 Conditions under which accommodation or other benefits such as meals on duty are supplied

Table 15   *Employee's statutory rights*

Statutory rights	When applicable
Itemised pay statements	Immediately on employment (see note 1)
Protection against dismissal on grounds of pregnancy	26 weeks (see note 1)
Written particulars of employment	13 weeks (see note 1)
Unfair dismissal	52 weeks (see notes 1,2)
Written statement of reasons for dismissal	26 weeks (see note 1)
Maternity pay	104 weeks (see note 1)
Right to return to work after child birth	104 weeks (see note 1)
Time-off to look for work if under notice of dismissal or redundancy	104 weeks (see note 1)
Redundancy payment	104 weeks (see notes 1, 3)
Protection against discrimination	Immediately on employment

Notes
1   Employees who work fewer than 16 hours a week (or fewer than 8 hours a week after five years' service) are excluded.
2   Employees over the normal retiring age for their particular job or, if there is none, who are aged 60 or over in case of a woman or 65 or over in case of a man, cannot claim for unfair dismissal, except where dismissal takes place because of trade union membership or activities. The qualifying period of 26 weeks does not apply.
3   Employees aged 60 or more, in case of a woman, or 65 or over in case of a man, are not entitled to claim.

2   Terms of joint (husband and wife) contracts
3   Right to search employees
4   Deductions from wages
5   Right to suspend employees
6   Responsibilities as to safety
7   Continuity of employment (especially to seasonal or casual staff)
8   Maternity rights

It is important to *check* whether staff understand what they have been told about your rules and procedures, especially if you employ foreign staff who may have language difficulties. In particular, check that they understand:

1   Disciplinary rules
2   Grievance procedure
3   Safety/fire/hygiene rules
4   Your attitude to trade union membership and consultation with staff

Dismissal

Every member of staff has a right 'not to be unfairly dismissed by his employer, and the remedy of an employee so dismissed . . . shall be by way of complaint to an industrial trinunal' says the Trade Union and Labour Relations Act, 1974. When such a claim is made, it is for the *employer* to satisfy the tribunal that he acted *reasonably* in the circumstances, i.e. that the dismissal was for a valid reason and was carried out correctly.

The Act lists reasons acceptable as 'fair':

1 Incompetence – lack of skill, technical, or academic qualifications
2 Conduct
3 Illegality (e.g. employing a driver without a licence, or a foreign worker without a work permit)
4 True redundancy
5 Other substantial reason

The Act also lists reasons that will definitely be classed as 'unfair', including dismissal caused by:

1 Being a member of an independent trade union, or proposing to join one
2 Taking part, or proposing to take part, in independent trade union activities at an appropriate time (outside work hours or during work time agreed by the employer for union activity)
3 Refusing to join or remain in a non-independent trade union
4 Unfair selection for redundancy

Constructive dismissal

An employee is regarded as having been dismissed if he or she terminates his or her own contract as a result of his or her employer's conduct. For example, if the work an employee is required to do is drastically changed without his or her prior agreement, or if his or her terms of employment are changed, for example by the withdrawal of some allowances and privileges, an employee may be entitled to resign and claim that he or she has been unfairly 'constructively' dismissed.

This means that employers who coerce employees to leave by making life difficult are liable to face an allegation of unfair dismissal. Similarly, a supervisor may, unbeknown to senior management, 'pick on' a member of staff so that he or she leaves; in such a case the senior manager may know nothing about the case until an unfair dismissal claim is sent to him by the industrial tribunal.

It is sensible to protect your organization by making managers and supervisors aware of the nature of constructive dismissal, and by ensuring that employees who leave are interviewed to establish the reason for their departure.

What is wrongful dismissal?

An employee is wrongfully dismissed if not given the proper period of notice (or wages in lieu) to which he or she is entitled under his or her contract of employment – unless he or she has so seriously misconducted himself or herself as to 'repudiate his or her contract', i.e. indicated an intention not to be concerned with his or her contractual duties, in which case he or she can be summarily dismissed. Stealing from a customer, or a flagrant breach of hygiene rules, might constitute grounds for summary dismissal – without notice or pay in lieu of notice. But the burden of showing that the employee has 'repudiated' his or her contract lies with you, and even if you succeed you could still face a claim for compensation for unfair dismissal. Summary dismissal is seldom warranted – at the very least, an employee should be given his notice or pay in lieu of notice, and the benefit of the doubt.

If you summarily dismiss an employee, but to avoid ill-will you decide to make some payment to him or her, short of paying his or her notice pay, ensure that you protect your position against a possible 'unfair dismissal' claim by sending a note with the payment saying that it is made 'without prejudice' to the company's right to dismiss summarily.

Statutory minimum notice periods

Under the Employment Protection Act an employee working sixteen hours/week (or eight hours/week after five years' service) is entitled to receive notice as follows:

> 1 week after 4 weeks' continuous service
> 2 weeks after 2 years' continuous service
> 3 weeks after 3 years' continuous service
> to maximum 12 weeks after 12 years' continuous service

The employee is required to give his or her employer one week's notice after four weeks' service.

Important exception

Employees who have a contract for twelve weeks or less (e.g. seasonal workers) are not entitled to a week's notice unless they actually work for more than twelve weeks. But this must be made clear at the time of engagement.

What should you do to protect your organization?

1 Never dismiss in anger
2 Get a second opinion before dismissing any employee who is eligible to claim unfair dismissal
3 If possible, do not dismiss without the presence of a witness
4 Follow an agreed discipline/dismissal procedure, which should contain provision for at least one written warning before dismissal. If possible keep

a record of all warnings, even verbal ones. The time limit for making a complaint is three months, but tribunals have discretion to hear complaints out of time where it was not reasonably practicable for the complaint to be made earlier

5   Make sure you understand the regulations on maternity leave, etc.

Must you give the reasons for dismissal?
The Employment Protection Act requires an employer to give a dismissed employee, on request, a written statement of the reasons for dismissal. The employee must have been employed for twenty-six weeks and the statement must be provided within fourteen days of the request, which need not be made in writing. Make sure that there is no chance of a verbal request being overlooked.

Source: *Industrial Relations Tribunal Handbook*: Hotel and Catering Industry Training Board.

Suggested reading

Personnel Management in the Hotel and Catering Industry, by Michael Boella, published by Hutchinson.

A Manual of Staff Management in the Hotel and Catering Industry, by Philip Magurn, published by Heinemann.

Employee Relations, Hotel and Catering Industry Training Board, £1.75 (plus 35p p&p).

Statutory Sick Pay (a training kit), Hotel and Catering Industry Training Board, £20 (plus £1.20 p&p)

Employing People in the Licensed Trade, Hotel and Catering Industry Training Board, £2.75 (plus 35p p&p)

Training Your Staff, Hotel and Catering Industry Training Board, £2.35 (plus 30p p&p)

A Guide to Systematic Training, Hotel and Catering Industry Training Board £2.35 (plus 25p p&p)

Training in Food Service, Hotel and Catering Industry Training Board, £10.95 (plus £1 p&p)

Training Aids in Customer Relations, Hotel and Catering Industry Training Board, £8.50 (plus £1 p&p)

Booklets and pamphlets on employment legislation are available from the local office of the Department of Employment, which can also provide the latest relevant Wages Council Orders.

12 Restaurants and bars

'Food, glorious food,' sang Oliver in Lionel Bart's musical but the hotelier needs to take a less joyous and more calculated attitude towards his food and beverage operation. A well-run restaurant can be highly profitable; a badly-operated unit can make a terrible loss. A good restaurant can be an excellent advertisement for your hotel and will get the establishment talked about in the town; a poor restaurant can give your hotel such a bad reputation that people will be deterred from staying with you altogether.

In no other department of the hotel does so much control have to be exercised and are there so many traps for the unwary. Food is a high cost perishable commodity and the competent staff needed to prepare it are a problem to recruit, expensive to employ and difficult to control. The difference between profit and loss is dependent on tight control in the kitchen, good purchasing procedures, skilled preparation and presentation and correct pricing. Owning a high class restaurant, whether it is a sole unit or whether it is part of a hotel, has undeniable attractions but the difficulties should never be underestimated.

Which market?

First you need to decide what kind of food and beverage operation you are going to run and whether a market exists for it in the area. Broadly speaking, there are three different markets for a hotel restaurant.

Haute cuisine, à la carte
A restaurant in this, the most difficult of all three markets, depends for its success entirely on the proprietor's ability to produce high quality food with an appropriate standard of service. His own personality will be an important factor in the restaurant's success and so will the atmosphere he is able to create in it. There are many examples of success in this field and most of them revolve around the cooking skills of the proprietor himself. Prices in these restaurants are high and the market is usually small. If there are no haute cuisine restaurants in your area there may be an opportunity to create one in your hotel or restaurant. However, the fact that one does not exist does not necessarily mean it is a wide-open market — others might have started in the past and failed. The market just may not exist. On the other hand, it is quite

likely that the area will support at least one high class restaurant that has the right food at the right prices. There may be a greater opportunity if other haute cuisine restaurants already exist in the area. This shows that locals have acquired the eating-out habit and, if they patronize other restaurants, they can be attracted to yours.

A more difficult achievement is to get them back after their first visit. The level of repeat business dictates the success of most restaurants. If other restaurants are successful, try to analyse why. What is it about them that attracts customers and what can you do differently that will create a demand for the type of food you want to serve? If there is a high class French restaurant, for example, the opportunity may exist for a restaurant specializing in English food. In marketing terms, you have to create your USP (unique selling proposition). This may be the food or the atmosphere or a combination of both. It could even be your own personality.

Cheaper, but high quality

A more common approach by most hotel restaurants is to offer a less expensive menu, with simpler, cheaper dishes – which might be themed – but with a high standard of cooking and service. This is often a sensible compromise. Running a high-class, de-luxe restaurant in a hotel will present difficulties because customers will expect the hotel itself to be of a similar standard of excellence. As most hotels are not in the de-luxe category it follows that a conflict of interests may arise. A hotelier can rarely divorce his food and beverage operation from his rooms; they must complement each other rather than draw attention to the other's shortcomings.

There are practical advantages in this second approach. The skills required are not as demanding in this kind of restaurant as those needed by a haute cuisine restaurant; at the same time, the food costs are lower and easier to control. In addition, the restaurant is likely to be attractive to overnight guests whereas an expensive restaurant would possibly deter many of them.

For these reasons, most hotels have chosen this middle course. This does not mean that they offer poor quality food (though that, regrettably, is often the case). Their objective should be to provide the highest possible quality that is compatible with the price and the market. Caviar and smoked salmon will not be on the menu but steak and kidney may be and would be of the highest standard. Aim to provide the highest quality food for the price charged and make the steak and kidney pie the best in town for the price. In this way, customers will readily appreciate that they are getting value for money, which must be every hotelier's prime objective. If customers believe they get value they will return again and again.

Simple table d'hôte menu

Many small hotels, particularly those in seaside resorts with little chance trade and where guests are on dinner, bed and breakfast terms, will find it difficult to expand their food and beverage operation, even if they want to. Anybody who wants to eat out in the town will be attracted to a hotel or a restaurant that has a more extensive menu. The possibility of building up the restaurant trade in a small resort hotel is remote. It may be better to recognize these limitations and not spend time and resources trying to attract a clientele that may not exist.

For the resident guests, the menu will be simple and brief – a choice of three or four starters and the same number of entrées and sweets. The quality will still need to be high, however, commensurate with the price being charged. Extensive use of convenience and frozen food will probably be made in this kind of establishment because the kitchen will have only basic cooking skills.

Choosing your level

Whatever type of hotel or restaurant you are operating, it is important to make sure that you maximize all opportunities for food sales. Don't assume, for example, that because the restaurant is busy there are no other sales opportunities. Do you serve bar snacks which could encourage a greater drinks turnover? If you have large public areas, could you serve morning coffee and afternoon tea? Hotels in busy shopping areas can build up a profitable trade with local shoppers. If you have an unused or undeveloped part of the building (especially with access to the main street) is it worth converting it into a coffee shop, fast food restaurant or a wine bar? With separate access from the street, it would be more worthwhile to use the space as a public bar and so build up a good lunch-time snack and bar trade. Cocktail bars are often grossly under-utilized; turning the area into a public bar may generate extra turnover and increase profits.

After your first visit to the hotel, you will know which of these developments are possible and which are not. Whether they will be profitable, however, will depend not only on the strength of the market and how successfully you can exploit it but how effectively, in technical and planning terms, you can operate the extra units. A bar or restaurant which is a long way from the kitchen presents enormous difficulties when serving food. The kitchen and restaurant needs to be adjoining and, ideally, should be on the same level with no steps for waiters to fall down. If you are expecting the kitchen to cope with an extra workload, is it big enough? The good design of a kitchen and restaurant operation is crucial to success, particularly for a popular or fast food restaurant.

After you have assessed your market, the next priority is to compile the menu. To begin with, this will be a trial and error exercise. You will probably have your own ideas of new and interesting dishes but you may have to compromise. The public, which is essentially conservative, tends to regard new dishes with suspicion. Long-established favourites, such as prawn cocktail, steak and roast meats, always sell well, usually to the detriment of more exotic dishes. Popular made-up dishes, like steak and kidney pie and shepherds pie are also very popular. If you offer roast sirloin of beef on a Sunday lunch, 85 per cent of the diners will choose it. This can be a frustrating experience for any proprietor who is anxious to introduce exciting dishes to his menu. He can only do this on an experimental basis. If he abandons all the well established dishes he may deter his clientele. Of course, some restaurants do offer unusual and exciting dishes and in doing so build up an enthusiastic following but they are the exception.

Whatever style of food you offer, the secret of success will be to offer a small number of high quality dishes rather than to create a large à la carte menu that the kitchen cannot cope with properly. A choice of five or six starters, an equal number of entrées, three or four sweets and some good cheeses is probably sufficient for most restaurants and for most occasions. A small menu is beneficial in other ways, too. It prevents the customer becoming confused when faced with an extensive à la carte menu and it helps to cut down mistakes in the service of the food. In the same way, a small wine list reduces the necessity of holding expensive stocks of little used wine and aids customer choice, particularly if you briefly describe the character of the wines on the list. Dishes should be similarly described if they are not obvious.

People are more ignorant about food and wine than many hoteliers realize and customers are often worried about making fools of themselves when ordering from a menu. A restaurant that insists on using French terminology in its menu without the necessary English translation runs the risk of deterring those many customers who will not want to display their ignorance by asking for a translation of a dish on the menu. The same problem, but greatly magnified, exists with the wine list. Here, even more mystique exists – often encouraged, it must be admitted, by proprietors themselves, many of whom foolishly believe it is good business to produce a wine list that is as informative to the layman as the average race card. Both the menu and the wine list are sales tools. Their prime aim is to promote restaurant sales and to encourage customers to buy more easily. They should not be viewed as an obstacle course which a customer has to overcome before he or she can choose his or her food. It is often good practice to suggest wines with a particular dish – many customers find such a recommendation helpful.

One word of warning. Don't forget the existence of the Trade Descriptions Act which protects the consumer against goods and services that are falsely or misleadingly described (see page 117). If you offer butter, for example, it must be pure butter and not a mixture of butter and margarine. The same applies to other items and dishes, though it is not clear whether an incorrectly prepared classical dish would be subject to the Act.

Not every dish will be popular and experience will soon tell you which items sell well. Those dishes that 'stick' (even though they may be your own personal favourites) should be taken off the menu. They take up space for dishes that could be more popular and therefore more profitable. Remember, the menu is a selection of dishes that you believe customers will want; whether or not you like the dishes yourself is immaterial.

If the restaurant is particularly busy, it might be worthwhile to invest in an electronic cash register (perhaps on lease) with pre-setting facilities. This simplifies control, speeds up the preparation of bills and automatically prints out the number of different dishes sold, thus giving you an accurate record of relative popularity. In a small restaurant, this can of course be done manually.

Costings

The price of your dishes will be dictated by your market and by your own costings. While it is true that you must prepare accurate costings for your dishes, and that the major items should give you a gross profit of at least 60 per cent and probably nearer 70 per cent, there is no point in preparing a dish that you have to sell at £12.50 to find that nobody wants it because it is too expensive. If the market demands dishes priced at £3, then you will have to create dishes at that price.

Your objective is for the kitchen to produce a gross profit of at least 65 per cent on its entire operation; some items, particularly starters and sweets, will yield a very much higher gross profit, some slightly lower.

Any restaurateur needs to prepare costings although there is a growing school of thought in the catering industry that too much emphasis is being placed on gross percentage profit and not enough on actual cash profit. Many operators now take the view that a rigid approach to gross percentages inevitably precludes a restaurant from serving popular but high cost items such as fillet steak or lobster. The price of these items becomes too high if the standard gross profit is imposed, so they are forced off the menu. To prevent this, some restaurants are now accepting a much lower gross profit – say 50 per cent – in the belief that it is better to make £3 profit on a lobster selling at £9 than nothing on a lobster priced at £12 which does not sell. A similar approach is being taken with wine, when the traditional 100 per cent mark up (i.e. twice the cost price) is being replaced by a more flexible pricing policy. Behind this thinking lies the belief that it is much easier to increase the volume of trade and level of profit by aggressive pricing than it is to squeeze extra profit out of existing business through ever-tighter cost control. The cash flow generated by the flexible approach to pricing should more than compensate for the lower margin. Some sample costings appear in Appendix 2.

An important prerequisite to any system of costing is the introduction of standard recipes so that the ingredients of dishes do not vary significantly every time they are prepared. This presumes close communication and agreement with the chef (who will be responsible for the gross profit). It also implies discipline on the part of both the chef and proprietor. In the early days of ownership, it is always a temptation to give extra value in a dish just to emphasize your good intentions and to encourage repeat business. This is natural but it is a dangerous practice. The extra quality, in terms of additional ingredients or bigger portion size, may attract customers in the beginning but dissatisfaction will soon occur when you eventually cut back to achieve your original targeted gross profit. Customers who have become accustomed to one standard of quality will not be happy with a lower standard at the same price. You must start as you mean to continue. A restaurant should succeed on the dishes that provide the customer with a satisfying meal and the operator with a reasonable profit. Trading up to a higher standard for promotional purposes only and then reducing quality at some later date is a dangerous practice.

It goes without saying that the reverse situation is equally dangerous. A hotelier can attempt to achieve a higher gross profit by cutting back on portion sizes or on the quality of the ingredients, but it is difficult to think of any action that would more successfully empty a restaurant. Regular customers instinctively recognize quality and value. Those who frequently eat out at expensive restaurants expect dishes of a quality commensurate with the price. A reduction in quality will be recognized immediately as cost cutting. No restaurant could withstand such an assault on its credibility. It would quickly lose trade and would not be able to pick up new customers lower down the market because they would still regard it as an expensive restaurant.

If you need to move your restaurant down market, do not casually reduce the quality of food and service. Make it obvious by introducing a new menu. You could also dress your staff differently, introduce a new décor and you should ensure that the message is hammered home by advertising, sales leaflets and other means.

Purchasing food

A small hotel has a special problem in buying food. It is not big enough to demand a high discount from local traders but travelling long distances to fresh meat and vegetable markets is a costly and time-consuming exercise. Often, therefore, a hotelier has to rely on the local cash and carry wholesaler or on retailers. Success in purchasing depends on the relationship you can build up. A wholesaler or retailer who realizes that you know exactly what you want, that you are willing to pay for it and that you will send goods back if they do not reach the required standard, will be more careful than if you accept anything that comes along.

Good purchasing depends on proper specifications combined with realistic pricing. You cannot expect to receive the finest fillet steak when you refuse to pay the price. But if you do pay the price, make sure the meat is precisely what you want in terms of weight and quality. If this is not the case send it back. There is inevitably a degree of bluff in food purchasing and some tradesmen will sooner or later try to palm off a poor quality item, hoping to get away with it. This might be carelessness or because the proper quality is not available but it could be dishonesty. You should be able to build up such a relationship with your suppliers that they will inform you if the required quality is not available. The chef must be responsible for accepting incoming food, which should always be inspected and weighed on receipt. Any system of food costing must start here because the recipes have been devised and costed on your specifications. A supplier who gets away with goods not up to specification on one occasion will certainly try it again – and again. Incidentally, and just as important, check incoming wet stocks. Always inspect beer, wine and spirit deliveries because shortages are a common occurrence.

The other major factor that affects gross profit is the level of skill in the kitchen. A skilled chef can always make sure that a realistic gross profit is achieved; an unskilled chef will never be able to do so. In a small hotel the chef's level of cooking skill may be high but he may not be adept with figures. If this is the case, he will need help. Even so, it would be wrong to take from him the responsibility for achieving his gross profit because that is one way to measure his efficiency – only one way, it must be emphasized. A good chef will know instinctively the cost of ingredients without referring to written costings. Sooner or later, so will you.

A good chef will get the most out of every item that is brought into the kitchen. A wasteful chef will only rarely hit his targets. A hotelier who allows expensive food to be thrown into the swill may be doing the pigs a good turn but he is ruining his own business. If too much food is going to the pigs directly from the kitchen, the chef is not preparing food carefully enough. If it is going into the swill from the plates of customers, the portions are too big or the quality is too poor. Whatever the cause, it needs investigating.

One way of helping the chef may be to utilize convenience and frozen foods. In doing this, the skills of preparation are removed from your kitchen and put into the hands of the manufacturer. There are advantages and disadvantages in this approach. If you use a high proportion of convenience and frozen foods, you effectively de-skill your kitchen operation. This may be desirable if you are not able to hire a worthwhile chef but it may also mean that you cannot hire a good chef in the future. Few competent chefs are attracted to a kitchen that does not give them the scope to create their own dishes and to put their own personality into their dishes. Another disadvantage is that you also introduce an element of factory-made food into the hotel. This may be perfectly acceptable – that is a decision you will have to make based on your own assessment of the market – but regular use of such commodities as soup mixes, tinned vegetables, tinned fruit and other ready-prepared commodities will give little individuality to your menu.

Many convenience and frozen foods are, however, perfectly adaptable. Best quality frozen vegetables can be better than the fresh variety and top class pre-cooked, frozen entrées are of a higher quality than the same dish prepared in all but the best kitchens. Few customers would be able to tell the difference and there are some restaurants that depend almost entirely on pre-cooked dishes, holding them in single portions or multi-portion packs in the freezer until required. They are reheated in a convection or a microwave oven, although some are reheated by the boil-in-the-bag process. There are professional caterers who believe that the introduction of frozen foods has downgraded professional catering, reducing a restaurant merely to a point of sale retail outlet; others regard the development as inevitable, particularly when high salaried chefs are so difficult to recruit and retain.

Whatever view you take about your hotel or restaurant must be coloured by the market you want to capture. A top-class hotel or restaurant will use mostly fresh products and little if any convenience and frozen foods; a middle market hotel will use a judicious mixture of fresh and frozen products. A popular restaurant will generally use convenience foods, buying in such items as frozen pizzas, hamburgers and other items to reheat on demand. All but the highest class restaurants take the view that it is permissible to have in the freezer one or two items that cannot be easily prepared in the kitchen. Typically, these are items requiring a high quality sauce and lengthy cooking times, such as duck à l'orange or boeuf bourguignon.

Used in these circumstances, convenience and frozen foods can considerably assist any restaurateur but there are disadvantages. A discriminating diner may be able to discern what can only be called the 'factory-made' taste while some frozen food portions are too small. For regular customers, menu fatigue may set in because the dishes will always taste the same; some dishes may lose popularity and the restaurant will thus lose custom. Cost, too, may be another drawback. Because of their high quality ingredients, the portion cost of many frozen entrées and other dishes is high. The restaurateur might save on labour, however, so he may not need such a high gross profit from the frozen item. Nevertheless, unless the restaurant is planned entirely as a frozen food operation, it will need staff to prepare the other dishes, so a saving on labour is often not achieved. Heavy dependence on frozen foods also demands extensive deep freeze facilities. Where space is at a premium, this could be a disadvantage. However, such dishes are very helpful as a service to guests late at night or when it is not economic to keep staff on duty.

Kitchen equipment

One further area which needs to be examined is the state of the kitchen and restaurant equipment. Because the hotel is a going concern, don't assume that the kitchen and restaurant are in a good state of repair. One hotelier who took over a hotel found that the vendor had taken away all the badged china and most of the cutlery; nor were there enough tables and chairs for the restaurant.

A chef does not want to spend expensive time and energy overcoming the problems of an inadequate kitchen. A well-designed kitchen should be light and airy. It does not need to be so big that the chef spends all his time walking about it but there must be adequate tabling and preparation areas and an efficient stove and deep fat fryer. The whole area needs to be compact but well planned. An efficient air extraction system should exist so that the hotel is not choked with cooking fumes day and night; a non-slip floor is essential. The still room needs adequate hot water for tea- and coffee-making together with a toast machine or griller. A bain-marie and hot plate is needed to keep plates and food hot before service. An efficient dish washer is important – not only does the Environmental Health Officer disapprove of washing crockery and cutlery by hand, but it is almost impossible to get anyone to work at a sink all day. There must be adequate cold room and freezer capacity. Depending on the size of the kitchen and the complexity of the menu, there ought to be a separate vegetable preparation area and a pastry section with its own oven. Most small kitchens will not have separate areas, but there should be adequate space for the storage and preparation of fresh vegetables and for the preparation of sweets.

There are kitchen hygiene regulations which require in broad terms that food premises be kept clean and in good condition with no risk of contamination by dirt, germs, insects, rodents or odours. Specific requirements include:

1   The provision of adequate lighting and ventilation and sufficient sinks with hot and cold running water so that food and equipment can be washed.
2   Wash hand basins must be provided with hot and cold running water, soap or other detergents, clean towels or other suitable drying facilities and nail brushes. These must not be used for any other washing purpose.
3   Adequate toilets with wash hand basins must be provided for the exclusive use of staff.
4   Staff should wear clean and washable overalls.
5   First-aid facilities must always be available and should include bandages, waterproof dressings and antiseptic.
6   Staff must not smoke or engage in any unhygienic practices.
7   All food must be stored at the correct temperatures, which especially applies to dishes containing, for example, meat, fish or gravy. Unless intended for immediate consumption (in which case they should be kept at a temperature of at least 145°F) these dishes should be kept in a refrigerator.
8   All floors, walls, ceilings, windows, doors and work surfaces must be properly constructed and maintained in a sound condition.
9   Surfaces should be smooth, impervious and easily cleaned.

All these requirements are contained in the Food Hygiene (General) Regulations 1970, a copy of which is obtainable from HMSO. The local Environmental Health Officer will help you interpret these regulations. If you are considering replanning or re-equipping the kitchen, ask his or her advice first. He or she can be contacted at your local council offices and will be able to advise you of any training courses for food handlers in the area.

If much equipment does need replacing the cost may be considerable. The larger kitchen equipment manufacturers provide a free kitchen planning service but, for a small restaurant, it is probably better to plan it yourself, preferably with the aid of your chef. Try to identify a work flow for items – in broadest terms, vegetables and other raw products need to come at one end and cooked items should appear at the other. There must be a system about the kitchen. Tables next to or nearby the stoves are essential so that dishes can be transferred. The dishwasher area needs space for storing dirty and clean plates; if a dishwasher is not installed, you will need a two sink system for crockery washing – one for washing, the other with water at a much higher temperature for sterilizing. Make sure that adequate provision is made for waste disposal and storage.

If you are in doubt about your plans pick the brains of a friendly local hotelier or restaurateur. Most of them will be pleased to advise and it is often the case that they will detect a flaw in a plan that escapes an inexperienced eye.

The same need for a systematic approach applies to the restaurant. Don't have tables all the same size – you need ones, twos, threes, fours and sixes so that they can be put together to make larger units. Make sure you have enough cutlery, china and glassware – all these items are easily stolen or broken. You will find cutlery in particular has a high pilferage rate.

The waiters' sideboards or tables need to be properly positioned so that they can take all the 'mise en place' that might be needed during service, such as spare plates and cutlery, condiments, etc. They must also provide space for the waiters to put down trays and dishes before service. Pay attention to frayed or worn carpets – they can be very dangerous. If you serve wine ensure that you have enough ice buckets. Don't put roast meat on the menu 'carved from the trolley' if you haven't got a suitable trolley or space to move it about in the restaurant – better to serve roast meat from the kitchen where it can be kept hot.

You will need to develop an accurate system of stock control, particularly liquor stock. This will become more and more important as you increase the number of bar and restaurant staff. Ideally, you need to take liquor stock every week, but monthly is usually sufficient. If only you and your wife and family are running the hotel, the need for regular stocktaking is reduced, but as soon as you start employing staff, it is important that you regularly check liquor and food stocks. Wastage and pilferage in a hotel need to be controlled. The importance of inspecting all deliveries cannot be over-emphasized.

The structure and the interrelationship of the kitchen and restaurant staff will also need your attention. The two teams should work together, but all too often they oppose each other. During the service this relationship is under great stress, so it is perhaps understandable that friction can occur. It can only be overcome if both kitchen and restaurant staff have complete confidence in each other. To ensure this, you have to ask some fundamental questions about the staff. Are they sufficiently skilled for the standard of operation you want to run? What other skills do they need? Do the restaurant staff need training in social skills – the ability to get on with the customers? Can the kitchen and the restaurant staff time the service properly or are there long gaps between courses which irritate customers? Do the waiters know anything about wine so that they can promote wine sales and do they know the menu so that they can answer questions about the dishes? These questions have to be answered before you can establish a food and beverage operation that is efficient, profitable and of the standard you require. The answers require thought, considerable planning and an accurate knowledge of your market and of your customers' requirements.

Suggested reading

A Guide to Improving Food Hygiene, by Graham Aston and John Tiffney, published by Hutchinson.
Clean Catering, 1972, HMSO.
An Approach to Food Costing, by Richard Kotas, published by Hutchinson.
Understanding Food Cost Control, by Michael Riley, published by Edward Arnold.
Theory of Catering, by Victor Ceserani and Ronald Kinton, published by Edward Arnold.
Food and Beverage Service, by Denis Lillicrap, published by Edward Arnold.
Practical Cookery, by Victor Ceserani and Ronald Kinton, published by Edward Arnold.
A Caterer's Guide to Drinks, by Conal Gregory, published by Hutchinson.

13 Repairs and renewals

There is a golden rule about owning a hotel or catering business: you must maintain the property in good order. No hotel or catering establishment will take care of itself. It needs a regular programme of redecoration and maintenance, what the professional hotelier calls Repairs and Renewals – R and R.

It is a common assumption by many people coming into the hotel industry that guests will take as much care of hotel property as they will of their own. Sadly, nothing is further from the truth. Except in a few isolated instances there is little intentional damage in a well-run hotel but customers will unintentionally damage hotel property in minor but irritating ways. They will burn holes in bedlinen and blankets, place burning cigarettes on shelves and leave scorch marks, and stamp out cigarette ends on carpets. They will accidentally tear curtains and drop keys or other heavy objects in the wash basin and damage tiles. They will scratch or mark lift doors and telephone booths and pull towels off the wall in public toilets. They will pilfer spoons and other pieces of cutlery to say nothing of more valuable pieces of furniture and fittings. The hotelier must take all this in his stride but the consequence is clear: a hotel's maintenance programme needs to be well-planned and realistic.

It is not only guest carelessness that costs money. A busy hotel, regularly filled with guests, experiences considerable natural wear and tear. Carpets are worn with heavy traffic, bed linen and tablecloths wear out in direct proportion to the number of times they are laundered; walls and paintwork become stained with cigarette smoke; chairs break with constant use. In any hotel, there is a normal cycle of renewal which is quite separate from the need to replace items damaged by careless guests.

There is no fixed sum that is commonly accepted by hoteliers as a suitable figure for repairs and renewals though three to four per cent of turnover is a figure often quoted. Infuriatingly for those who want specific advice, everything depends on the type and character of the establishment. If it is a modern hotel, the need to spend large sums of money on R and R is unlikely to be as great as it would be in an older hotel, where whole systems may need renewal. For example, the electrical circuit of any hotel over thirty years old must be frequently inspected. On the other hand, some buildings constructed seventy or more years ago may be in better structural shape than those built since the last war though plumbing and electrical systems will almost certainly need attention. They were more solidly constructed which, indeed, may present problems now if you want to alter the interior layout of rooms, for Victorian buildings can be expensive to convert. The advantage of modern buildings is that services – pipes and cables – have special access chambers making them easily accessible.

Planning

The best course of action in planning your maintenance programme is to go round the hotel and draw up a list of essential tasks giving them an order of priority. It is unlikely that you will be able to afford everything that needs doing because the result of your critical investigation will almost certainly show up the need to redecorate every area and to renew every piece of furniture! You will have to concentrate on the most important areas at the beginning. Behind the scenes, there is a similar need for constant attention to be given to items like boilers, kitchen equipment, the cleaning of trunking and canopies, drains. Regular maintenance contracts on these essential pieces of equipment are important if they are not to need replacing before the end of their expected life.

The scope of your repairs programme depends on the hotel style, character and business. Priority areas should be those that yield the greatest revenue although you may need to re-equip the kitchen as the first priority or put in a new boiler and central heating system. If the hotel caters primarily for businessmen and the bedrooms are in poor shape, it would be sensible to bring the rooms up to standard before you begin to work on public areas. An overnight businessman needs a clean room, comfortable bed and adequate bathroom facilities. He may not enter the lounge area during his stay. If a large proportion of revenue comes from the bars and restaurant, those areas should be given priority and the bedrooms should be left until later. Plan the programme carefully because it is important that you keep operating while the redecoration is under way. The more rooms you have off, the less revenue you will be earning to pay for the renovations.

Schedule the programme over the next three to five years if possible, making sure that short-term activities will not be negated by long-term objectives. For example, you may plan to install a bathroom in every bedroom. As this is a major operation which will disrupt the whole hotel, don't spend money redecorating a bedroom in the first year if, by the end of the second year, the builders are going to install bathrooms. Good planning will help you finance the programme more easily and will prevent waste of money.

Planning is also required in deciding on the type of repairs and renewals you undertake. Unless the need is so urgent that swift action is imperative, think carefully about what you want to do. One way of reducing staff costs is to invest some capital in plant and equipment so plan the programme partly with the aim of making staff more productive. In redecorating a bedroom, for example, consider how it can be more quickly cleaned by staff. Wallpapers should be washable and preferably vinyl so that they resist marks; carpets must be of the best appropriate quality and not shag pile which cannot be easily cleaned. Cleaning will be made easier if you dispense with corners and crevices in favour of rounded edges and if you introduce fitted furniture. The bathroom floor should be easily washed and should preferably not be lino or vinyl tiles which tend to rise if they get soaked. A drain hole in the bathroom floor is useful in case guests leave bath water running so that it overflows or do not draw the curtain when they have a shower. It is possible to get a plastic floor laid in liquid form. Do not renew baths unless they are badly damaged: it is much more economical to get them resurfaced and the result is almost as good as a new bath although the enamel will not stay polished if staff are allowed to clean it with an abrasive cleaner. If you have to install a new ring main, a skirting board that incorporates new wiring will help prevent too much disruption caused by the need to lift floorboards. When rewiring make sure each bedroom has sufficient power points – for the electric kettle, perhaps, that you are intending to install as an extra service and for the hair dryer by the mirror. If you are renewing carpets, inspect floorboards and joists for woodworm.

If you have to get floorboards and carpets up, it would be the right time to think about central heating if the hotel does not have it installed already. The capital cost of a gas fired system (far preferable to oil) will be high and it could be more economic to install electric heating which reduces the installation costs substantially but which is more expensive to run. The cost of light and power is inevitably going to increase substantially in the coming years and hoteliers will have to think very carefully about their heating bills. One thing is certain, whatever system is used it needs to be flexible enough for the heat to be turned off in bedrooms when it is not required. Conventional radiators or electric heaters should be turned down by the room-maids during the day and only turned up at night by the guest when the room is in use. In the future hoteliers must take advantage of every opportunity to save energy costs. It is possible to obtain a grant from the Department of Energy to help pay for the cost of an investigation into a hotel's heating system by an engineer. Such an investigation can be well worth while and the outlay can be recouped by savings made in fuel consumption. In addition, grants are available for insulation.

Even from this necessarily brief list, it is clear that a lot of thought must go into an ordinary bedroom refurbishing scheme. Don't forget to test all the beds and mattresses to check that they do not need renewing; that there are sufficient mirrors (including one full length mirror) and that they are properly lit, particularly the one that will be used for ladies' make-up purposes. There should be sufficient shelves in the bathrooms and an ashtray by the washbasin or toilet. When re-equipping bedrooms and public areas, purchase the most appropriate fittings. Don't obtain cheap furniture in the belief that you are saving money. It will wear out much more quickly. The same maxim applies to carpets and chairs. A heavy duty Wilton carpet, 80 per cent wool 20 per cent nylon or 100 per cent Acrilan will appear ruinously expensive but, in the long term, it is cheapter to buy than a poorer quality carpet. With regular maintenance such a carpet can be expected to last anything between five and ten years in the main public areas where there is heavy traffic. In bedrooms, where there is less wear, a lighter duty carpet can be installed. The same principle applies to furniture. As, in a renovation scheme, the carpet is usually the most expensive item to purchase, it is advisable to start with that and design the rest of the redecoration scheme around it.

Resist the temptation to drive to the nearest major retail store to purchase the goods immediately because this will be an expensive way of buying new capital items. There are hotel and catering buying organizations that specialize in hotel and catering equipment and you should take advantage of them. Their addresses appear on page 201.

As the most expensive item in any hotel redecoration scheme is labour, many couples who buy a hotel believe they will be able to do their own redecoration. A do-it-yourself approach is feasible in a resort hotel where the establishment is closed in the winter, giving the owner time to carry out his own redecoration. Even in a busy year-round hotel, there are days which can be spent redecorating. If you do this, however, you are diverting yourself from other possibly more important activities, such as sales calls.

Most hoteliers accept the need to use an outside decorator, although if the programme is big enough it may be more economical to employ your own handyman. In getting quotes from three or more decorating firms, remember that the cheapest estimate may not always be the most suitable. What is important is the time the decorator will take. Valuable revenue will be lost every day a bedroom is out of operation and it can never be recovered. A decorator who gives a cheap quote may work on the bedrooms on an 'as and when' basis, using workmen when they become available from other projects. This would be highly unsatisfactory because the rooms would be out of action for a longer period than if a more diligent decorator were employed. The loss of your room revenue for an extra week could mean that the firm giving the cheapest estimate is by far the most expensive.

Cost benefit exercises

Begin any maintenance and redecoration scheme or extension programme by assessing its cost benefit although it can be difficult to estimate in precise financial terms what benefit will accrue by spending money on a bedroom redecoration scheme. The primary consideration may be the certain knowledge that if the rooms are not brought up to standard, there will be a disbenefit in that you will begin to lose trade because people will not want to stay in them.

The same difficulty presents itself in other areas. It is not always possible to assess the extra revenue that will be generated as a result of some schemes. On the other hand, it is generally accepted that a hotel that does not continually renew its facilities and amenities will lose out to those hotels that do invest money in modernization schemes.

However, a cost benefit exercise must be undertaken before the construction of new bedrooms or the installation of bathrooms or showers into existing bedrooms. Unless you have raised capital at the outset, you are unlikely to have the resources to consider building an extension immediately on take-over, but the installation of bathrooms or showers and toilets en suite may be an important factor in your marketing plan.

In theory, there is no difficulty in working out the sums for installing bathrooms but in practice problems can occur. A substantial element of the cost will be dictated by the run of plumbing pipes. If existing soil and water pipes can be conveniently tapped the cost of installing private bathrooms will not be as great as if new pipes have to be laid. Unless you have experience in the building or architectural professions a builder and/or an architect will be necessary to assess the likely cost of the project. With a simple scheme a good builder may be sufficient; he will be able to carry out the design and construction work providing both of you are absolutely clear about the objectives. Once you have laid your plans (and had them approved by the local authority) don't change them because that is when high extra costs are incurred. The builder will advise you on the number of rooms that should be converted at any one time. It is important that you install as many bathrooms as you can afford at the same time but, because of the plumbing, the rooms might have to be converted in stacks, above each other, rather than on one floor. The latter is more convenient as the floor can be closed off, thus minimizing guest disruption.

The four major considerations in any scheme to install bathrooms are:

1   How many bedrooms do you lose to make room for the bathrooms?
2   How much extra occupancy will be generated by the new facilities?
3   How much extra can you charge for the rooms with the private facilities; and over what period of time will the investment be recouped?
4   How much revenue will you lose while the rooms are out of commission?

It is important that these sums are worked out carefully. If you lose bedrooms to make space for the new bathrooms, the loss of potential revenue has to be set against the extra revenue that you will be able to obtain from the new rooms with private facilities. Assuming your current levels of occupancy you can work out how long it will take you to repay the costs of conversion.

This will be your worst estimate because it is correct to assume that the new facilities will attract more business and thus increase occupancy levels. Estimate the number of extra guests, the revenue they will generate and the length of time it will take to repay the loan you will have to raise to finance the project. This will be your best estimate. Somewhere between the two extremes lies a realistic compromise.

Having worked out both sums, the project may still be only marginally profitable because you lose too many bedrooms to fit in the bathrooms. Even the most optimistic occupancy projections may not make the conversion pay within the period of the loan. If that is the case, you may have to reconcile yourself to running a hotel with rooms without private facilities. This will limit your marketing policies but you will have a price advantage over hotels in the locality that have private bathrooms. If you are in a situation in which private bathrooms are required and you cannot offer them, then business will inevitably decline. Take this fact into account and re-examine the figures. The two relevant questions that then need answering are:

1   If private bathrooms are not installed what will be the occupancy in five
    years' time and how much revenue will the hotel be producing (assuming a
    given rate of inflation)?
2   Will this provide as much profit as the hotel would have earned if it had
    not been converted?

In other words, because bedrooms with bathrooms are now widely expected you may lose far more trade by not converting than you would gain by converting. In this case it would make economic sense to go ahead with the conversion, repaying the finance over a long period, in the optimistic expectation that you can increase occupancy to even higher levels than you previously estimated. Inflation will help because you can increase tariffs year by year.

As a very approximate guide, conversion costs are likely to be in the region of £3,000–£4,000 per room and it is possible to charge anything from £3–£7 a night extra for a room with bathroom, depending on location and competition. The premium tariff that can be charged usually makes the addition of private bathrooms an economic proposition.

Basically, the same exercise must be undertaken with an extension. Being a much more costly undertaking and one that will undoubtedly require considerable extra finance it will need to be much more sophisticated. A new bedroom block added to an existing hotel in the provinces would cost between £10,000 and £20,000 per room, depending on the style of hotel and its facilities. In London the cost would be much higher.

A project of this nature would demand a separate budget and the need to raise substantial finance to build the extension would take it out of the R and R account and into a new developments account; even installing new bathrooms will demand extra finance which, on a short term basis, your bank would normally be prepared to consider though you will need profit projections to support your application.

Repairs and renewals, however, should be budgeted out of revenue and a specific amount is best set aside every year, sufficient to meet your current and future needs. A carpet that costs £1,000 to install and is estimated to last five years will require a sum of £200 per year to be credited to the R and R account for a replacement in five years' time. In fact, more needs to be set aside because an item that costs £1,000 now may cost £1,500 in five years' time. In practice, your accounts may not work out as simply as this but in a small business there is much to be said for putting aside, perhaps into a deposit account, the money that you will need to meet furniture and equipment renewals. There are bound to be times when unexpected emergencies arise which will need immediate attention and financial outlay. If you plan realistically for the expected you will be in a better position to cope with the unexpected.

Buying organizations

Best Western Hotels, 26 Kew Road, Richmond, Surrey
Inter-Hotel, 29 Harrington Gardens, London SW7 4JT
Minotels, 11 Palmeira Mansions, Church Road, Hove, East Sussex BN3 2GA
British Federation of Hotels, Guest House and Self-Catering Associations, Central Purchasing Authority, 3 Green Lane, Ashwell, Herts.

These organizations are primarily marketing consortia but all of them operate a purchasing scheme to members. Best Western has a separate purchasing company that does not require membership of the marketing organization (see Chapter 10).

Appendix 1 Minimum standards of accommodation

The following minimum standards for hotels and guest houses, including hotels and inns, were drawn up by the British Tourist Authority, the English Tourist Board, the Scottish Tourist Board and the Wales Tourist Board. The BTA regards adherence to the minimum standards as a basic criterion for the inclusion of establishments in its publications.

Minimum standards for accommodation in all licensed establishments and all other establishments with four or more letting bedrooms

Please note: conversions are approximate.

A Bedrooms

1 All bedrooms must conform to, or exceed, the following minimum dimensions for floor areas excluding private bath or shower areas:

   (a) Single bedrooms: 5.60 m²   (60 sq ft)
   (b) Double bedrooms: 8.40 m²   (90 sq ft)
   (c) Twin-bedded rooms: 10.20 m²   (110 sq ft)
   (d) Family rooms:
   Minimum floor area of 2.80 m² (30 sq ft) plus:
   5.60 m² (60 sq ft) for each double bed and/or
   3.70 m² (40 sq ft) for each single adult bed and/or
   1.85 m² (20 sq ft) for each cot

2 All bedrooms must have reasonable free space for movement and for easy access to doors, drawers and beds.

3 All beds, other than those for use by children, must conform to, or exceed, the following minimum dimensions:
   (a) Single beds: 183 cm × 76 cm   (6 ft × 2 ft 6 in)
   (b) Double beds: 183 cm × 122 cm   (6 ft × 4 ft)

4 All mattresses must be spring interior, foam or of similar quality, and in sound condition. Bedding must be clean, and in sufficient quantity.

5 Beds must be made daily. Linen must be changed at least once per week and for every new resident guest.

6 All bedrooms must be equipped with a wash basin, having both hot and

cold running water, either in the bedroom or in a private bathroom. A mirror must be above, or adjacent to, the wash basin.

7 All bedrooms (or bathrooms) must be equipped with an electric shaver point.

8 All bedrooms must be supplied, for every new resident guest, with fresh soap and a clean towel and these must be replenished or changed as required.

9 All bedrooms must be provided with:
   (a) Dressing table or equivalent, and mirror
   (b) Wardrobe, or clothes hanging space, equipped with at least four hangers per person
   (c) Adequate drawer space
   (d) Bedside table, or equivalent
   (e) One chair, or equivalent, per person (minimum of two in family rooms)
   (f) Wastepaper container
   (g) Ashtray
   (h) One drinking vessel per person (minimum of two in family rooms)

10 All bedrooms must be equipped with bedside rugs or mats, where no carpet is provided.

11 All bedrooms must have at least one window and be adequately ventilated.

12 All bedrooms must be equipped with opaque curtains or blinds on all windows.

13 All bedrooms must be adequately heated, according to season, at no extra charge.

14 All bedrooms must be adequately lit, to the following minimum levels, with a light controlled from the bed:
   (a) Single bedrooms: 100 watts or equivalent
   (b) Other bedrooms: 150 watts or equivalent

15 All bedrooms must be fitted with a lock that will ensure privacy for guests and security for their property. Guests must be provided with a key to their bedrooms, duplicate or master keys being kept by the management.

16 All resident guests must be allowed access to their bedrooms at all reasonable times.

B Bathrooms

1 The establishment must have at least one bathroom, equipped with a bath or shower, for every fifteen resident guests (other than guests in bedrooms with private bathrooms).

2 Hot water must be available at all reasonable times, with no extra charge for baths or showers.

3 All private bathrooms must be equipped with a WC and either a bath or shower.

C WCs

1 The establishment must have at least one WC for every ten resident guests (other than guests in bedrooms with private bathrooms).
2 Where there is only one WC, it must not be in a bathroom.
3 All WCs, including those in private bathrooms, must be equipped with toilet paper and a disposal bin.

D General

1 The establishment must provide a residents' lounge or lounge area, appropriate to the type of establishment.
2 All public areas must be adequately heated, according to season, at no extra charge.
3 All public areas must be adequately lit for comfort and safety.
4 A telephone must be available for residents' use at all reasonable times.
5 The establishment must be kept clean throughout, and all exterior and interior decorations, furnishings, floor coverings and fittings must be maintained in good condition

E Optional standard: Disabled guests

The establishment may or may not be able to accommodate severely disabled guests (e.g. those in wheelchairs). Those that welcome disabled guests, and wish to be so designated in publications, must conform to the following minimum requirements:

1 At least one entrance must either have no steps or be equipped with a ramp whose gradient does not exceed 1 in 12.
2 All doors (including those of WCs, private bathrooms, etc.) must have a clear opening width of at least 74 cm (29 in) with a head-on approach.
3 All essential accommodation, if not on the ground floor, must be served by an adequately sized lift
4 Lift gates must be at least 80 cm (31.5 in) wide; lifts must be at least 122 cm (48 in) deep and 91 cm (36 in) wide.
5 At least one bedroom and one public WC must be suitable for disabled guests.
6 In the bedrooms, private or public bathrooms and WCs used by the disabled, the clearance around beds, and to reach wash basins, WCs, etc must be at least 75 cm (29.5 in) and there must be turning space of 122 cm (48 in) by 122 cm (48 in).
7 The establishment must accept guide dogs, but may exclude them from dining or restaurant areas.

Note: Although not required as minimum standards, it is strongly recommended that:

1 All beds, other than those for use by children, conform to, or exceed, the following dimensions:

Single beds: 190 cm or 6 ft 3 in × 90 cm or 3 ft
Double beds: 190 cm or 6 ft 3 in × 135 cm or 4 ft 6 in.

2   There be at least one bathroom for every ten resident guests (other than those with private bathrooms).
3   There be at least one WC for every eight resident guests (other than those with private bathrooms).

Code of conduct for establishments providing tourist accommodation and designed to ensure a fair deal for all guests
In addition to fulfilling its statutory obligations, the management undertakes to observe the following code of conduct:

1   To ensure high standards of courtesy, cleanliness, catering and service appropriate to the type of establishment.
2   To describe fairly to all visitors and prospective visitors the amenities, facilities and services provided by the establishment, whether by advertisement, brochure, word of mouth or any other means and to allow visitors to see accommodation, if requested, before booking.
3   To make clear to visitors exactly what is included in all prices quoted for accommodation, meals and refreshments, including service charges, taxes and other surcharges. Details of cancellation procedures and charges for additional services or facilities available should also be made clear. In the case of establishments with four bedrooms or more, to adhere to the Hotel Industry Voluntary Code of Booking Practice.
4   To adhere to, and not to exceed, prices current at time of occupation, for accommodation or other services.
5   To advise visitors at the time of booking, and subsequent to any change, if the accommodation offered is in an unconnected annexe, or similar, or by boarding out and to indicate the location of such accommodation and any difference in comfort and amenities from accommodation in the main establishment.
6   To give each visitor, on request, details of payments due, and a receipt, if required.
7   To deal promptly and courteously with all enquiries, requests, reservations, correspondence and complaints from visitors.

Appendix 2 Menu costings

These sample costings are not intended to reflect up-to-date prices – merely the way in which they should be compiled. It is important that costings are undertaken regularly so that fluctuations in the price of raw materials do not materially affect your gross profit. Inevitably, there will be seasonal variations in prices; these should be noted and, if they reduce your gross profit dramatically or if they appear to be permanent price increases, you will have to increase your selling prices to maintain gross profit.

Chilled fruit juice (20p) *1 portion*

Ingredients	Quantity	Cost (£)
Bottled juice (Orange, pineapple, grapefruit or tomato)	4fl oz	0.01
		0.10

Food cost = 50 per cent. Gross food profit = 50 per cent.

Grapefruit cocktail (40p) *4 portions*

Ingredients	Quantity	Cost (£)
Canned segments	1 tin	0.34
Cherries (jar)	4	0.04
		0.38

Portion cost 0.095

Food cost = 23.75 per cent. Gross food profit = 76.25 per cent.

Egg mayonnaise (50p) *1 portion*

Ingredients	Quantity	Cost (£)
Standard eggs	2	0.08
Ready made mayonnaise	2 fl oz	0.03
Round lettuce	2 leaves	0.01
Paprika pepper	pinch	0.005
		0.125

Food cost = 25 per cent. Gross food profit = 75 per cent.

Chilled melon (70p) *1 portion*

Ingredients	Quantity	Cost (£)
Honeydew melon	1/3 melon	0.14
Jaffa orange	1 slice	0.015
Cherries (jar)	1	0.01
		0.165

Food cost = 23.57 per cent. Gross food profit = 76.43 per cent.

Prawn cocktail (80p) *1 portion*

Ingredients	Quantity	Cost (£)
Grade M frozen prawns	2 oz	0.13
Ready made cocktail sauce	2 fl oz	0.02
Round lettuce	1 leaf	0.005
Lemon	$\frac{1}{4}$	0.015
Cucumber	1 slice	0.005
Brown bread and butter	1 slice	0.015
Paprika pepper	pinch	0.005
		0.195

Food cost = 24.38 per cent. Gross food profit = 75.62 per cent.

Avocado pear with prawns (£1.05) *1 portion*

Ingredients	Quantity	Cost (£)
Avocado pear	1	0.27
Grade M frozen prawns	2 oz	0.13
Ready made cocktail sauce	2 fl oz	0.02
Paprika pepper	pinch	0.005
Double cream	1 tspn	0.01
		0.435

Food cost = 41.43 per cent. Gross food profit = 58.57 per cent.

Fried fillet of plaice (£1.60) *1 portion*

Ingredients	Quantity	Cost (£)
Frozen, breadcrumbed fillet	6–7 oz	0.30
Frozen peas	3 oz	0.04
Frozen chips	6 oz	0.06
Lemon	$\frac{1}{4}$	0.015
Tomato	$\frac{1}{2}$	0.03
Parsley butter	$\frac{1}{3}$ oz	0.01
Cooking oil	1 fl oz	0.03
Seasoning, sauce, etc		0.01
		0.495

Food cost = 30.94 per cent. Gross food profit = 69.06 per cent.

Deep fried scampi (£2.30) *1 portion*

Ingredients	Quantity	Cost (£)
Frozen, breadcrumbed scampi	8 oz	0.90
Frozen peas	3 oz	0.04
Frozen potato croquettes	4 oz	0.06
Cucumber	4 slices	0.02
Oil, other garnish, seasoning	as for plaice	0.095
		1.115

Food cost = 48.48 per cent. Gross food profit = 51.52 per cent.

Grilled rainbow trout (£2.30) *1 portion*

Ingredients	Quantity	Cost (£)
Frozen trout	7–9 oz	0.60
Frozen chips	6 oz	0.06
Oil, other veg, garnish and seasoning	as for scampi	0.135
		0.795

Food cost = 34.57 per cent. Gross food profit = 65.43 per cent.

Poached salmon cutlet (£2.60) *1 portion*

Ingredients	Quantity	Cost (£)
Frozen cutlet of salmon	8 oz	0.73
Frozen peas	3 oz	0.04
Frozen chips	6 oz	0.06
Tomato	½	0.03
Cucumber	4 slices	0.02
Lemon	¼	0.015
		0.895

Food cost = 34.42 per cent. Gross food profit = 65.58 per cent.

Grilled rump steak (£2.88) *1 portion*

Ingredients	Quantity	Cost (£)
Portioned rump steak	8 oz	1.01
Frozen peas	3 oz	0.04
Frozen chips	6 oz	0.06
Tomato	½	0.03
Parsley butter	⅓ oz	0.01
Cooking oil	1 fl oz	0.03
Seasoning		0.01
		1.19

Food cost = 41.32 per cent. Gross food profit = 58.68 per cent.

Grilled sirloin steak (£2.95) *1 portion*

Ingredients	Quantity	Cost (£)
Portioned sirloin steak	8 oz	1.00
Vegetables, garnish, oil and seasoning	as for rump steak	0.18
		1.18

Food cost = 40 per cent. Gross food profit = 60 per cent.

Mixed grill (£2.90) *1 portion*

Ingredients	Quantity	Cost) (£)
Rump steak	4 oz	0.505
Pork chop	2–3 oz	0.19
Kidney	2 oz	0.10
Bacon rasher	1	0.06
Sausage	1	0.05
Standard egg	1	0.04
Vegetables, garnish, oil and seasoning	as for rump steak	0.18
		1.125

Food cost = 38.79 per cent. Gross food profit = 61.21 per cent.

Grilled gammon with egg and pineapple ring (£2.35) *1 portion*

Ingredients	Quantity	Cost (£)
Gammon slice	8 oz	0.37
Standard egg	1	0.04
Canned pineapple ring	1	0.03
Vegetables, garnish, oil and seasoning	as for rump steak	0.18
		0.62

Food cost = 26.38 per cent. Gross food profit = 73.62 per cent.

Home made steak and kidney pie (£1.90)
24 portions

Ingredients	Quantity	Cost (£)
Pie beef	10 lb	6.90
Kidney	2½ lb	1.90
Onion	2 lb	0.24
Self-raising flour	2 lb	0.17
Cooking fat	½ lb	0.095
Margarine	½ lb	0.105
Milk	½ pt	0.055
Standard egg	1	0.04
Gravy mix	4 oz	0.065
Seasoning		0.03
		9.60
	Portion cost	0.40

1 portion

Frozen peas	3 oz	0.04
Frozen chips	6 oz	0.06
		0.50

Food cost = 26.32 per cent. Gross food profit = 73.68 per cent.

Grilled lamb chops (£2.00) *1 portion*

Ingredients	Quantity	Cost (£)
Two lamp chops, NZ	4 oz each	0.60
Frozen peas	3 oz	0.04
Frozen chips	6 oz	0.06
Mint sauce		0.02
Garnish, oil and seasoning		0.08
		0.80

Food cost = 40 per cent. Gross food profit = 60 per cent.

Grilled pork chop with baked apple (£2.00)
1 portion

Ingredients	Quantity	Cost (£)
Pork chop	8 oz	0.52
Apple	½	0.01
Frozen peas	3 oz	0.04
Frozen chips	6 oz	0.06
Garnish, oil and seasoning		0.08
		0.71

Food cost = 35.50 per cent. Gross food profit = 64.50 per cent.

Fried onion rings (50p) *1 portion*

Ingredients	Quantity	Cost (£)
Frozen battered onion rings	4 oz	0.125
Oil		0.02
		0.145

Food cost = 29 per cent. Gross food profit = 71 per cent.

Cauliflower (50p) *1 portion*

Ingredients	Quantity	Cost (£)
Frozen florettes	6 oz	0.16
Seasoning		0.01
		0.17

Food cost = 34 per cent. Gross food profit = 66 per cent.

Fresh pineapple (60p) *1 portion*

Ingredients	Quantity	Cost (£)
Fresh pineapple	¼	0.25
Double cream	1 fl oz	0.05
Orange	1 slice	0.015
Maraschino cherry	1	0.01
		0.325

Food cost = 54.17 per cent. Gross food profit = 45.83 per cent.

Baked egg custard (60p) *4 portions*

Ingredients	Quantity	Cost (£)
Standard eggs	4	0.16
Caster sugar	2 oz	0.02
Milk	1 pt	0.12
Grated nutmeg		0.005
		0.305
	Portion cost	0.076

1 portion

Double cream	1 fl oz	0.05
		0.126

Food cost = 21 per cent. Gross food profit = 79 per cent.

Lemon meringue pie (60p) *18 portions*

Ingredients	Quantity	Cost (£)
Meringue pie mix	1 pkt	0.99
Self-raising flour	12 oz	0.06
Cooking fat	2 oz	0.02
Margarine	4 oz	0.053
Caster sugar	6 oz	0.06
Milk	¼ pt	0.025
Salt	pinch	0.005
		1.213
	Portion cost	0.067

1 portion

Double cream	1 fl oz	0.05
		0.117

Food cost = 19.50 per cent. Gross food profit = 80.50 per cent.

Fresh fruit salad (60p) *10 portions*

Ingredients	Quantity	Cost (£)
Apples	2 lb	0.24
Oranges	3	0.24
Bananas	1 lb	0.17
Pears	1 lb	0.13
Black grapes	½ lb	0.26
Caster sugar	1 oz	0.01
Cointreau	2 ml	0.37
Peaches	3	0.40
		1.82
	Portion cost	0.182

1 portion

Double cream	¼ fl oz	0.05
		0.232

Food cost = 38.67 per cent. Gross food profit = 61.33 per cent.

Home made apple tart (60p) *9 portions*

Ingredients	Quantity	Cost (£)
Cooking apples	3½ lb	0.28
Self-raising flour	12 oz	0.06
Cooking fat	2 oz	0.02
Margarine	4 oz	0.053
Caster sugar	2 oz	0.02
Demerara sugar	1 oz	0.01
Milk	¼ pt	0.025
Standard egg	1	0.04
		0.508
	Portion cost	0.056

1 portion

Double cream	1 fl oz	0.05
		0.106

Food cost = 17.67 per cent. Gross food profit = 82.33 per cent.

The cheese board (55p) *1 portion*

Ingredients	Quantity	Cost (£)
Cream cracker biscuits	1 oz	0.04
Butter	1 oz	0.03
Cheddar cheese	2 oz	0.12
Stilton cheese	2 oz	0.20
Cheshire cheese	2 oz	0.14
Danish blue cheese	2 oz	0.16

Respective food costs, portion costs and gross profits:
Cheddar: £0.19; 34 and 66 per cent.
Stilton: £0.27; 49.09 and 50.91 per cent.
Cheshire: £0.21; 38.18 and 61.82 per cent.
Danish Blue: £0.23; 41.81 and 58.19 per cent.

Coffee (25p) *1 portion*

Ingredients	Quantity	Cost (£)
Coffee	¹⁄₁₆ oz	0.03
Single cream	1 fl oz	0.04
Brown sugar	½ oz	0.025
Petits fours		0.02
		0.115

Food cost = 46 per cent. Gross food profit = 54 per cent.

Index